D0099939

Published by
The Junior League of Jackson, Inc.
Jackson, MS

Designed and edited by
Communication Arts Company
Jackson, MS

Studio and Location
Photography by
Patricia Brabant
© Patricia Brabant Studios
Photo Assistance by
M.J. Murphy

Food Styling by
Robert Lambert

Copyright © 1991, 1993 by
The Junior League
of Jackson, Inc.
All rights reserved

This book, or any portions
thereof, may not be reproduced in
any form without written permission
of The Junior League of Jackson, Inc.

Any inquiries about this book
or additional copies should be
directed to:
The Junior League of Jackson, Inc.
P.O. Box 4709
Jackson, MS 39296-4709

Printed in Japan

Library of Congress
Catalog Card Number
91-60406

Come On In:
Recipes from the Junior League
of Jackson, Mississippi

ISBN 0-9606886-1-7

JUNIOR
LEAGUE
OF JACKSON
MISSISSIPPI

The Junior League
is an organization of women
committed to promoting
voluntarism and to improving
the community through the
effective action and leadership
of trained volunteers.
Its purpose is exclusively
charitable.

Come On In!

Recipes from the Junior League
OF JACKSON, MISSISSIPPI

PHOTOGRAPHY
Patricia Brabant

FOOD STYLING

Robert Lambert

TABLE OF CONTENTS

Our cover and introductory photo series feature the home of Carleton "Chip" Billups, Jr., and his wife, Debra, on Eastwood Road in Jackson, Mississippi. The 50s-era tract house has been continually reinterpreted through the years, with the current owners adding this airy, sun-dappled entranceway. As enthusiastic supporters of Mississippi arts, Chip and Debra have made their home an eclectic, exuberant celebration of valued antiques and handcrafted treasures.

D O O R W A Y S
TO THE HOSPITALITY OF THE SOUTH

Here in the South, doors symbolize our famous gift for hospitality—a legend which just happens to be true. As a matter of fact, in earlier times, the hospitality began even before the door was reached. In the heat of the day, visitors were invited up on the front porch to sit a spell, enjoy some lemonade or iced tea, and catch a breeze. Later, after dinner, guests and hosts would take their coffee and dessert back out to the porch, where a rhythmic rocking chair or a gently creaking swing proved to be a remarkably effective aid to digestion.

In today's air-conditioned South, if a house has any sort of front porch at all, it's usually a token gesture at best. Indeed, the modern front door itself has taken on a character that is usually more symbolic than functional. Friends know that they should enter through the garage or "come on around back." The front door bell is likely to announce the newspaper carrier seeking the monthly payment you forgot to mail, a high school student selling magazine subscriptions to finance a band trip to some exotic destination, or a candidate for the town council promising to clean up the mess in city hall.

Since you're our guest, however, we invite you to choose any door you like:

~ The imposing entranceway to an antebellum mansion, framed by Greek Revival pillars and promising an elegant candlelit dinner served on richly gleaming china, silver, and crystal.

~ The latticed gate to a private garden where minted tea and tiny frosted cakes wait on a filigreed wrought iron table.

~ The squeaky door of a screened porch leading to a kitchen from which drift the down-home aromas of catfish, hushpuppies, and turnip greens.

~ The simple, stately door of a small country church where, in the Fellowship Hall, long tables and folding chairs are set up and ready for Wednesday night's pot luck supper.

~ The expansive tailgate of a big four-wheel-drive (thoroughly cleaned and washed after last week's fishing trip), laden with covered baskets and colorful plastic jugs, ready to fortify the fans for the biggest game of the season.

Southern doors welcome family members to the warm reassurances of home, hearth, and dinner table. They reunite friends and introduce strangers at graceful receptions and raucous get-togethers. Whenever and wherever Southerners gather together, fine Southern cooking is almost always the center of attention. In fact, Southern hospitality and Southern food are virtually inseparable. And Southern doors lead the way to both.

Our door is always open, so don't bother to knock; just come on in!

§

As you leaf through
the pages of
Come On In!,
you will often find this
symbol: §
Whenever you do,
congratulations—
you've discovered one of
our Southern Secrets!
These are some of our
most cherished recipes,
our most time-tested
techniques, and our
most treasured tales.
They've been handed
down through the
generations and passed
around from family
to family, bringing
special pleasures and
providing unforgettable
memories.

~

Southern Secrets
form the foundation on
which the South's
legendary reputation for
food and hospitality has
been built, and we're
proud to be able to share
some of them with
our readers.

9

PHOTO (left): *Dignitaries such as Henry Clay and William Jennings Bryan, Theodore Roosevelt and John F. Kennedy, Eudora Welty and Margaret Walker Alexander have all been guests at the Mississippi Governor's Mansion. William Nichols, Mansion architect, said that his intent was "to avoid a profusion of ornament and to adhere to a plain republican simplicity as best comporting with the dignity of the state." Original construction was completed in 1842, with renovations in 1908 and 1975. The building has been designated a National Historic Landmark.*

PHOTO (overleaf):

Onion Sandwiches
Grilled Pork Tenderloin with Tomato Mint Salsa on
Cornbread Cutouts

A P P E T I Z E R S

Grilled Pork Tenderloin with Tomato Mint Salsa
Serves 8-12

Marinade:

½ cup	extra virgin olive oil
¼ cup	red wine vinegar
6 cloves	garlic, minced
½ tsp	dried thyme, crumbled
2 lbs	pork tenderloin
~	Tomato Mint Salsa (see accompanying recipe)
~	Cornbread Cutouts (page 176)

Whisk together olive oil, vinegar, garlic, and thyme. Place tenderloin in a plastic storage bag and pour in marinade. Seal and refrigerate at least 4 hours. Grill pork tenderloin until internal temperature reaches 160-165° on meat thermometer. Slice and serve with salsa and Cornbread Cutouts.

Tomato Mint Salsa

Yields 1 qt

2 bunches	watercress, tops, coarsely chopped
4	ripe tomatoes, seeded, coarsely chopped
⅔ cup	fresh mint, minced, or 2 tsp dried basil
½ cup	extra virgin olive oil
¼ cup	red wine vinegar
4 cloves	garlic, minced
1 tsp	salt
1 tsp	freshly ground black pepper

Combine watercress, tomatoes, and mint. Whisk together olive oil, vinegar, garlic, salt, and pepper and add to vegetable mixture.

Beef Tenderloin with Tomato Basil Vinaigrette
Serves 6-8

Tomato Basil Vinaigrette

Yields 3 1/2 cups

2	fresh tomatoes, (8 oz canned), diced
1/4 cup	minced fresh basil (1 Tbs dried)
1 1/2 cups	extra virgin olive oil
1 cup	balsamic vinegar
1 tsp	salt
1 tsp	freshly ground black pepper

Combine all ingredients and refrigerate.

2 1/2 lbs	beef tenderloin, center cut, trimmed
1/2 tsp	freshly ground black pepper
1/2 tsp	garlic powder
1 tsp	paprika
1/2 tsp	celery salt
1/4 tsp	rubbed sage
2 Tbs	extra virgin olive oil
~	Tomato Basil Vinaigrette (see accompanying recipe)
2 lbs	fresh spinach, washed and julienned
1 cup	freshly grated Parmesan cheese
~	freshly ground black pepper for garnish

Rub beef with pepper, garlic powder, paprika, celery salt, and sage. Refrigerate 2 to 4 hours. Remove beef from refrigerator 1 hour before cooking. When ready to cook, heat 2 tablespoons olive oil at medium temperature 3 to 4 minutes. Add beef and cook on all sides, 2 minutes per side for rare. For each degree of doneness past the rare stage, add 8 minutes of cooking time. After cooking, allow meat to cool and refrigerate. To serve, nestle a large handful of julienned spinach in the center of each dinner plate. Slice meat across the grain as thinly as possible. Arrange meat medallions in a circular fashion, overlapping on spinach all around. Spoon the vinaigrette over meat and sprinkle with cheese. Serve cold, garnished with freshly ground black pepper.

Al Roberts, owner and chef, Amerigo Italian Restaurant, Jackson, MS

Peppered Beef
Serves 20

¼ cup	coarsely ground black peppercorns
5 lbs	beef brisket

Marinade:

²/₃ cup	soy sauce
½ cup	vinegar
1 Tbs	catsup
1 tsp	paprika
1 clove	garlic, pressed
½ cup	red wine

Spread black pepper on a sheet of wax paper. Firmly press beef into pepper, covering both sides, and place in a large plastic storage bag. Combine remaining ingredients and pour into bag with beef. Seal and refrigerate overnight, turning occasionally. To cook, remove beef from marinade, wrap in foil, and bake in a shallow baking pan at 300° for 3 hours. Slice thinly against the grain to serve.

This boldly flavored beef appetizer, which can also be smoked on the grill, is a great favorite among the guys, especially when it's served on homemade rolls with fiery, coarse-grained mustard.

Grilled Venison Tenderloin with Sour Cream Mustard Sauce
Serves 6

1	venison tenderloin
~	freshly ground black pepper
2 cloves	garlic, minced
1 Tbs	fresh rosemary (1 tsp dried)
½ cup	dry red wine
2 Tbs	soy sauce
½ cup	vegetable oil

~	Sour Cream Mustard Sauce (see accompanying recipe)

Rub venison on all sides with black pepper, garlic, and rosemary. Combine red wine and soy sauce and thoroughly coat meat. Add oil and coat meat again. Cover and marinate at room temperature for at least 1 hour, turning occasionally. To grill, sear meat on both sides over hot coals, then cook until medium-rare, approximately 10 minutes (do not overcook). Allow meat to rest 10 minutes before slicing into ¼" rounds. Serve warm or at room temperature with Sour Cream Mustard Sauce for dipping.

Sour Cream
Mustard Sauce
Yields 1 cup

1 cup	sour cream
2 Tbs	Creole mustard

Blend ingredients thoroughly.

Venison Sausage Balls
Yields 75

1 ½ lbs	ground venison or ground round
1 lb	hot sausage
1 cup	sour cream
1 jar	Major Grey chutney (8 oz), chopped
½ cup	sherry

Combine venison and sausage and form into balls. Cook meatballs over medium heat, draining off fat. In a saucepan, blend sour cream, chutney, and sherry. Add meat balls and heat thoroughly. If mixture thickens too much, add extra sherry. Serve hot in chafing dish. Sausage balls may be made ahead and reheated.

This slightly sweet and spicy hot game dish makes a remarkable entree when served over wild rice.

Smoked Cinnamon Duck
Serves 8

½ cup	vegetable oil
3 Tbs	Worcestershire sauce
3 Tbs	fresh lemon juice
8	duck breast fillets, skinned
~	ground cinnamon
~	lemon pepper seasoning
~	crackers
~	coarse-grained mustard

Blend oil with Worcestershire sauce and lemon juice. Cover duck breasts with oil mixture and marinate 2 to 3 hours. To cook, place duck breasts on charcoal grill away from fire and cover liberally with cinnamon and lemon pepper seasoning. Close grill and cook 10 to 12 minutes, depending on heat. Turn fillets, baste with oil mixture, and cover again with cinnamon and lemon pepper seasoning. Close grill and cook 10 to 15 minutes more (do not overcook—juices should run clear when duck is sliced). Slice very thinly and serve with crackers and coarse-grained mustard.

Grilled Marinated Doves

Serves 8

Marinade:

1/3 cup	vinegar
1/3 cup	fresh lemon juice
1/4 cup	soy sauce
1 1/2 cups	vegetable oil
1 Tbs	Worcestershire sauce
6 dashes	Tabasco Sauce
2 cloves	garlic, minced
1/4 tsp	pepper
1/4 tsp	paprika
1 cube	chicken bouillon, dissolved in 1 cup water
25	doves, breasted and deboned
13 slices	bacon, halved

Thoroughly blend all marinade ingredients. Pour marinade over doves, cover, and refrigerate overnight. To grill, wrap two dove breasts together with half-slice of bacon and secure with toothpick. Grill over hot charcoal, being careful not to overcook and basting frequently with marinade. Medium rare delivers full flavor and juiciness.

Curried Chicken Kabobs

Yields 25

3 lbs	boneless, skinless chicken breasts
1 cup	vermouth
1 1/2 tsp	salt
1/2 tsp	curry powder
1 medium	onion, sliced
2 stalks	celery, coarsely chopped
1	cantaloupe, in bite-sized chunks or balls
~	curly leaf lettuce, in bite-sized pieces
~	Curry Sauce (see accompanying recipe)

Cook chicken in enough water to cover with vermouth, salt, curry powder, onion, and celery added. Refrigerate chicken in cooking liquid until well chilled, then drain and cut into cubes. On wooden skewers, alternate 2 pieces of chicken, 2 pieces of lettuce, and 1 piece of cantaloupe. Curried Chicken Kabobs may be served alone or with Curry Sauce.

Curry Sauce

Yields 1 1/2 cups

1 cup	mayonnaise
2 Tbs	Durkee's Sauce
1/2 tsp	Worcestershire sauce
1 tsp	celery seed
1/4 tsp	garlic powder
1 Tbs	prepared horseradish
1 tsp	curry powder
1 tsp	seasoned salt
~	Tabasco Sauce to taste
~	freshly ground black pepper to taste

Combine all ingredients and chill.

Crab Cakes Dijon
Serves 4

Dijon Sauce
Yields 1 ¼ cups

½ cup	plain yogurt
3 Tbs	Dijon mustard
¼ cup	mayonnaise
1 Tbs	chopped onion
2 Tbs	dill relish
2 tsp	balsamic vinegar

Whisk together all ingredients. Serve at room temperature. Refrigerate sauce if not using immediately.

½ cup	vegetable oil, divided
1 Tbs	chopped green pepper
4 Tbs	chopped green onion
1 lb	fresh lump crabmeat, picked
1 large	egg, beaten
1 Tbs	mayonnaise
6 Tbs	dry bread crumbs
1 tsp	dry mustard
¼ tsp	black pepper
¼ tsp	cayenne pepper
1 tsp	seasoned salt
~	Dijon Sauce (see accompanying recipe)

Sauté green pepper and onion in 2 tablespoons oil until wilted. Drain and mix with crabmeat, egg, mayonnaise, bread crumbs, mustard, peppers, and salt. Chill 20 minutes. Form chilled mixture into 8 flat cakes. Sauté crab cakes in ⅓ cup oil until golden, 5 to 8 minutes on each side. Drain on paper towels. Serve warm with Dijon Sauce.

Lemon Dill Crabmeat Salad on Cucumber
Serves 4-6

Red Pepper Flowers
- Tiny red chili peppers
- Basil leaves, Italian parsley or cilantro leaves

Make tiny slits from the tip of the pepper almost to the stem. Drop in ice water and store in refrigerator overnight or up to two days. Use with basil leaves, Italian parsley or cilantro leaves for a decorative garnish. The same technique also works with green onions.

½ lb	fresh crabmeat, picked
1	green onion, finely chopped
2 Tbs	chopped fresh dill (2 tsp dried)
1 tsp	grated lemon zest
¼ cup	mayonnaise
⅛ tsp	cayenne pepper
~	salt and pepper to taste
1	cucumber, 10-12", scored, sliced in ¼" rounds
~	paprika to taste
~	fresh dill for garnish
~	Red Pepper Flowers for garnish (see accompanying recipe)

Combine crabmeat, onion, dill, lemon zest, mayonnaise, and cayenne and chill for 1 hour. Sprinkle cucumber slices with salt and pepper. Mound crabmeat salad onto each cucumber round, sprinkle with paprika, and garnish with sprig of dill.

Crab Strudels

Serves 15

5	green onions, chopped
½ cup	unsalted butter
1 cup	dry vermouth
1 lb	fresh crabmeat, picked
4 oz	cream cheese, room temperature
4	anchovy fillets, finely chopped
¼ cup	minced fresh parsley
4 large	egg yolks
1 tsp	salt
½ tsp	pepper
12	frozen phyllo sheets, thawed
~	unsalted butter, melted
1 large	egg, beaten
~	parsley for garnish

Sauté onions in butter for 3 minutes. Add vermouth, heat to boiling, and continue boiling until liquid is reduced by half, 3 to 5 minutes. Remove from heat and add crabmeat, cream cheese, anchovies, parsley, egg yolks, salt, and pepper. Stir until cream cheese is melted, then cool. Preheat oven to 350°. On a kitchen towel, layer 4 phyllo sheets, one on top of the other, brushing each with melted butter. Mound ⅓ of crab mixture lengthwise on phyllo, keeping mixture 2 inches from sides. Starting from long side nearest filling, use towel to roll up phyllo jelly-roll fashion, forming a cylindrical shape. Place completed strudel on buttered shallow baking pan. Repeat with remaining phyllo and crab mixture to make 3 strudels in all. Brush tops with melted butter and beaten egg. Bake at 350° for 15 minutes. To serve, cut each strudel crosswise into 10 slices. Garnish with parsley and serve warm.

Crab Strudels are an elegant first course. They may be pre-baked and frozen for up to one week in advance. After baking, cool the strudels completely, wrap them first in plastic wrap, then in foil, and freeze. At serving time, bake the strudels uncovered at 350° until thoroughly heated.

Mustard Crab Claws
Serves 6

¼ cup	unsalted butter
1 clove	garlic, minced
1 medium	onion, finely chopped
¼ cup	chopped fresh parsley
2 tsp	Creole mustard
60	crab claws
½ tsp	salt
½ tsp	pepper
4 Tbs	brandy (optional)

In a large skillet, melt butter and sauté garlic, onion, parsley, and mustard 5 to 7 minutes, being careful not to brown. Add crab claws and simmer 5 minutes, turning gently until evenly heated and coated with mustard sauce. Season with salt and pepper. Pour brandy over crab claws and flame, if desired. Serve immediately.

Creole Shrimp and Leek Soufflé
Serves 6

4 Tbs	unsalted butter
¾ lb	small shrimp, peeled (1 cup)
1 bunch	leeks, chopped (2 cups)
¼ cup	anise-flavored liqueur
1 pt	heavy cream
2 large	egg yolks
~	Tabasco Sauce to taste
~	salt and pepper to taste
4 large	egg whites
⅛ tsp	salt
1 pinch	cream of tartar
6 thin slices	white bread, cut into triangles and toasted in 250° oven

Preheat oven to 350°. Melt butter in skillet and sauté shrimp until just pink. Remove shrimp and set aside. Sauté leeks in butter. Deglaze with anise-flavored liqueur, add cream, and reduce until thickened. Add shrimp back to sauce and remove from heat. Puree 1 cup of shrimp mixture in food processor. Blend in egg yolks and season with Tabasco, salt and pepper. Beat egg whites with salt and cream of tartar until stiff. Fold beaten egg whites into puree. To assemble, place toast points into 6 small gratin dishes. Spoon unpureed shrimp mixture onto toast and top with soufflé mixture. Bake 8 to 10 minutes.

Joe Middleton and Lee Barnes, developed for Pontchartrain Hotel, New Orleans, LA

Basic Boiled Shrimp
Yields 2 lbs

2 qts	water
½	lemon
½	onion, quartered
1	bay leaf
~	shrimp boil (optional)
2 lbs	shrimp, unpeeled

Bring water with lemon, onion, bay leaf, and shrimp boil (if desired) to a boil and continue to boil for 15 minutes. Add shrimp. Return to a boil, then quickly remove from heat, cover, and allow to rest 5 to 10 minutes. Drain shrimp, cover with ice to cool, and peel.

Mustard Marinated Shrimp
Serves 8-10

Mustard Marinade:

¼ cup	tarragon vinegar
¼ cup	red wine vinegar
1 tsp	black pepper
¼ cup	dry mustard
1 tsp	hot red pepper flakes
2 tsp	salt
¼ cup	vegetable oil
¼ cup	extra virgin olive oil
¼ cup	finely chopped fresh flat-leaf parsley
2 cloves	garlic, minced
6	green onions, chopped
¼ cup	capers, drained
1	lemon, quartered
1	garlic clove, flattened
1 pkg	shrimp boil (3 oz)
2 ½ lbs	medium shrimp, uncooked, peeled
~	crackers and chilled cucumber slices

Whisk together vinegars, black pepper, dry mustard, red pepper flakes, and salt. Slowly pour in oils, continuing to whisk until mixture thickens slightly. Stir in parsley, garlic, green onions, and capers. For the shrimp, boil lemon, garlic, and shrimp boil in 3 quarts water for 5 minutes. Add shrimp to boiling water and cook uncovered just until pink, 1 to 2 minutes. Drain shrimp, cool, and combine with marinade. Cover and refrigerate overnight or up to 2 days. Drain marinade from shrimp and serve with crackers and chilled cucumber slices.

If there is such a thing as haute cuisine in Southern cooking, Basic Boiled Shrimp is not it. Replace that treasured linen tablecloth with spread-out newspapers. Make available plenty of cold beer for sipping, horseradish-laced cocktail sauce for dipping, lemon wedges for squeezing, and paper napkins for quick and frequent clean-ups. Add some conveniently placed trash receptacles for discarded shells, and you're in the party business good and proper.

Shrimp Secret

The most important thing to know about cooking shrimp is when to stop. They're done when they just turn pink. Be extremely vigilant to avoid overcooking.

Garlic Stuffed Jumbo Shrimp
Serves 8

Explaining
Deveining

When deveining is necessary,
shrimp should be uncooked with
shells on. Counting 2 to 3 shell
sections from head end, insert a
toothpick from the side between
two shell plates and through meat
near top outer edge. Lift out the
entire vein, keeping the
meat intact.

40	jumbo shrimp
4 Tbs	unsalted butter, divided
16 cloves	garlic, pressed
1 cup	soft French bread crumbs
1 Tbs	fresh chopped parsley
2 Tbs	finely chopped green onion
1 large	egg, beaten
~	salt and pepper to taste
~	white wine and/or fresh lemon juice to taste
~	parsley or herbs for garnish

This is a lightly textured,
more delicate variation on
traditional recipes for stuffed
shrimp.

Peel, devein, and butterfly 32 shrimp, leaving tails on. Peel and devein remaining 8 shrimp completely. Preheat oven to 400°. Sauté 8 fully peeled shrimp in 2 tablespoons butter over low heat until pink , 2 to 3 minutes. Remove from pan and chop. Blend chopped shrimp with garlic, bread crumbs, parsley, onions, and egg. Toss lightly to coat. Add butter from sauté pan, then salt, pepper, and wine or lemon juice (stuffing should be lightly moistened, not dense or compacted). Place rounded teaspoon of stuffing onto widest part of each butterflied shrimp. Bring tail fin over and press lightly into stuffing. Arrange 4 shrimp in each of 8 buttered ramekins. Drizzle with additional melted butter and bake 5 to 10 minutes, until shrimp are pink and stuffing juices appear. Sprinkle with fresh parsley or herbs and serve immediately.

Shrimp Paté with Horseradish Sauce
Yields 8 cups

Horseradish Sauce

Yields 1 cup

1 cup	catsup
2 Tbs	horseradish
2 tsp	fresh lemon juice

Thoroughly blend all
ingredients and chill.

4 lbs	medium shrimp, cooked, peeled, and chopped
1 medium	white onion, finely chopped
1/2 cup	unsalted butter, melted
2/3 cup	mayonnaise
5 Tbs	fresh lemon juice
~	Tabasco Sauce to taste
~	garlic salt to taste
~	Horseradish Sauce (see accompanying recipe)
~	wheat crackers

Combine shrimp and onion with melted butter. Add mayonnaise, lemon juice, Tabasco, and garlic salt and mix well. Coat paté mold with mayonnaise, fill with shrimp mixture, and refrigerate until firm. To serve, unmold chilled paté onto serving plate and pour Horseradish Sauce over. Serve with crackers.

Seafood in Salsa

Serves 6

3	fresh tomatoes, peeled, seeded and diced, or 1 can whole tomatoes (16 oz), drained, diced
½ cup	fresh lime juice
1 Tbs	sugar
1 tsp	salt
10 drops	Tabasco Sauce
½ tsp	cumin
1 clove	garlic, minced
2 Tbs	extra virgin olive oil
1 medium	red onion, finely diced, chilled
½ medium	green bell pepper, finely diced, chilled
1	jalapeño pepper, chopped (optional)
24 large	oysters, uncooked, shucked, chilled and/or shrimp, cooked, peeled, chilled
~	fresh cilantro or parsley for garnish

Puree tomatoes, lime juice, sugar, salt, Tabasco, cumin, garlic, and olive oil in food processor. Blend onion, bell pepper, and jalapeño into tomato sauce. Chill. To serve, place four oysters and/or shrimp in cocktail glass. Pour sauce over seafood and garnish with cilantro or parsley.

Grilled Oysters Busche-Style

Serves 6

½ cup	unsalted butter, melted
1 small	onion, finely chopped
3 cloves	garlic, minced
1 tsp	lemon pepper seasoning
2 Tbs	chopped, fresh parsley
24	oysters, uncooked, shucked

Combine melted butter, onion, garlic, lemon pepper and parsley. Fill muffin tins ⅓ full with onion mixture and top with 1 large oyster or 2 small ones. Place muffin tins on grill and cook 5 to 10 minutes or until oysters turn white and barely curl at edges.

Some Pearls of Wisdom About Oysters

The old wives' tale about eating oysters only during "R" months is outdated. Today's oysters are in season almost 11 months a year due to good private reefs and refrigeration. Oysters are not available when they are spawning during the heat of late summer— generally, the first 10 days of July and the last 10 days of August.

~

When purchasing oysters in the shell, look for tightly closed shells or shells that close tightly when tapped, indicating that the oysters are alive. Open shells mean that the oysters are dead or inedible.

~

Shucked oysters should be plump and creamy. Their liquor should be clear instead of milky, and the odor should be fresh and mild. Always keep oysters chilled.

~

One pint of shucked oysters equals two dozen oysters.

Seafood Coquille

Serves 4

6 Tbs	unsalted butter, divided
12	oysters, uncooked
12 large	shrimp, uncooked, peeled, deveined
½ cup	chopped fresh parsley
5 medium	green onions, chopped
1 small	onion, chopped
1 cup	white wine
1 Tbs	all-purpose flour
~	salt and pepper to taste
8	fresh mushrooms, chopped
2 Tbs	fresh lemon juice
2 large	egg yolks
½ cup	half & half
~	Parmesan cheese, freshly grated

Seafood Coquille can be prepared a day in advance and refrigerated, but be sure to bring it to room temperature before broiling. This recipe should not be frozen.

In medium saucepan, melt 4 tablespoons butter and cook oysters, shrimp, parsley, and onions over high heat at first, then medium heat, for 5 minutes. Add wine, lower heat, and simmer 5 minutes. Strain seafood, saving pan juices. Add 1 tablespoon butter and flour to pan juices and cook, stirring constantly, 5 minutes. Return seafood to pan, heat for 1 minute, then add salt and pepper. Cover and set aside to cool. In a separate saucepan, sauté mushrooms in 1 tablespoon butter for 2 minutes. Add lemon juice and simmer 3 minutes. To the cooled seafood mixture, add egg yolks beaten into half & half. Cook seafood mixture over low heat until thickened (do not boil). Combine seafood and mushroom mixtures, spoon into coquille shells or ramekins, and sprinkle with freshly grated cheese. Brown under broiler and serve hot.

Soft-Shell Crawfish in Praline Sauce

Serves 4

12	soft-shelled crawfish
1 can	artichoke bottoms (14 oz), drained
1 cup	buttermilk
½ tsp	salt
½ tsp	pepper
2 cups	all-purpose flour, seasoned with salt and pepper
6 Tbs	unsalted butter
~	Praline Sauce (see accompanying recipe)
2 Tbs	chopped pecans for garnish

Remove heads from crawfish. Soak crawfish and artichoke bottoms for 30 minutes in buttermilk that has been seasoned with salt and pepper. Drain and dredge in seasoned flour. Pan fry crawfish and artichoke bottoms in butter until golden brown, about 5 minutes each side, and drain on paper towels. On individual plates, arrange crawfish atop artichokes. Spoon over Praline Sauce, garnish with pecans, and serve immediately.

Crawfish Cardinale

Serves 8-10

1 lb	crawfish tails
8 Tbs	unsalted butter, divided
1 medium	white onion, chopped (1 cup)
3 Tbs	all-purpose flour
1 Tbs	tomato paste
½ pt	half & half
¼ cup	white wine
2 Tbs	chopped fresh parsley
½ tsp	salt
½ tsp	white pepper
¼ tsp	cayenne pepper
~	Melba rounds and crackers for serving
~	chopped fresh parsley for garnish
~	paprika

Sauté crawfish in 4 tablespoons butter for 10 minutes and set aside. In remaining butter, sauté onion for 10 minutes, then add flour and tomato paste and blend well. Add half & half, wine, parsley, crawfish, salt, and peppers. Continue cooking 5 minutes. Serve in chafing dish with Melba rounds and crackers. Garnish with fresh parsley and paprika.

Praline Sauce

Yields 1 ½ cups

1 Tbs	minced shallots
1 Tbs	minced garlic
¼ cup	clarified unsalted butter
¼ cup	pecans, chopped
3 sprigs	fresh thyme (½ tsp dried)
1 ½ tsp	black peppercorns
4 sprigs	fresh mint , whole
⅓ cup	dry white wine
2 Tbs	praline-flavored liqueur
2 cups	heavy cream
2 sprigs	fresh mint , chopped

Sauté shallots and garlic in butter over medium heat until golden. Add pecans, thyme, peppercorns, and whole mint sprigs and sauté 1 minute. Add wine and cook 1 minute, stirring. Heat liqueur in a small pan over low heat until warm. Ignite and pour quickly over shallot mixture. Boil until reduced by half. Stir in cream and reduce by half again. Add chopped mint sprigs and keep warm to serve immediately or store refrigerated.

Crawfish Cardinale also has excellent entreé potential when ladled over a half-pound of cooked spinach fettucine— serves 6.

Salmon and Vegetable Smorgasbord
Serves 10-12

Spread:

2 pkgs	cream cheese (16 oz total), room temperature
½ cup	unsalted butter, room temperature
2 Tbs	heavy cream
1 Tbs	Hungarian paprika

Toppings:

2 bunches	green onions, finely chopped (2 cups)
2 pkgs	radishes, finely chopped (2 cups)
2 medium	cucumbers, finely chopped (2 cups)
2 cups	capers, drained
1 lb	smoked salmon, sliced
~	lettuce leaves or alfalfa sprouts for garnish
~	dark pumpernickel bread in small slices

This dish is an effective icebreaker at parties. Guests can't help but engage in conversation as they attempt to determine just how many tempting toppings can be stacked on a single slice of pumpernickel. Before you know it, conviviality will be bursting out all over!

Blend cream cheese, butter, and heavy cream until smooth. Add paprika and refrigerate several hours or overnight. To serve, place cheese mixture in bowl in center of serving platter. Surround with separate beds of lettuce or alfalfa sprouts for mounds of green onions, radishes, cucumbers, capers, and salmon. Accompany with pumpernickel slices.

Dilled Caper Sauce for Seafood
Yields 1 ½ cups

VERY GOOD

1 cup	mayonnaise
2 Tbs	Dijon mustard
2 Tbs	capers, drained
1 Tbs	fresh lemon juice
1 Tbs	chopped fresh dill (1 tsp dried)
~	smoked salmon, cooked shrimp or crab claws
~	crackers for serving

Try adding a pound of picked lump crabmeat to create a delightful dip for crackers, Melba toast, or raw vegetables.

Combine mayonnaise, Dijon mustard, capers, lemon juice and dill. Serve with salmon, shrimp, or crab claws and crackers.

HOLIDAY COCKTAIL BUFFET

Peppered Beef and Yummy Rolls

~

Herb Cheese Cake

~

Brie with Cranberry Marmalade and Fresh Fruit Slices

~

Snow Peas with Honey Mustard and Pecans

~

Tortellini with Parsley-Caper Sauce

~

Oyster-Artichoke Dip

~

Mustard Crab Claws

~

Chocolate Paté with Short'nin' Bread

~

Grand Marnier Custard Squares

"Life in the
Mississippi executive
mansion during the
[Governor William]
McWillie residency
[1857-1859] gave no
indication of the
impending crisis [the
Civil War]. McWillie's
inaugural reception and
dinner must rank as one
of the grand affairs for
which the mansion was
by then well known and
its reputation well
deserved. Included on
the menu were
three gallons of rum,
15 gallons of brandy,
two gallons
of champagne,
20 pounds of cheese,
33 pounds of mutton,
28 pounds of beef,
10 dozen oysters,
10 large cakes, and an
unspecified quantity of
small cakes, candy,
bread, crackers, etc."

A History of
the Mississippi Governor's Mansion
by David G. Sansing
and Carroll Waller

PHOTO:
This doorway opens onto
the dining room at the
Mississippi Governor's Mansion.
The lavish carvings were modeled
after examples in
Beauties of Modern Architecture
by Minard Lafever,
published in 1835.

Herb Cheese Cake

Serves 50

Crust:

1 cup	all-purpose flour
1/2 cup	unsalted butter, chilled
1/2 tsp	salt
1 large	egg yolk
2 tsp	grated lemon zest

Filling:

2 cloves	garlic
1 large	onion, coarsely chopped
2/3 cup	chopped fresh parsley
3 oz	freshly grated Parmesan cheese (3/4 cup)
3 pkgs	cream cheese, room temperature (24 oz total)
3 Tbs	all-purpose flour
4 large	eggs
2 tsp	salt
1/2 tsp	Tabasco Sauce
2 Tbs	fresh lemon juice
1 Tbs	chopped fresh oregano (1 tsp dried)
1 Tbs	chopped fresh tarragon (1 tsp dried)
1 Tbs	chopped fresh basil (1 tsp dried)
1/2 Tbs	chopped fresh rosemary (1/2 tsp dried)
1/2 cup	chopped pepperoni
~	fresh herbs for garnish
~	wafer crackers for serving

For the crust, in food processor, blend flour, butter, salt, egg yolk, and lemon zest to a cornmeal-like consistency. Remove dough from bowl and knead lightly. Shape into ball, wrap in waxed paper, and refrigerate until slightly chilled. Evenly press 1/3 of dough into bottom of 8" springform pan and press remaining dough around sides. Store in freezer while preparing filling.

Chop garlic in processor, add onion, then parsley and Parmesan cheese. Add cream cheese, one package at a time, and process. Add flour and 1 egg and continue processing until smooth. Add remaining 3 eggs, one at a time, blending well after each addition. Add salt, Tabasco, lemon juice, and herbs, processing just until blended. Stir in pepperoni and pour into dough-lined pan. Bake at 400° for 10 minutes, reduce temperature to 325°, and bake 50 minutes longer. Let stand 1 hour before serving. Garnish with fresh herbs and serve with plain wafer crackers.

An adaptation of a classic by Shirley Corriher, food chemist and cooking instructor, Atlanta, GA

Apple and Havarti Quesadilla

Serves 12

1 large	Granny Smith apple, peeled, cored, and thinly sliced
1/4	red bell pepper, chopped
3	green onions, chopped
1 1/2 Tbs	unsalted butter
1/4 tsp	cayenne pepper
1/4 tsp	salt
2 tsp	cider vinegar
1 clove	garlic, minced
1 tsp	brown sugar
4	flour tortillas (9")
8 oz	Havarti cheese, thinly sliced
1 large	egg, beaten
2 Tbs	unsalted butter

Over medium heat, sauté apple, bell pepper, and onions in butter until softened. Add cayenne pepper, salt, vinegar, garlic, and brown sugar. Heat to blend, 2 to 3 minutes. Preheat broiler. Place tortillas on rack and heat until softened, 30 seconds to 1 minute. Arrange cheese slices over half of each tortilla, leaving 1/2" border. Top cheese with apple mixture. Brush tortilla edge with egg and fold each tortilla in half, pressing to seal. In a skillet over medium heat, melt butter and cook quesadillas in batches until golden brown, 1 1/2 minutes on each side. Drain on paper towels, cut into eighths. Serve warm—may be reheated.

Cheddar Walnut Toasts

Yields 64

12 oz	sharp cheddar cheese, shredded
4 Tbs	unsalted butter, room temperature
1/4 cup	medium dry sherry
1/2 tsp	salt
~	Tabasco Sauce to taste
1 1/2 cups	walnuts, lightly toasted, finely chopped
8	whole wheat pita loaves (6"), halved horizontally, cut into wedges, and toasted

Substituting pecans for the walnuts will give this dish a more pronounced Southern accent.

Cream together cheese, butter, sherry, salt, and Tabasco, then stir in walnuts. Spread cheese mixture on toasted pita wedges and broil 1 to 2 minutes, until topping is lightly browned and bubbly.

Brie with Cranberry Marmalade
Serves 12

Marmalade:

1 pkg	cranberries (12 oz)
3/4 cup	firmly packed, light brown sugar
1/3 cup	dried currants
1/3 cup	water
1/4 tsp	dry mustard
1/4 tsp	ground allspice
1/4 tsp	ground cloves
1/4 tsp	ground ginger
1 wheel	Brie cheese, 8" diameter
~	crackers and fruit slices for serving

Combine all ingredients except Brie in heavy non-aluminum saucepan. Cook over medium-high heat, stirring frequently, until most berries burst, 5 minutes. Cool to room temperature, cover, and refrigerate (may be stored up to 3 days at this point). Cut a circle in top rind only of Brie, leaving a 1/2" border of rind on top. Place cheese on foil-lined cookie sheet and spread with cranberry marmalade. Cover and refrigerate up to six hours. Preheat oven to 300°. Bake cheese until soft, about 12 minutes. Serve on platter surrounded with crackers and fruit slices.

Parmesan Rounds
Yields 150

2 loaves	thinly sliced white bread
~	unsalted butter
2 pkgs	cream cheese (16 oz total), room temperature
1/2 cup	unsalted butter, room temperature
1/3 cup	mayonnaise
6	green onions, chopped
~	freshly grated Parmesan cheese

Cut four 1 1/2" circles from each bread slice. Butter one side of each circle and arrange in single layer, buttered side up, on baking sheet. Broil until lightly toasted, then turn and toast unbuttered sides. Cool on rack. Combine cream cheese, butter, mayonnaise, and green onions. Spread 1 teaspoon cream cheese mixture over buttered sides of bread circles and dip into Parmesan cheese. Preheat broiler and arrange rounds on baking sheet. Broil until bubbly and golden, 5 minutes, and serve immediately.

Cheddar Beef Crisps
Serves 6-8

4 oz	cheddar cheese, shredded
2 1/2 oz	dried beef or dried pastrami, chopped
1 cup	mayonnaise
1 small can	pitted ripe olives (3 1/4 oz), sliced
~	crisp rye crackers

Blend cheese, beef, mayonnaise and olives. Preheat oven to 375°. Spread on crackers and bake for 3 to 5 minutes or until cheese is bubbly. Cheese mixture may be prepared ahead of time and refrigerated, then spread on crackers just before baking.

Four-Cheese Fritters
Serves 20

8 oz	Swiss cheese, shredded
8 oz	mozzarella cheese, shredded
8 oz	Parmesan cheese, grated (2 cups)
6 oz	cottage cheese
10 large	eggs, lightly beaten
~	pepper to taste
1/2 bunch	fresh parsley, chopped
1 Tbs	cayenne pepper
1 Tbs	salt
1 cup	all-purpose flour
~	vegetable oil for deep frying

Combine all ingredients except vegetable oil and mix well. For each fritter, carefully drop 1 heaping tablespoon of cheese mixture into hot oil. Fry until fritters are golden, 3 minutes. Drain and serve immediately with a marinara sauce.

§ Coon Cheese Squares
Yields 80

1 loaf white sandwich bread, thinly sliced
1/4 cup unsalted butter
10 oz coon cheese
3 large egg whites, stiffly beaten

~

Remove bread crusts and cut slices into quarters. Over low heat, melt butter and cheese together, then remove from heat. While cheese mixture is hot, fold in beaten egg whites. Dip bread quarters into cheese mixture, place on wax paper, and refrigerate overnight. Broil until golden brown on each side.

~

The overnight refrigeration period is necessary for this dish. It can also be prepared up to the cooking point and stored in the freezer for quick and easy snacks.

Delta Cheese Rolls
Yields 24

1 lb	extra sharp cheddar cheese, shredded
1/3 cup	mayonnaise
2 Tbs	milk
1 Tbs	dried parsley
6	green onions, finely chopped
1 Tbs	Worcestershire sauce
1/2 tsp	Tabasco Sauce
1/2 tsp	onion powder
1/2 tsp	garlic powder
1/2 tsp	seasoned salt
1/2 tsp	black pepper
1/2 tsp	cayenne pepper
1 loaf	sliced white bread, crusts removed
1/2 cup	unsalted butter, melted

These are a Mississippi Delta tradition at lunch with soup or salad, as a savory accompaniment to tea, or for a good, hot bite at a cocktail party.

Combine all ingredients except bread and melted butter. For each roll, flatten one slice of bread with a rolling pin and spread with cheese mixture. Roll bread diagonally and secure with a toothpick. Place rolls on cookie sheet and brush with melted butter. Bake at 375° until cheese is melted and bread is golden brown, 10 to 12 minutes .

Bulldog Blitz
Yields 40

8 oz	sharp cheddar cheese, shredded, room temperature
1/2 cup	unsalted butter, room temperature
1 1/2 cups	cake flour
1/2 tsp	salt
1/2 tsp	cayenne pepper
2 Tbs	cold water (if needed)
1 pkg	pitted dates (16 oz)
40	pecan halves

Named in honor of the Mississippi State University Bulldogs football team, these chewy/crunchy treats make an unusual holiday confection when one end is dipped in melted chocolate to resemble acorns.

They will keep for several weeks in a closed container, and freeze well.

Preheat oven to 400°. Cream together cheese and butter and blend in flour, salt, and pepper. If dough is too stiff, add 2 tablespoons cold water. Stuff dates with pecan halves and cover with dough to make balls. Arrange on ungreased cookie sheet and bake 10 to 15 minutes.

Stuffed Tomatoes with Spinach and Ricotta

Yields 48

3 tsp	extra virgin olive oil
1 medium	yellow onion, finely chopped
1 pkg	frozen spinach (10 oz), thawed, drained, and squeezed to remove moisture
~	salt and pepper to taste
1/8 tsp	nutmeg
1 cup	ricotta cheese (8 oz)
2 large	egg yolks
1/2 cup	pine nuts
1 oz	freshly grated Parmesan cheese (1/4 cup)
1/2 cup	chopped flat-leaf parsley
48	Cherry Tomato Cups (see accompanying recipe)
~	Parmesan cheese for topping

Cherry Tomato Cups

Remove tops of tomatoes and scoop out seeds and partitions, being careful not to pierce sides. Salt cavities and allow to drain upside down on paper towel for 30 minutes.

Cook onion in olive oil over low heat, covered, until tender and lightly colored, 15 minutes. Chop spinach and add to onions. Season with salt, pepper, and nutmeg. Cover and continue to cook on low heat for 10 more minutes, stirring occasionally. Beat together ricotta cheese and egg yolks thoroughly. Add spinach mixture, pine nuts, Parmesan cheese, and parsley. Season with salt and pepper. Preheat oven to 350°. Blot tomato cup cavities with paper towel, spoon spinach mixture into each one, and top with Parmesan. Bake in upper third of oven until hot and bubbly, 10 minutes.

Onion Sandwiches

~	firm white bread, thinly sliced
~	mayonnaise
~	sweet mild onions, thinly sliced
~	freshly ground black pepper to taste
~	minced fresh parsley

Cut bread into circles—do not use the crust. Thinly coat one side of each circle with mayonnaise. For each sandwich, place 1 onion slice on a bread circle, sprinkle with salt and pepper, and top with another circle. Brush the edge of each sandwich with mayonnaise, then roll the edge in minced parsley. Arrange sandwiches on a platter and cover with a damp dish towel until serving time.

These delectable Onion Sandwiches perfectly illustrate the virtues of simplicity. Be sure to make plenty, because we guarantee there won't be enough.

Tortellini with Parsley-Caper Sauce
Serves 6-10

The Italians have produced an almost infinite assortment of pasta in various sizes and clever shapes. Tortellini, "little hats," come stuffed with a variety of fillings.

1 clove	garlic
2 Tbs	sunflower seeds, without hulls
1 oz	freshly grated Parmesan cheese (¼ cup)
2 Tbs	capers, drained
¾ cup	flat-leaf parsley, tightly packed
½ cup	extra virgin olive oil (or more)
~	salt and pepper to taste
½ lb	small tortellini, meat or cheese, cooked

For the sauce, process garlic clove in food processor 10 seconds. Add sunflower seeds, grated cheese, capers, and parsley and process to a coarse puree. With machine running, add ½ cup olive oil in a thin stream. Salt and pepper to taste. Combine tortellini with sauce and heat thoroughly, tossing to coat. Serve in a warm, shallow bowl with toothpicks or small skewers.

Snow Peas with Honey Mustard and Pecans
Yields 50

Yogurt Cheese

Yields 1 ½ cups

2 cups	plain yogurt
~	cheese cloth

Place a colander inside a large bowl and line with cheesecloth. Spoon yogurt into colander and allow to drain overnight in refrigerator.

Yogurt Cheese may be used as a substitute for sour cream or cream cheese.

1 ½ cups	pecan halves
¼ cup	unsalted butter, melted
½ tsp	cayenne pepper
¼ tsp	salt
1 ½ cups	Yogurt Cheese (see accompanying recipe)
4 tsp	honey mustard
2 tsp	brown sugar
~	salt to taste
~	cayenne pepper to taste
50	snowpeas, stemmed, strings removed, blanched

Preheat oven to 300°. Toss pecan halves in melted butter, cayenne, and salt and toast in oven until lightly golden, 5 to 10 minutes (do not overcook—pecans will darken as they cool). Finely chop cooled pecans and place in shallow dish. Combine Yogurt Cheese, mustard, brown sugar, salt, and cayenne and spoon mixture into pastry bag. Slice each snowpea open along straight side and pipe yogurt mixture into pea pods. Dip stuffing edge of each pea pod into chopped pecans. Arrange pea pods on serving platter, cover, and refrigerate until ready to serve.

Pesto Stuffed Mushrooms

Yields 25

Pesto:

4 ½ cups	fresh basil, loosely packed
1 cup	extra virgin olive oil
½ cup	pine nuts
5 cloves	garlic
2 tsp	salt
4 oz	freshly grated Parmesan cheese (1 cup)
~	fresh mushrooms, cleaned, stems removed
~	cream cheese

For the pesto sauce, puree basil, olive oil, pine nuts, garlic, and salt in food processor until smooth. Stir in freshly grated Parmesan cheese and refrigerate if not to be used immediately. To assemble, fill each mushroom cap with cream cheese and top with dollop of pesto sauce. Heat under broiler until hot and bubbly.

Pesto Ideas

Pesto is a versatile sauce with many applications. Here are two more:

~

Layer cream cheese, pesto, and sun-dried tomatoes in a small loaf pan or 6" springform pan. Chill and turn out to serve as a spread with firm, salty crackers.

~

Top halved French bread with cream cheese, pesto, and sun-dried tomatoes. Heat at 450° for 5 minutes, cut into wedges, and serve as an appetizer.

Mushroom Puffs

Yields 48

2 pkgs	crescent dinner rolls
1 pkg	cream cheese (8 oz), room temperature
1 can	mushrooms (4 oz), drained, chopped
2	green onions, chopped
1 tsp	seasoned salt
1 large	egg, beaten
2 Tbs	poppy seeds

Preheat oven to 375°. Lay out crescent roll dough and press perforations to seal. Mix cream cheese, mushrooms, onions, and salt and spread over dough. Roll up jelly roll fashion and slice into 1" pieces. Brush with egg, sprinkle with poppy seeds, and bake at 375° for 10 minutes. Serve hot.

This recipe can be prepared ahead up to the baking point and then frozen until time to cook. In fact, the mushroom roll is easier to slice if it's frozen.

Autumn Pumpkin Tureen
Serves 8

1	pumpkin (4 lb), washed and dried
2 Tbs	vegetable oil
2 cloves	garlic, minced
6 oz	baby Swiss cheese, shredded
4 slices	white bread, toasted, crumbled
2 oz	mozzarella cheese, shredded
1 pt	half & half
1 tsp	salt
½ tsp	pepper
½ tsp	freshly grated nutmeg
~	French bread fingers, buttered, toasted, for dipping

Preheat oven to 350°. With serrated knife, cut 2" slice from top of pumpkin and reserve. Remove seeds and fibers. Blend oil and garlic and rub into interior of pumpkin, then place in a large roasting pan. Alternate layers of toast crumbs and cheeses inside pumpkin. Combine half & half, salt, pepper, and nutmeg and pour over layers. Replace top and bake pumpkin 2 hours, gently stirring contents after 1 ½ hours. For a fondue, accompany with French bread fingers for dipping. By using a larger pumpkin, the recipe may be doubled.

The visually distinctive presentation of this dip can also add flair to a dinner table. When serving as a side dish, scoop out pumpkin flesh along with cheese mixture.

Caramelized Onion Dip
Serves 6

VERY GOOD !

1 Tbs	unsalted butter
1 Tbs	peanut oil
1 large	red onion, quartered, thinly sliced
½ cup	sour cream
½ cup	mayonnaise
¼ tsp	salt
¼ tsp	cayenne pepper
1 tsp	red pepper flakes
⅛ tsp	Tabasco Sauce
~	crackers for serving

Sauté onion in butter and oil until caramelized (golden brown), 20 minutes. Cool and combine with remaining ingredients. Mix well and chill for at least 1 hour. Serve with crackers.

Vidalia Onion Cheese Dip

Serves 12-15

3 large	Vidalia onions, coarsely chopped
2 Tbs	unsalted butter
1 cup	mayonnaise
8 oz	sharp cheddar cheese, shredded
½ tsp	Tabasco Sauce
1 clove	garlic, minced
~	tortilla chips or crackers for serving

Preheat oven to 375°. Sauté onions in butter. Blend with mayonnaise, cheese, Tabasco, and garlic. Pour into buttered casserole and bake at 375° for 25 minutes. Serve with tortilla chips or crackers.

There seem to be some mystical properties in the soil and climate around Vidalia, Georgia, where the supremely sweet Vidalia onion is grown. These large, pale yellow onions, which can be eaten out of the hand like an apple, are generally available in the South from May through June. Mail order has made possible the enlightenment of palates in more distant regions.

Zucchini Cheese Spread

Yields 2 cups

4 oz	sharp cheddar cheese, shredded
1 small	zucchini, grated (1 cup)
¾ cup	mayonnaise
½ cup	toasted walnuts, chopped
1 tsp	fresh lemon juice
1 Tbs	fresh oregano, chopped (1 tsp dried)
6 drops	Tabasco Sauce
~	crackers or crudités for serving

Combine all ingredients and refrigerate for 1 hour or overnight. Serve with firm, salty crackers or crudités.

Monterey Jack Salsa

Serves 4-6

1 can	green chilies (4 oz), chopped
1 can	black olives (3 ¼ oz), chopped
4	green onions, chopped
¼ lb	Monterey Jack cheese, shredded
1	tomato, chopped
½ cup	Italian salad dressing
¼ cup	chopped fresh cilantro
~	tortilla chips for serving

Blend all ingredients and serve with tortilla chips.

Herb Dip with Asparagus
Serves 6

Herb Hints

To dry fresh herbs in the microwave, first clean and air them dry. Then place them on a paper towel and cook 4 minutes on HIGH. If herbs are still moist, turn them and dry a few minutes more. They should be bright green with lots of essence.

~

Freezing is an easy way to preserve herbs. In fact, some herbs that do not dry well, such as basil, fennel, dill, parsley, chives, and tarragon, will freeze very successfully. Some darkening may occur, but the flavor will remain intact.

1 pkg	cream cheese (8 oz), room temperature
1/3 cup	sour cream, or more
3	green onions, chopped
2 Tbs	capers, drained
2 Tbs	finely chopped fresh parsley
1 Tbs	Dijon mustard
1/8 tsp	dried tarragon
1/8 tsp	dried basil
1/8 tsp	dried marjoram
~	salt and pepper to taste
1 tsp	lemon pepper seasoning
2 lbs	thin asparagus, blanched, for dipping

VERY GOOD

Combine all ingredients except asparagus and blend until smooth, using just enough sour cream to achieve a soft consistency. Cover and chill. Serve with blanched asparagus for dipping.

Dijon Dip
Yields 1 cup

VERY GOOD

2 cloves	garlic
1 Tbs	chopped onion
4 Tbs	Dijon mustard
3 Tbs	red wine vinegar
1 Tbs	white wine vinegar
1/4 tsp	salt
1 Tbs	fresh basil or oregano (1 tsp dried)
1/8 tsp	black pepper
2 drops	Tabasco Sauce
1/4 cup	safflower oil
~	fresh basil or oregano for garnish
~	raw vegetables for dipping

In food processor, finely chop garlic and onion. Add mustard and vinegars; blend well. Then blend in salt, basil, pepper, and Tabasco. With machine running, add oil very slowly. Refrigerate until ready to serve. Garnish with fresh herbs and serve with vegetables for dipping.

Blue Cheese Avocado Dip

Serves 6-8

2 Tbs	chopped onion
2	avocados, peeled, pitted
1 ½ tsp	fresh lemon juice
1 ½ cups	sour cream (12 oz total)
¼ cup	blue cheese, crumbled
~	salt and pepper to taste
~	tortilla chips, crackers, or crudités for serving

Puree onion, avocados, and lemon juice in food processor. Blend with sour cream, cheese, salt, and pepper. Chill 1 hour. After chilling, adjust seasoning to taste and serve with tortilla chips, crackers, or crudités.

Place avocado pit in dip while chilling to maintain fresh green color.

Oyster Artichoke Dip

Serves 30

¼ cup	unsalted butter, melted
⅓ cup	extra virgin olive oil
¾ cup	all-purpose flour
6 cloves	garlic, minced
3 stalks	celery, chopped
5 cans	artichoke hearts (70 oz total), drained, chopped
1 tsp	dried thyme
1 tsp	dried oregano
1 tsp	dried basil
½ gallon	oysters, drained, their liquor reserved
1 pt	whipping cream
2 Tbs	chopped fresh parsley
~	salt to taste
~	crushed red pepper to taste
~	firm, salty crackers for serving

Make a roux by combining melted butter with olive oil and flour. Microwave on HIGH until golden brown, stirring every 1 ½ minutes. Add garlic and celery and microwave on HIGH until soft, about 2 minutes. Add oyster liquor and microwave on HIGH until thickened, stirring at 1 ½ minute intervals. Add artichoke hearts, thyme, oregano, and basil and microwave on HIGH for 1 ½ minutes. Add oysters, cream, parsley, salt, and red pepper. Microwave on HIGH for 1 ½ minutes or until oysters barely curl. Serve hot with firm, salty crackers.

PHOTO (left): *Quiet, tree-shaded Gillespie Street, where the home of Frank and Ivey Alley is located, lies within Jackson's Belhaven area, an 80-year-old monument to architectural diversity and neighborhood preservation.*

PHOTO (overleaf):

Chilled Shrimp and Dill-Cucumber Bisque

Cucumber Avocado Bisque with

Roasted Red Pepper Soup

S O U P S

Chilled Shrimp and Dill-Cucumber Bisque
Serves 4-6

2 large	cucumbers, peeled, coarsely chopped
¼ cup	red wine vinegar
1 Tbs	sugar
1 tsp	salt
1 lb	medium shrimp, uncooked, peeled
2 Tbs	unsalted butter
¼ cup	dry white vermouth
1 Tbs	fresh lemon juice
½ tsp	salt
½ tsp	pepper
1 ½ cups	buttermilk, chilled
⅓ cup	chopped fresh dill (1 Tbs dried)
~	additional fresh dill for garnish

Toss cucumbers with vinegar, sugar, and salt. Let stand 30 minutes. Sauté shrimp in butter just until pink, 2 to 3 minutes. Remove shrimp and reserve. Add vermouth and lemon juice to skillet and boil until reduced to a few spoonfuls. Pour sauce over shrimp and season with salt and pepper. Drain cucumbers and process briefly in food processor. Add buttermilk and continue processing until smooth. Add fresh dill and process 1 second more. Combine soup with shrimp and sauce, cover, and refrigerate until very cold. Adjust seasonings and serve in chilled bowls. Garnish with additional fresh dill.

Joe Middleton, executive chef, Nick's Restaurant; former executive chef, MS Governor's Mansion, Jackson, MS

More Herb Hints

Pick fresh herbs in the morning, just after the dew has dried.

~

Always snip your herbs with scissors.

~

Dried and fresh herbs may be used interchangeably in most recipes. Three units of fresh herbs equals one unit of dried.

~

To release full flavor of herbs, gently crush desired amount before adding to recipe.

~

To avoid overcooking and insure fullest flavor, add herbs only in the last 30 minutes of cooking.

Spinach-Oyster Soup
Serves 8

1/4 cup	unsalted butter
1/2 medium	onion, chopped
2 cloves	garlic, minced
1/2 cup	all-purpose flour
2 1/2 cups	half & half, heated
1 cup	chicken stock
1 pkg	frozen chopped spinach (10 oz), thawed, drained
1 pt	oysters, drained, chopped
~	salt, black pepper, cayenne pepper to taste

Sauté onion and garlic in butter over medium heat. Add flour and cook, stirring, 3 minutes. Add half & half and continue to cook, stirring, until smooth, 2 to 3 minutes. Remove from heat. Mix chicken stock and spinach in blender and combine with onion mixture. Add oysters and simmer until oysters begin to curl. Season to taste and serve hot.

Fresh Corn and Crab Bisque
Serves 6

1/2 cup	unsalted butter
1/2 cup	all-purpose flour
3 cups	shrimp stock or clam juice
2 cups	chicken stock
1 tsp	liquid crab boil
4 ears	fresh yellow corn, kernels and juice
1/2 pt	heavy cream
1 lb	fresh lump crabmeat, picked
~	salt and pepper to taste
1 Tbs	Creole seasoning
1 tsp	lemon pepper seasoning
1 bunch	green onions, chopped, divided

Melt butter in saucepan, add flour, and cook, stirring constantly, until flour sticks to pan. Add stocks and crab boil. Bring to a boil, stirring constantly, then lower heat and simmer 15 minutes. Add corn kernels and juice and continue simmering 15 minutes more. Add cream and blend well. Gently add crabmeat, salt and pepper, Creole seasoning, lemon pepper, and 1/2 cup green onions. Remove from heat and let stand for 15 minutes. To serve, ladle bisque into bowls and top with remaining green onions.

Cream of Crawfish Soup

Serves 8-10

½ cup	unsalted butter
1 large	onion, chopped
4 stalks	celery, chopped
2 Tbs	seafood seasoning
2 lbs	crawfish tails, cooked, divided
2 cups	shrimp stock or clam juice
~	salt and pepper to taste
2 pts	half & half
½ cup	white wine
~	lime slices for garnish

Sauté onion and celery in butter 10 minutes over medium heat. Add seafood seasoning and cook, stirring, 5 minutes. Add 1 pound crawfish tails and shrimp stock and cook 5 minutes. Puree mixture and season to taste. Add half & half, reheat, and add wine and remaining crawfish tails. Serve hot, garnished with lime slices.

JoAnn Hanson, owner and chef, The Plantation Café, Pass Christian, MS

Salmon Chowder

Serves 8-10

4 large	potatoes, diced
4	carrots, diced
2 large	white onions, diced
1 ½ qts	water
½ lb	bacon, cooked, diced
1 tsp	freshly ground black pepper
½ tsp	cayenne pepper
1 lb	salmon, bones and skin removed, in bite-sized pieces
1 pt	heavy cream
1 can	creamed corn (17 oz)
½ cup	unsalted butter
1 ½ tsp	salt
~	chopped fresh parsley for garnish

In a covered pot, boil potatoes, carrots, and onions in water 20 minutes. Add bacon and boil 10 more minutes. Add peppers and boil 10 more minutes. Add salmon, reduce heat, and simmer 20 minutes. Add cream, corn, butter, and salt and continue to simmer until well blended and heated through (do not allow to boil). Garnish with parsley and serve.

Crawfish Facts

Crawfish are generally in season from December to June.

~

Six pounds of whole crawfish equal one pound of tail meat.

~

Crawfish do not freeze well. Whole crawfish can be frozen for only 4 to 5 weeks before the fat turns rancid. Crawfish tails can be frozen after being blanched, deheaded, and washed, but quality is lost during the freezing process.

~

Vacuum-packed, shelled crawfish tails are available at fish markets and work well in most dishes. These crawfish tails have already been blanched, so they are ready for use in recipes calling for cooked tails. They can also be sautéed, fried, etc. Vacuum-packed crawfish tails maintain their freshness for 7 to 10 days in the refrigerator.

Chicken Tortilla Soup
Serves 6-8

2 Tbs	vegetable oil
1 small	onion, chopped
1 can	green chilies (4 oz), chopped
2 cloves	garlic, pressed
1 cup	canned tomatoes, chopped, liquid reserved
1 can	beef stock (10 ¾ oz)
1 can	chicken stock (10 ¾ oz)
1 ½ cups	water
1 ½ cups	spicy vegetable juice cocktail
1 tsp	cumin
1 tsp	chili powder
1 tsp	salt
⅛ tsp	pepper
2 tsp	Worcestershire sauce
1 Tbs	Heinz 57 Sauce
½ lb	chicken, boneless, cut into strips
3	flour tortillas cut into strips
4 oz	cheddar cheese, shredded

Sauté onion, chilies, and garlic in oil until soft. Transfer to large kettle and add tomatoes with liquid, stocks, water, vegetable juice cocktail, cumin, chili powder, salt, pepper, Worcestershire, and steak sauce. Bring to a boil, then lower heat and simmer 1 hour. Add chicken strips and simmer 45 minutes longer. Add tortilla strips and simmer 5 minutes more. To serve, place cheese in bowls and ladle soup over.

Chicken Leek Soup

Serves 12

1	chicken (2 ½ lbs)
2 ½ qts	water
1 ½ tsp	salt
½ tsp	freshly ground black pepper
¼ tsp	dried thyme
1	bay leaf
2 cloves	garlic, minced
¼ cup	unsalted butter
¼ cup	all-purpose flour
2	carrots, julienned
1	leek, julienned
2 stalks	celery, julienned
½ cup	potatoes, peeled, julienned
¼ cup	onions, julienned
~	fresh chopped parsley for garnish

Cook chicken in water with salt, pepper, thyme, bay leaf, and garlic until done. Remove chicken from stock and cool; strain and reserve stock. Remove chicken meat from bones and cut into bite-size pieces. Cook butter and flour together over medium heat to make a light brown roux. Add the reserved stock gradually, stirring until smooth. Simmer 30 minutes. Add vegetables to soup. Simmer until tender but not overcooked. Add chicken meat and continue simmering until chicken is heated through. Serve garnished with chopped fresh parsley.

Nick Apostle, owner, Nick's and 400 East Capitol Restaurants, Jackson, MS

Basic Roux

A basic roux is composed of equal parts butter and flour.

~

Conventional Roux

Melt butter in heavy skillet over medium heat. Add flour and cook, whisking constantly for 1 to 2 minutes until flour is desired color of brown.

~

Microwave Roux

In a microwavable dish, combine butter and flour. Microwave on HIGH, stirring every 1 ½ minutes until flour is desired color of brown.

~

Be careful not to burn! If flour is browning too quickly, remove from heat and whisk until cooking has slowed. If black specks appear, burning has occurred—start over.

Wild Rice Soup

Serves 12

3 cups	chicken stock
2 large	potatoes, peeled and diced
9 slices	bacon, in small pieces
1 medium	onion, chopped
1 ½ cups	cooked wild rice
2 pts	half & half
8 oz	American cheese, shredded
~	salt and pepper to taste
~	chopped green onion for garnish

Cook potatoes in chicken stock until tender. Puree in food processor. Sauté bacon, add onion, and cook until tender. Combine bacon mixture with wild rice in saucepan. Add half & half, potato puree, and cheese and heat gently, stirring until cheese melts. Add salt and pepper to taste. Garnish with chopped green onions.

Three cans of cream of potato soup (30 oz total) may be substituted for potato-chicken stock puree.

Spicy Venison Stew

Serves 4-6

Spicy Seasoning Mix

Yields 3 1/2 Tbs

2 tsp	ground cumin
2 tsp	ground coriander
2 1/2 tsp	chili powder
2 tsp	dried oregano, crumbled
1 1/2 tsp	dried thyme, crumbled
1/4 tsp	ground cloves
1/4 tsp	ground allspice
1/4 tsp	cinnamon

Combine all ingredients and blend thoroughly.

1 cup	dried pinto beans, rinsed and picked over
1	venison roast (3 lbs), well trimmed, in 1 1/2" cubes
~	salt and pepper to taste
~	Spicy Seasoning Mix (see accompanying recipe)
3 Tbs	all-purpose flour
7 Tbs	vegetable oil, divided
2 large	onions, diced
6 cloves	garlic, minced
2	hot chili peppers with seeds, minced
3 Tbs	tomato paste
1 1/2 cups	red zinfandel wine
2 cups	beef stock
2 cups	chicken stock
1 can	tomatoes (28 oz), drained, quartered
1	smoked ham hock
1/2 tsp	dried red pepper flakes (optional)
2	red bell peppers, in 1 1/2 " pieces
2	zucchini, in 1" thick wedges
2	yellow squash, in 1" thick wedges
~	fresh cilantro, minced, for garnish

Very well-trimmed beef chuck roast can substitute for the venison in this recipe. Or try adding 3/4 of a pound of cooked smoked sausage along with the squash and zucchini.

Cover beans with cold water and bring to a boil. Remove from heat, cover, let stand 1 hour, maintaining water level, then drain. Season venison with salt, pepper, and 2 teaspoons of Spicy Seasoning Mix and toss well. Add flour and toss again to coat. In heavy, 4-quart Dutch oven, brown venison in 3 tablespoons oil over medium-high heat. Remove meat, add 2 tablespoons oil to pot, and reduce heat to medium. Add onions and all but 2 teaspoons Spicy Seasoning Mix. Toss to coat. Add garlic, hot peppers, and tomato paste and stir 1 minute. Add wine to deglaze. Add stocks, tomatoes, ham hock, and red pepper flakes (if desired) and bring to simmer. Add meat, beans, and remaining Spicy Seasoning Mix. Cover partially and simmer, stirring occasionally, until beans and meat are tender, 1 1/2 hours. Skim grease from stew and remove ham hock. Discard fat and bone from hock, cut meat into pieces, and return to stew. In remaining 2 tablespoons of oil, sauté bell pepper, zucchini, and yellow squash over medium-high heat until crisp-tender, 5 to 6 minutes. Stir vegetables into stew and continue to simmer until just tender, 5 to 10 minutes. Ladle stew into serving bowls and sprinkle with fresh cilantro.

Crusty New Orleans French bread and cold beer make hearty cohorts for this hot and spicy stew.

Pine Nut Chili

Serves 8

3 Tbs	extra virgin olive oil
5 medium	yellow onions, sliced
3 cloves	garlic, chopped
3 lbs	ground beef, browned, drained
3 cans	tomatoes (60 oz total)
1 cup	dry red wine
1/2 tsp	Tabasco Sauce
6 Tbs	chili powder
2 tsp	dried oregano
~	salt and pepper to taste
1/2 cup	sour cream
1/2 cup	pine nuts, toasted
1/2 cup	pitted black olives, chopped

Sauté onions and garlic in oil until tender but not browned. Add ground beef, tomatoes, wine, Tabasco, chili powder, oregano, salt, and pepper. Continue to cook over medium heat 1 hour. Adjust seasonings and serve individual portions topped with sour cream, pine nuts, and olives. The full flavor of this chili improves if made a day ahead.

Bacon, Lettuce, and Tomato Soup

Serves 6-8

6 strips	bacon, cooked, crumbled
1 Tbs	bacon drippings, strained
1	yellow onion, finely chopped
2 cloves	garlic, minced
1 can	plum tomatoes (16 oz), with liquid, chopped
3 Tbs	tomato paste
1 Tbs	chopped fresh basil (1 tsp dried)
3 Tbs	all-purpose flour
4 cups	chicken stock
1/4 tsp	sugar
1 tsp	salt
1/2 tsp	pepper
1/4 head	lettuce, shredded

Sauté onion and garlic in bacon drippings 5 minutes. Stir in tomatoes, tomato paste, and basil and cook 2 to 3 minutes more. Sift in flour and whisk to blend. Add stock, sugar, salt, and pepper and simmer 15 minutes. Just before serving, add bacon and lettuce. Serve warm.

Herbed Tomato Soup
Serves 8

¾ cup	unsalted butter, divided
2 Tbs	extra virgin olive oil
1 large	onion, thinly sliced
4 sprigs	fresh thyme (1 tsp dried)
4 large	basil leaves, chopped (1 tsp dried)
~	salt and freshly ground black pepper to taste
2 ½ lbs	fresh tomatoes, peeled, cored
	or 1 can tomatoes (35 oz), with liquid
3 Tbs	tomato paste
⅓ cup	all-purpose flour
4 cups	chicken stock, divided
1 tsp	sugar
½ pt	heavy cream
~	croutons for garnish

Melt ½ cup butter in a large saucepan and add olive oil. Add onion, thyme, basil, salt, and pepper and cook, stirring occasionally, until onion is wilted. Add tomatoes and tomato paste and stir to blend. Simmer 10 minutes. Place flour in a small mixing bowl and add 5 tablespoons of stock, stirring to blend. Combine flour mixture with tomato mixture. Add remaining stock and simmer 30 minutes, stirring frequently to prevent scorching. Puree soup in food processor, then return to heat and add sugar and cream. Simmer, stirring occasionally, 5 minutes. Swirl in remaining butter. Serve hot or cold, garnished with croutons.

Cucumber Avocado Bisque
Serves 6

For "burpless" cucumbers, cover sliced cucumbers in salted water, refrigerate for at least an hour, and drain.

1 medium	cucumber, peeled, seeded
½ medium	avocado, peeled, pitted
3	green onions, chopped
1 cup	chicken stock
1 cup	sour cream
2 Tbs	fresh lemon juice
½ tsp	salt
~	paprika or chopped fresh parsley for garnish

Blend all ingredients except garnish in food processor for 10 to 15 seconds. Cover and chill. Serve in chilled mugs or soup bowls garnished with paprika or chopped fresh parsley.

SATURDAY FARE

Green Salad
with
Beth's Salad Dressing

~

Fresh Corn and Crab Bisque

~

Crusty French Bread

~

Glazed Raspberry-Chocolate Cakes

~

Wine

*"Listen and I'll tell you
what Miss Nell served
at the party," Loch's
mother said softly, with
little waits in her voice.
She was just a glimmer
at the foot of his bed.
"Ma'am."
"An orange scooped out
and filled with orange
juice, with the top put
back on and decorated
with icing leaves, a
straw stuck in. A slice of
pineapple with a heap of
candied sweet potatoes
on it, and a little handle
of pastry. A cup made
out of toast, filled with
creamed chicken, fairly
warm. A sweet peach
pickle with flower petals
around it of different-
colored cream cheese.
A swan made of a cream
puff. He had whipped
cream feathers, a pastry
neck, green icing eyes.
A pastry biscuit the size
of a marble with a little
date filling." She sighed
abruptly.
"Were you hungry,
Mama?" he said.*

from "June Recital"
by Eudora Welty

PHOTO:
*A bookcase in the Governor's
Mansion displays works by many of
the extraordinary literary figures
that the State of Mississippi
has produced.*

Jarlsberg Vegetable Bisque
Serves 6-8

3 Tbs	unsalted butter
3 Tbs	all-purpose flour
4 cups	chicken stock
1 lb	fresh broccoli, coarsely chopped
2	carrots, chopped
1 stalk	celery, chopped
1 small	onion, chopped
1 clove	garlic, minced
1/4 tsp	dried thyme
1/2 tsp	salt
1/8 tsp	pepper
1/2 pt	heavy cream
1 large	egg yolk
8 oz	Jarlsberg Swiss cheese, shredded

In a large, heavy saucepan, melt butter, add flour, and cook several minutes, stirring constantly. Remove from heat and gradually blend in stock, then bring mixture to a boil while stirring. Add broccoli, carrots, celery, onion, garlic, thyme, salt, and pepper. Cover and simmer until vegetables are tender, 8 minutes. Blend cream and egg. Gradually blend several tablespoons of soup into egg mixture, then add egg mixture to soup and cook, stirring until thickened. Blend in cheese. Can be served hot or cold.

Roasted Red Pepper Soup
Serves 4-6

3 large	red bell peppers, roasted, peeled, seeded
2 cans	stewed tomatoes (32 oz), drained
3 Tbs	extra virgin olive oil
2 cloves	garlic, minced
3 cups	chicken stock
~	salt and pepper to taste

For a truly spectacular presentation, serve this bright red soup in the same bowl with another soup of contrasting color —spinach, for example. The trick is to put each soup in a separate pitcher and pour both pitchers into the bowl simultaneously. The result is called Harlequin Soup.

Puree peppers and tomatoes in food processor, being careful not to overprocess. Gently heat garlic in olive oil, but do not brown (browned garlic is bitter). Stir in pepper puree and chicken stock and bring to a boil. Season with salt and pepper to taste. Serve hot or cold.

Cream of Carrot Soup

Serves 6

½ cup	chopped fresh cilantro or parsley (2 Tbs dried)
1 lb	carrots, finely chopped
2 medium	onions, finely chopped
2 stalks	celery, finely chopped
3 Tbs	unsalted butter
1 Tbs	all-purpose flour
4 cups	chicken stock
3 large	egg yolks
½ cup	heavy cream
¼ tsp	freshly ground black pepper
~	chopped fresh cilantro or parsley for garnish

Sauté chopped cilantro and vegetables in butter until tender, 10 to 15 minutes. Stir in flour and cook 2 to 3 minutes. Stir in chicken stock, cover, and cook over medium heat until carrots are soft, 15 to 20 minutes. Strain cooked vegetables and return stock to pan. Process vegetable mixture, 2 cups at a time, until smooth. Add puree to stock, stirring until smooth. Process egg yolks and cream until blended. With processor running, gradually add 1 cup hot soup. Stir egg yolk mixture gradually into remaining hot soup. Stir in pepper and simmer until slightly thickened and hot—do not boil. Just before serving, sprinkle with chopped cilantro or parsley.

Cauliflower Soup

Serves 4-6

2 Tbs	chopped onion
4 Tbs	unsalted butter
½ tsp	salt
1 pt	half & half
1 large	egg yolk
2 Tbs	shredded cheddar cheese
½ head	cauliflower, cooked, pureed
½ lb	bulk sausage, cooked, drained

Sauté onion in butter. Add salt and half & half and heat gently—do not boil. Whip egg yolk into cream mixture. Stir in cheese and cauliflower puree. Continue stirring to blend flavors. When ready to serve, pour into tureen or individual bowls and top with sausage.

Mexican Corn Soup
Serves 6-8

5 ears	fresh corn, kernels off cob, or 4 cups frozen corn kernels
1 cup	chicken stock
¼ cup	unsalted butter
2 ½ cups	milk
1 clove	garlic, pressed
1 tsp	dried oregano
~	salt and pepper to taste
½ tsp	cinnamon
3 Tbs	chopped mild green chilies
4 oz	Monterey Jack cheese, cubed
2 medium	tomatoes, diced
~	fresh parsley for garnish

In food processor, blend corn and stock 15 seconds. Over medium heat, simmer corn mixture in butter 5 minutes, stirring frequently. Blend in milk, garlic, oregano, salt, pepper, and cinnamon and bring to a boil. Reduce heat, add chilies, and simmer another 5 minutes. Remove soup from heat and stir in cheese until melted. Divide diced tomatoes among serving bowls, pour soup over tomatoes, and garnish with parsley. Serve immediately.

Black Bean Soup
Serves 6

Marinated Onions

Yields 1 ½ cups

1 large	red onion, finely chopped
2 cloves	garlic, minced
3 Tbs	white vinegar
~	salt and pepper to taste
½ cup	extra virgin olive oil

Combine all ingredients and allow to marinate for several hours.

2 cups	dried black beans
2 Tbs	extra virgin olive oil
2 medium	onions, chopped
1	bell pepper, seeded, chopped
1	bay leaf
½ tsp	dried oregano
1	ham hock
~	salt and pepper to taste
~	Marinated Onions (see accompanying recipe)

Soak beans overnight in enough water to allow for swelling. Drain and rinse. Sauté onions, bell pepper, bay leaf, and oregano in olive oil. Combine sautéed onion mixture with beans and ham hock in stock pot. Add water to cover and simmer, covered, at least 5 hours or all day, adding water if necessary. Add salt and pepper to taste. Serve soup topped with marinated onions.

Good Luck Soup

Serves 6

1 lb dried black-eyed peas (do not soak)
2 qts chicken stock
1 ham hock
$^1/_3$ lb smoked ham, in 1" cubes
2 medium yellow onions, chopped
1 green bell pepper, chopped
1 stalk celery, chopped
2 cloves garlic, minced
3 dried chili peppers or $^1/_2$ tsp ground red pepper
1 pkg frozen cut okra (10 oz), thawed
$1^1/_2$ tsp salt

~

In a large saucepan, combine peas, stock, ham hock, ham,
onions, bell pepper, celery, garlic, and chili peppers.
Cover and bring to a boil over high heat, stirring occasionally.
Reduce heat to low and simmer 1 hour, stirring occasionally.
Stir in okra and salt, and simmer, covered, for 30 minutes,
stirring frequently to prevent scorching.
Remove cover and cook, stirring, until creamy thick, 10 minutes.
Remove ham hock and chili peppers.
Serve hot.

§

*Black-eyed peas
(sometimes known as
cowpeas) originated in
Africa, though they've
been fundamental to the
Southern diet for at least
three centuries.
Southerners believe that
those who eat black-eyed
peas on New Year's Day
will have good luck
throughout the
coming year.*

*Good Luck Soup
is best made a day ahead,
and that will give you
time to sit back and
enjoy the holiday with
friends.*

*Serve with plenty of hot,
buttered cornbread,
and your luck can only
get better.*

Vichyssoise

Serves 6

4 Tbs	unsalted butter
1 medium	yellow onion, sliced
2	leeks, chopped
1 stalk	celery, chopped
1	bay leaf
1/8 tsp	dried thyme
1/8 tsp	cayenne pepper
~	ham bone
1 qt	milk
1 lb	potatoes, peeled and sliced
1 large	egg yolk, beaten
~	salt to taste
1/2 pt	heavy cream
~	chopped chives and parsley for garnish

Sauté onion, leeks, celery, bay leaf, thyme, and cayenne in butter. Add ham bone and simmer 5 minutes. Add milk and potatoes and simmer until potatoes are tender. Remove ham bone and bay leaf and process vegetable mixture until smooth. Blend in egg yolk, salt, and heavy cream. Serve chilled, garnished with chives and parsley.

Joe Middleton, executive chef, Nick's Restaurant; former executive chef, MS Governor's Mansion, Jackson, MS

Fancy Cantaloupe Soup

Serves 6

Rules for Ripeness

A perfectly ripe cantaloupe has a sweet, fruity odor, a thick, raised netted surface, and is a bit soft at the blossom end.

2 medium	cantaloupes, well ripened, halved and seeded
1/4 cup	sugar
1/3 cup	fresh orange juice
1 Tbs	fresh lime juice
1/3 cup	apple juice
1/4 cup	dry sherry
1 Tbs	fresh lemon juice
1/4 tsp	vanilla extract
1/8 tsp	ground ginger
1/4 cup	chopped macadamia nuts
~	thin lime slices

Scoop pulp from 3 cantaloupe halves. Cut remaining cantaloupe half into melon balls and reserve. Thoroughly combine cantaloupe pulp, sugar, orange juice, lime juice, apple juice, sherry, lemon juice, vanilla extract, and ginger. Process mixture in 2-cup batches, 30 seconds per batch or until smooth. Pour into large non-metal bowl, cover, and chill several hours or overnight. Serve in shallow bowls garnished with melon balls, macadamia nuts, and lime slices.

Cold Squash Soup

Serves 6-8

¼ cup	unsalted butter
2 medium	white onions, chopped
5 medium	yellow squash, sliced
2 cups	chicken stock
¼ tsp	sugar
1 pt	heavy cream
~	salt and white pepper to taste
¼ tsp	freshly grated nutmeg (⅛ tsp ground)
~	fresh chives, dill, or mint for garnish

Sauté onions in butter. Add squash, stock, and sugar and continue to cook until done. Cool squash mixture, then puree. Blend in cream, salt, pepper, and nutmeg and chill for several hours. Correct seasonings and serve in wine goblets or mint julep glasses, garnished with fresh chives, dill, or mint.

Basic Homemade Stock

Yields 1 qt

Common ingredients:

2 quarts	cold water
1 medium	onion, quartered
1 clove	garlic, quartered
1 stalk	celery, in large pieces
1	carrot, peeled, in large pieces
1	bay leaf

For shellfish stock:

Add 1 ½ lbs rinsed shrimp heads and/or shells, or crawfish heads and/or shells, or oyster liquor, or any combination.

For chicken stock:

Add 1 ½ lbs backs, necks, and/or bones from chicken.

For beef stock:

Add 1 ½ lbs beef shank or other beef bones.

For a richer beef stock, roast beef bones and vegetables at 350° until thoroughly browned, 30 to 40 minutes. Add to water, bring to boil, then use small amount of boiling water to deglaze roasting pan. Return deglazing liquid to stock pot and proceed as directed.

Place all ingredients in stock pot or saucepan. Bring to boil over high heat, then reduce heat and simmer, partially covered, at least 4 hours. Add additional water when necessary to maintain 1 quart liquid. After cooking, strain, cool, and refrigerate or freeze stock until ready for use. If you find that you don't have 4 hours of simmering time available, just keep this motto in mind: A 30-minute stock is at least half an hour better than plain water.

PHOTO (left): *The architectural firm of Barlow & Plunkett Ltd currently occupies the Mims-Dreyfus House on North State Street in Jackson. Originally constructed in 1905, the building was renovated in 1964 without altering its exterior appearance.*

PHOTO (overleaf)·

Fresh Corn and Black-Eyed Pea Salad
Grilled Chicken in Artichoke Salad
Crab Mango Salad

S A L A D S

Crab Mango Salad
Serves 4

1 medium	onion, finely chopped
2 stalks	celery, chopped
1 lb	fresh lump crabmeat, picked
~	salt and pepper to taste
½ cup	vegetable oil
⅓ cup	cider vinegar
½ cup	ice water
3	mangoes
3	avocados
2 Tbs	fresh lime juice, combined with 1 cup water
~	lime wedges

Spread half of onion on bottom of serving bowl. Add layers of celery, crabmeat, and remaining onion. Salt and pepper to taste. Stir together oil, vinegar, and water and pour over salad layers. Marinate for one day or longer. Peel and slice mangoes and avocados into ½", half-moon shaped pieces. Dip slices in lime juice and water. Drain crab mixture and serve over mango and avocado slices. Squeeze a lime wedge over each serving.

Mango Memo

Look for plump, slightly soft mangoes with a fresh smell and a smooth skin that has at least begun to color. Avoid those that are bright green, rock-hard, shriveled, bruised, or discolored. Mangoes can be refrigerated for a day or two, but only when they are completely ripe. The flavor is best when mangoes are served very cold.

Crawfish Salad
Serves 4

1 lb	fresh crawfish tails, cooked
1 ½ Tbs	mayonnaise
1 tsp	brown Creole mustard
2	green onions, chopped
2 Tbs	capers, drained
1 tsp	fresh lemon juice
~	salt and pepper to taste
~	leafy lettuce, sliced avocado, tomato wedges, or crackers

Combine crawfish tails, mayonnaise, mustard, green onions, capers, lemon juice, salt, and pepper. Serve over lettuce with avocado and tomatoes or as a dip with crackers.

Shrimp Salad
Serves 8

Garlic Chili Sauce

Yields 2 ½ cups

¼ cup	garlic vinegar
1 tsp	salt
¼ cup	Worcestershire sauce
1 medium	onion, grated
1 tsp	paprika
⅔ cup	chili sauce
⅓ cup	sugar
¾ cup	vegetable oil

Blend vinegar, salt , Worcestershire, onion, paprika, chili sauce, and sugar. Gradually add oil while stirring. Chill.

~	Garlic Chili Sauce (see accompanying recipe)
6 oz	cream cheese, room temperature
1 Tbs	Worcestershire sauce
3	green onions, chopped
½ tsp	garlic salt
8 slices	Holland rusk
2 large	tomatoes, peeled, sliced
1 large	head of lettuce, torn
2 lbs	medium shrimp, cooked, peeled, deveined, chilled

Combine cream cheese, Worcestershire, green onions, and garlic salt and blend well.

To serve, spread cream cheese mixture on each slice of Holland rusk. Center rusks on serving plates and cover each with slice of tomato. Place torn lettuce over tomato slice and top with shrimp (about 4 ounces per serving). Spoon Garlic Chili Sauce over each salad.

Grilled Chicken in Artichoke Salad

Serves 2

2 large	fresh artichokes, trimmed, cooked and choked
~	salt and freshly ground white pepper to taste
¼ cup	extra virgin olive oil
2 Tbs	wine vinegar
4	boneless, skinless chicken breast halves, grilled and cubed
4 oz	Swiss cheese, cubed
1 tsp	capers, drained
2	green onions, chopped
¼	red bell pepper, chopped
¼	yellow bell pepper, chopped
1 tsp	Dijon mustard
¼ cup	mayonnaise

Approaching Artichokes

Choose firm, dark green, spotless artichokes with tightly closed leaves. Wash in cool water and cut stems flush with base. Trim thorny outside leaves with scissors and rub cut edges with lemon juice to prevent discoloration. Boil or steam until tender, 40 minutes.

~

To open, place cooled artichoke on plate. Using heel of hand, strike artichoke sharply on top. Gently remove center leaves and use a spoon to remove the fibrous "choke," leaving heart and bottom intact.

Place each artichoke on a serving plate, arranging leaves around edge. Shake together olive oil and vinegar, pour over artichokes, and set aside. Combine chicken, cheese, capers, green onions, bell peppers, and mustard, adding mayonnaise to desired consistency. To serve, stuff center of each artichoke with salad.

Chicken Pasta Salad

Serves 8

Dressing:

½ cup	mayonnaise
3 Tbs	soy sauce
2 Tbs	sherry
⅛ tsp	ground ginger
¼ tsp	pepper
1 cup	spiral pasta, cooked, drained
2 cups	cubed cooked chicken
2 cups	fresh snow peas, stringed and blanched
2	green onions, sliced
½ cup	water chestnuts, sliced
¼ cup	slivered almonds, toasted, for garnish

Prepare dressing by thoroughly blending mayonnaise, soy sauce, sherry, ginger, and pepper. Combine pasta, chicken, snow peas, green onions, and water chestnuts and toss with dressing. Refrigerate overnight. Sprinkle with toasted almonds before serving.

Chutney Chicken Salad
Serves 6

1 cup	mayonnaise
½ cup	Major Grey chutney
8	chicken breast halves, cooked, in bite-sized pieces
2 stalks	celery, coarsely chopped
4	green onions, coarsely chopped
1	Granny Smith apple, unpeeled, coarsely chopped, sprinkled with lemon juice
½ cup	red seedless grapes, sliced
½ cup	chopped pecans, toasted
2 cups	cooked brown rice

Thoroughly blend mayonnaise and chutney. Combine with chicken, celery, onions, apple, grapes, pecans, and rice. Serve chilled.

Layered Turkey and Broccoli Pasta Salad
Serves 8-10

Ricotta Yogurt Dressing

Yields 2 cups

1 cup	plain yogurt
½ cup	ricotta cheese
2 Tbs	white wine vinegar
4 cloves	garlic, minced
¼ cup	chopped fresh basil or 1 Tbs dried
½ tsp	sugar
1 tsp	salt
~	freshly ground black pepper to taste

Blend all ingredients.

12 oz	corkscrew pasta, cooked, drained
2 Tbs	extra virgin olive oil
1 lb	fresh spinach, washed, stemmed, dried, torn into pieces
2 cups	cooked turkey breast, cubed
1 bunch	broccoli, blanched, broken into pieces
4 medium	tomatoes, peeled, seeded, chopped
~	salt and pepper to taste
~	Ricotta Yogurt Dressing (see accompanying recipe)

Mix pasta with olive oil and chill. In a large serving bowl, using half of the total amount of each ingredient, alternate layers with a light sprinkling of salt and pepper. Start with spinach, followed by pasta, turkey, broccoli, tomato, and then Ricotta Yogurt Dressing. Repeat sequence using remaining half of each ingredient. Chill thoroughly.

Smoked Duck Confetti Salad

Serves 4

	duck breast halves with skin
	salted water for soaking
⅓ cup	balsamic vinegar
Tbs	fresh lemon juice
	salt and pepper to taste
⅓ cup	extra virgin olive oil
½ lb	angel hair pasta, cooked, drained
	vegetable oil for deep frying
large	carrot, sliced
¼ each	red, yellow, and green bell peppers,
	cut in triangles, squares, slivers
¼ cup	chopped fresh parsley
½ cup	seedless grapes, halved
large	orange, peeled, sectioned

To smoke duck, submerge in salted water for several hours. Prepare smoker, using contained smoke unit. Smoke duck slowly, 2 ½ to 3 hours. Remove and reserve duck skin for cracklings. Slice meat into bite-sized pieces and set aside. For cracklings, slice reserved duck skin into tiny slivers. Roast in oven until crisp, draining excess fat during cooking. Prepare vinaigrette by blending vinegar, lemon juice, salt, and pepper. Slowly whisk in olive oil and set aside. Deep-fry cooked pasta in hot oil (375°) until crisp, 15 to 30 seconds. To assemble salad, arrange fried pasta on serving plates. Toss carrot, bell peppers, parsley, grapes, orange sections, and duck in vinaigrette. Mound salad over pasta and top with cracklings.

Joe Middleton, executive chef, Nick's Restaurant; former executive chef, MS Governor's Mansion, Jackson, MS

---

§

Frosty Tomato Salad

Serves 8

1 Tbs gelatin
¼ cup cold water
2 cups tomato juice
1 can crushed pineapple
(8 oz), drained
½ cup small curd
cottage cheese, pureed
⅛ tsp dry mustard
¼ tsp dry ginger
⅛ tsp cayenne pepper,
or to taste
1 tsp onion juice
¾ tsp salt
Tabasco Sauce to taste
½ cup mayonnaise

~

Blend all ingredients,
adding mayonnaise last.
Pour into oblong dish
and place in freezer.
Stir three times at
30-minute intervals to
keep ingredients
thoroughly mixed.
Remove from freezer
30 minutes
before serving, cut into
squares, and place on
lettuce leaves. Top with
a dollop of homemade
mayonnaise.

*Served in the dining room
of the Memphis Country Club.*

Salad with Asparagus and Creamy Garlic Dressing

Serves 16

Creamy Garlic Dressing:

4 cloves	garlic
1 tsp	salt
1 tsp	freshly ground black pepper
½ tsp	dry mustard
1 tsp	Dijon mustard
1 large	egg
1 Tbs	fresh lemon juice
¼ cup	balsamic vinegar
¼ cup	extra virgin olive oil
½ cup	vegetable oil

3 heads	fresh salad greens, washed and dried
1 lb	fresh asparagus, blanched, in 1 ½" pieces
1 medium	zucchini, grated
3	red or yellow bell peppers, roasted, peeled, seeded, chopped
½ cup	sunflower seeds, without hulls

For the dressing, thoroughly blend garlic, salt, pepper, mustards, egg, lemon juice, vinegar, and oils. Refrigerate until ready to assemble salad. Combine lettuce, asparagus, zucchini, peppers, and sunflower seeds. Toss with dressing.

Broccoli Cauliflower Salad

Serves 10

1 bunch	broccoli, florets only, in small pieces
1 bunch	cauliflower, florets only, in small pieces
1 small	red onion, grated
4 oz	cheddar cheese, shredded
1 pkg	bacon (12 oz), cooked, crumbled

1 cup	mayonnaise
¼ cup	sugar
2 Tbs	wine vinegar

Combine broccoli, cauliflower, onion, cheese and bacon. In separate bowl, blend mayonnaise, sugar, and vinegar and mix well. Pour dressing over salad, toss, and chill several hours before serving.

SUMMER MENU

Cucumber Avocado Bisque

~

Shrimp Salad

~

Lemon Butter Buns

~

Orange Ginger Sorbet

~

Iced Tea

"Southern porches
have been used to
entertain, to prepare food,
to wash clothes and
bodies, and to provide
sheltered play space
for children, but their
most important ongoing
use is to transmit folklore.
Children continue to
invent games designed
around the architecture of
a particular porch style,
and fabled Southern
storytellers gather with
family and friends on
porches to benefit from
any possible breeze and
to regale each other with
tales. Today's older
Southerners, unwilling to
adjust to ubiquitous air-
conditioning, pass family
lore to children and
grandchildren on
ancestral porches."

by Sue Bridwell Beckham from
Encyclopedia of Southern Culture, co-
edited by Charles Reagan Wilson and
William Ferris

PHOTO:

Mrs. Dean Morris Alexander's
two-story Classic Revival home
at 505 North State Street
in Jackson, Mississippi, was built
by Joseph Henry Morris
around the turn of the century.
Mrs. Alexander, a former president
of the Junior League of Jackson
(1968-69), often takes a glass of
minted iced tea out to her shady
back porch to escape the brutal
Mississippi summers.
"For generations," she writes,
"the porches of 505 have reached out
to enfold guests
in gentle hospitality."

Mixed Greens and Strawberries with Balsamic Vinaigrette
Serves 10-12

¼ cup	balsamic vinegar
½ tsp	salt
½ tsp	freshly ground black pepper
¾ cup	extra virgin olive oil
7 cups	mixed salad greens, torn into small pieces
1 ½ cups	sliced celery
⅓ cup	pine nuts, lightly toasted
½ cup	coarsely grated Parmesan cheese
1 pt	strawberries, halved

Add some grilled chicken or lamb to this salad, and luncheon is served.

Whisk together vinegar, salt, and pepper. Add oil in a thin stream, whisking until emulsified. Just before serving, combine greens, celery, pine nuts, cheese, and strawberries. Toss dressing with salad, using just enough to coat but not wilt the greens. Serve on a clear glass plate.

Crunchy Romaine Toss
Serves 10-12

EXCELLENT!

Sweet and Sour Dressing

Yields 2 ½ cups

1 cup	vegetable oil
1 cup	sugar
½ cup	wine vinegar
1 Tbs	soy sauce
~	salt and pepper to taste

Blend all ingredients.

1 cup	walnuts, chopped
1 pkg	Ramen Noodles, uncooked, broken up (discard flavor packet)
4 Tbs	unsalted butter
1 bunch	broccoli, coarsely chopped
1 head	romaine lettuce, washed, broken into pieces
4	green onions, chopped
1 cup	Sweet and Sour Dressing (see accompanying recipe)

Brown walnuts and noodles in butter; cool on paper towels. Combine noodles and walnuts with broccoli, romaine, and onions. Pour Sweet and Sour Dressing over and toss to coat well.

Lemon Dill Potato Salad

Serves 8

24	new potatoes, unpeeled
~	salt and freshly ground black pepper, to taste
2 tsp	lemon zest
2 Tbs	fresh dill, chopped (2 tsp dried)
1 small	red onion, chopped
½ cup	sour cream
½ cup	mayonnaise
2 Tbs	fresh lemon juice

Cover potatoes with cold salted water. Bring to a boil and cook until tender but firm, 10 minutes. Drain and refrigerate. Quarter and season cooled potatoes with salt, pepper, lemon zest, dill, and onion. Blend in mayonnaise, sour cream, and lemon juice. Cover and refrigerate at least 3 hours. Toss again and adjust seasoning before serving.

Walnut and Roquefort Salad

Serves 8

½ cup	walnut halves
5 Tbs	white wine vinegar
½ tsp	salt
½ tsp	pepper
½ cup	extra virgin olive oil
1 head	romaine lettuce, torn into pieces
1	avocado, peeled, pitted, sliced, dipped in lemon juice
2	green onions, chopped
4 oz	Roquefort cheese, crumbled

Toast walnut halves in heavy skillet until golden, 5 to 8 minutes, and cool. Mix vinegar, salt, and pepper. Add oil in thin stream, whisking continuously until dressing is smooth and thoroughly blended. Combine romaine, avocado, green onions, and cheese with walnuts in salad bowl. Toss with dressing and serve.

Old-Fashioned Potato Salad

Serves 6

4 cups diced, cooked
red potatoes
3 stalks celery, sliced
5 green onions, diced
3 medium radishes, sliced
2 Tbs snipped fresh
parsley
½ to 1 cup mayonnaise
1 Tbs vinegar
2 tsp prepared mustard
1 tsp celery seed
1 tsp salt
¼ tsp pepper

~

Combine all ingredients
and refrigerate
overnight.

*Justin Wilson,
the world-famous Cajun
storyteller and television cook,
has a recipe for potato salad
that uses leftover French fries.
But you'll have to get it
from him, not us.*

Fresh Corn and Black-Eyed Pea Salad

Serves 6

If the season isn't right for fresh ingredients, one 10 oz package each of frozen corn and black-eyed peas, cooked, can substitute.

1/3 cup	balsamic vinegar
1 Tbs	hot, sweet mustard
1/4 cup	chopped fresh parsley
1/2 tsp	salt
1/4 tsp	freshly ground black pepper
1/2 tsp	Creole seasoning
1/4 cup	extra virgin olive oil
2 ears	fresh corn, cooked, kernels off cob (1 1/2 cups)
1/2 lb	shelled fresh black-eyed peas, seasoned, cooked with ham or bacon
1 medium	red bell pepper, chopped
1 medium	Vidalia or red onion, chopped
3 stalks	celery, chopped

This salad is a natural for outdoor occasions featuring grilled chicken, pork, or hamburgers. It even makes a great dip with corn chips.

Blend vinegar, mustard, parsley, salt, pepper, and Creole seasoning. Whisk in oil and set aside. Combine corn, peas, bell pepper, onion, and celery. Toss dressing with vegetables and refrigerate until ready to serve, but not longer than 12 hours.

Cornbread Salad

Serves 8

1 pkg	cornbread mix (8 1/2 oz)
1 large	egg
1/3 cup	milk
4 medium	tomatoes, peeled, chopped
1	green bell pepper, chopped
1/2 small	onion, chopped
1/2 cup	chopped sweet pickles
9 slices	bacon, cooked, crumbled
1 cup	mayonnaise
1/4 cup	sweet pickle juice

Combine cornbread mix, egg, and milk. Spoon into 8" square pan and bake at 400° for 20 minutes. Cool, crumble, and set aside. Combine tomatoes, bell pepper, onion, pickles, and bacon. Toss gently. Combine mayonnaise and pickle juice, stir well, and set aside. Layer 1/2 each of cornbread, tomato, and mayonnaise mixtures in large glass bowl. Repeat layers with remaining mixtures, making six layers in all. Cover and chill 2 hours before serving.

White Bean and Feta Salad

Serves 8-10

1 lb	dried small white navy beans, soaked in cold water overnight, drained
6 cups	water
3	carrots, in ¼" dice
2	bay leaves
2 cloves	garlic, minced
1 ½ Tbs	coarse-grained mustard
⅓ cup	fresh lemon juice
1 ¼ cups	extra virgin olive oil
~	salt and freshly ground black pepper to taste
1 medium	red onion, chopped
4 oz	feta cheese, crumbled
½ cup	pine nuts, toasted
1 bunch	parsley, chopped

Combine beans, water, carrots, and bay leaves in large saucepan. Heat to boiling, skimming foam from surface. Reduce heat and simmer uncovered until beans are tender but not mushy, 25 to 30 minutes. Remove from heat and drain, discarding carrots and bay leaves. Mix garlic, mustard, and lemon juice in small mixing bowl. Whisk in oil and add salt and pepper to taste. Toss warm beans with dressing. Add onion, cheese, pine nuts, and parsley. Toss to combine well. Serve at room temperature.

Lemon Mint Slaw

Serves 8

1 head	cabbage, thinly sliced
~	salt and pepper to taste
2 cloves	garlic, pressed
¼ cup	fresh lemon juice
¼ cup	extra virgin olive oil
2 Tbs	chopped fresh mint

Season sliced cabbage with salt and pepper. Add garlic, lemon juice, olive oil, and mint and mix well. Serve chilled.

§

Spiced Peach Salad

Serves 6

¾ cup sugar
¼ cup vinegar
1 stick cinnamon
½ tsp whole cloves
1 can peach halves (16 oz),
drained
2 pkgs cream cheese
(6 oz total)
¼ cup chopped nuts
lettuce
mayonnaise for garnish
~
Combine sugar, vinegar, cinnamon and cloves and simmer 5 minutes. Remove from heat, strain, and reserve ¼ cup syrup. Pour remaining syrup over peach halves and chill 4 hours. Blend cream cheese, chopped nuts, and ¼ cup syrup. Drain chilled peaches, reserving liquid, and place peaches on lettuce. Fill peach centers with cheese mixture. Garnish each with dollop of mayonnaise thinned with small amount of spiced liquid from peaches.

A tiny but widely praised barbecue restaurant in Texas uses the liquid from spiced peaches as the closely guarded secret ingredient in its barbecue sauce.

Don't tell anybody we told you.

§

Chaminade Cranberry Salad
Serves 8-10

1 lb fresh cranberries
1 orange,
peeled and seeded
2 cups sugar
2 cups pineapple juice
4 Tbs unflavored gelatin
1/2 tsp salt
2 stalks celery, chopped
1 cup pecans, chopped
4 slices pineapple, diced

~

*Process cranberries
and orange in food
processor. Add sugar
and let stand one hour.
Bring pineapple juice to
a boil. Dissolve gelatin
in juice and combine
with cranberry mixture.
Add salt, celery, pecans,
and pineapple.
Pour into 9" x 13"
casserole dish or large
salad mold and chill.*

*Since fresh cranberries freeze
very well, you can enjoy this
refreshing treat all year round.*

~

*The Chaminade Club
is a group of accomplished
musicians who have been meeting
regularly at the Jackson
Municipal Art Gallery since
1940. The members take turns
providing a musical program for
each meeting, and this cranberry
salad is often served at their
luncheons.*

Fresh Orange-Cranberry Salad
Serves 8

2 large	navel oranges
1 pkg	fresh cranberries (12 oz), washed and picked over
1 cup	walnuts, chopped
3/4 cup	sugar

With vegetable peeler or zester, remove and reserve orange zest (outermost orange layer only). Peel and section oranges. In food processor, combine zest, cranberries, oranges, walnuts, and sugar. Pulse until coarsely chopped.

Fresh Fruit Salad with Citrus Sauce
Serves 12

2 Tbs	fresh orange juice
2 Tbs	fresh lemon juice
2 Tbs	fresh lime juice
2/3 cup	sugar
1/3 cup	water
2 medium	fresh peaches, sliced
1 cup	fresh pineapple, sliced or in chunks
1 cup	honeydew melon, sliced or in chunks
2 medium	nectarines, sliced
1 cup	blueberries
1 cup	strawberries
2 medium	bananas

Prepare sauce by thoroughly blending juices, sugar, and water. Combine peaches, pineapple, honeydew, nectarines, and blueberries. Pour dressing over fruit. Slice bananas and add with strawberries just before serving.

Beth's Salad Dressing

Yields 1 ½ cups

2 cloves	garlic
⅓ cup	fresh lemon juice
1 tsp	Dijon mustard
1 Tbs	balsamic vinegar
⅛ tsp	cayenne pepper
½ cup	extra virgin olive oil
½ cup	vegetable oil
~	salt and freshly ground black pepper to taste

In food processor, combine garlic, lemon juice, mustard, vinegar, and cayenne. With machine running, add oils slowly in a thin stream until thoroughly combined. Add salt and pepper to taste and refrigerate until ready to serve.

Buttermilk Blue Cheese Dressing

Yields 2 cups

1 large	egg
3 cloves	garlic
1 cup	vegetable oil
¼ cup	buttermilk
½ tsp	salt
½ tsp	white pepper
¼ tsp	cayenne pepper
8 oz	blue cheese, coarsely crumbled
2	green onions, tops only, finely chopped

For a lighter blue cheese dressing, thoroughly combine an 8-ounce carton of plain yogurt with 1 teaspoon onion salt and 2 tablespoons of crumbled blue cheese. Season with freshly ground black pepper to taste. Yields 1 cup.

In food processor, blend egg and garlic until smooth. With machine running, add oil slowly in a thin stream. Add buttermilk, salt, and peppers and process a few seconds more until well mixed. Remove to bowl and add cheese and green onions. Break up large lumps of cheese, but maintain chunky texture. Refrigerate.

Creamy Greek Salad Dressing

Yields 2 cups

3 cloves	garlic
4	anchovy fillets in olive oil
2 Tbs	red wine vinegar
1 tsp	dried oregano
1 cup	extra virgin olive oil
1/2 cup	plain yogurt
~	freshly ground black pepper to taste
8 oz	feta cheese, crumbled

In food processor, blend garlic, anchovies, vinegar, oregano, and olive oil until smooth, 30 to 45 seconds. Add yogurt and blend a few seconds longer. Remove to bowl and add pepper and cheese. Refrigerate at least 3 hours before serving. Will keep refrigerated for weeks.

Onion Basil Vinaigrette

Yields 1 qt

1 tsp	salt
2 tsp	freshly ground black pepper
2 tsp	dry mustard
2	shallots, pureed
1/4	yellow onion, pureed
2 cups	vegetable oil
1 cup	red wine vinegar
1/4 cup	chopped fresh basil (1 tsp dried)
1	green onion, chopped
2 Tbs	chopped fresh parsley

Combine salt, pepper, mustard, and shallot and onion purees in a bowl. Blend well with a little of the oil. Slowly add remaining oil and vinegar while constantly blending. Mix in basil, green onion, and parsley.

Nosa Agho, owner and chef, Colours Restaurant, Jackson, MS

All About Olive Oil

Olive oils are graded according to the amount of acid they contain. Lower acidity means better oil.

Cold-pressed, extra virgin olive oils have the finest and fruitiest flavor. These superior oils range in color from pale yellow to bright green. The deeper the color, the more intense the flavor.

Lesser grades, in descending order, are superfine, fine, and pure (or virgin).

"Light" olive oil is not lighter in calories but lighter in olive flavor. It is intended for use in baking and other recipes where the obvious taste of olive oil would be undesirable. Light olive oil can also be used in high-heat frying because it has a higher smoking point. The "pure" grade of olive oil is also suitable for high-heat frying. The flavor of the more expensive, extra virgin oils, however, will break down under high temperatures.

These oils should be used in low- to medium-heat cooking or in salad dressings and marinades.

~

Store olive oil in a cool, dark place for 6 months, or in the refrigerator for 1 year. Chilled olive oil is cloudy and thick, but it will clarify if left at room temperature.

Mimi's Shrimp Salad Dressing

Yields 2 ½ cups

1 tsp	pepper
1 tsp	dry mustard
⅛ tsp	paprika
1 Tbs	Worcestershire sauce
~	Tabasco Sauce to taste
½ cup	vegetable oil
½ cup	catsup
1 medium	onion, grated
2 Tbs	water
2 Tbs	fresh lemon juice
1 cup	mayonnaise
2 cloves	garlic, minced

Thoroughly blend all ingredients and chill.

Sweet Celery Seed Dressing

Yields 2 cups

⅓ cup	sugar
1 tsp	dry mustard
½ tsp	salt
2 tsp	celery seed
1 tsp	fresh lemon juice
¼ cup	white vinegar
1 cup	vegetable oil, chilled

This sweet yet refreshing dressing is especially flavorful over grapefruit, avocado, and red onion slices.

Thoroughly combine sugar, mustard, salt, celery seed, lemon juice, and vinegar until well blended. Slowly add oil and blend until thickened. Chill thoroughly and serve over fruit salad.

PHOTO (left): *The home of Lois and Charles L. Scott on East Hill Drive in Jackson invokes the gracious Georgian style of the antebellum South, even though it was completed in early 1990.*

PHOTO (overleaf): *Catfish Mardi Gras*

E N T R E E S

Catfish Mardi Gras
Serves 6-8

⅓ cup	fresh lemon juice
⅔ cup	extra virgin olive oil
1 can	anchovy fillets (2 oz), drained
2 cups	fresh parsley or basil, lightly packed
1 tsp	dried oregano
8	catfish fillets (small to medium)
~	Greek seasoning to taste
~	salt and pepper to taste
~	large spinach leaves for wrapping fillets
½	yellow bell pepper, julienned
½	green bell pepper, julienned
½	purple bell pepper, julienned
~	extra virgin olive oil for sautéing

Prepare marinade by processing lemon juice, olive oil, anchovies, parsley, and oregano. Season catfish fillets with Greek seasoning, salt, and pepper. Pour marinade over fillets, cover, and refrigerate at least 3 hours or overnight. When ready to cook, preheat oven to 375°. Drain fillets, reserving marinade. Wrap fillets in spinach leaves, return to marinade, and cover tightly with foil. Poach in oven until done (check after 30 minutes—cooking time depends on size of fillets). Lightly sauté pepper strips in olive oil until warm but still crisp. Decorate fillets with pepper strips.

Yellow, green, and purple are the official colors of New Orleans' world-famous Mardi Gras celebration, hence the title for this recipe.

If, however, purple bell peppers are difficult to find, official permission is hereby granted to substitute red. Should you have any leftovers, puree the catfish and refrigerate overnight. Then mold the chilled puree into a fish shape (half-rounds of fluted yellow squash make nifty scales) and present as an impressive cold hors d'oeuvre.

Catfish Fillets with Crawfish Sauce
Serves 4

The Catfish:
From the Bottom
to the Top

For a long while, the catfish—
that poor old bottom-feeding
scavenger—garnered little if any
respect outside the Southland.
In the mid-1960s, however,
farmers in the Mississippi Delta
began to raise catfish as a cash
crop. By constructing crystal-
clean ponds and using grain as
feed, they were able to produce a
catfish that is cleaner and
healthier, with more eye-appeal.
It's delicious, high in protein, low
in fat and cholesterol, and so
versatile that some of the world's
greatest chefs have created new
dishes in its honor.
The catfish is finally getting the
respect it deserves—the respect
that we Southerners have been
giving it all along.

Crawfish Sauce:

1 bunch	green onions, chopped
8 Tbs	unsalted butter
⅓ cup	all-purpose flour
½ pt	half & half
½ cup	grated Parmesan cheese
⅓ cup	white wine
4 Tbs	chopped fresh parsley
~	salt and pepper to taste
3 Tbs	paprika
2 Tbs	Creole seasoning
½ tsp	garlic powder
1 lb	fresh crawfish tails, cleaned
6	fresh catfish fillets
8 Tbs	unsalted butter
4 Tbs	fresh lemon juice
3 Tbs	chopped fresh parsley
1 tsp	Creole seasoning
1 tsp	paprika
~	salt and pepper to taste
~	lemon slices and fresh parsley for garnish

For the sauce, sauté green onions in butter until soft. Gradually stir in flour until well blended. Slowly add half & half and stir well. Blend in cheese. Add wine, parsley, salt, pepper, paprika, Creole seasoning, and garlic powder. Add crawfish and mix thoroughly. Simmer 10 minutes, then set aside. To prepare the fish, lay catfish fillets in baking dish. In saucepan, melt butter and blend in lemon juice, parsley, Creole seasoning, paprika, salt, and pepper. Brush fillets with butter mixture and broil 10 minutes. Turn fish, brush with butter mixture, and broil until fish is flaky, 5 more minutes. Top fish with crawfish sauce and broil 3 to 4 minutes longer. Serve garnished with lemon slices and fresh parsley.

Stuffed and Skewered Catfish with Lemon Sauce
Serves 4

Caper Stuffing:

¼ cup	freshly grated Parmesan cheese
2 cloves	garlic, minced
3 Tbs	capers, drained, chopped
½ cup	unseasoned bread crumbs
1 Tbs	fresh lemon juice
~	salt and pepper to taste
8	thin catfish fillets
~	extra virgin olive oil to coat fish
3	tomatoes, quartered, or 12 cherry tomatoes
~	lemons, quartered
~	white wine
~	Lemon Sauce (see accompanying recipe)

Lemon Sauce

Yields ¹/₂ cup

1 clove	garlic, minced
4 Tbs	fresh lemon juice
¼ cup	extra virgin olive oil
¼ tsp	pepper
1 tsp	Dijon mustard
1 Tbs	grated lemon zest

Combine all ingredients in food processor and blend well. Serve at room temperature.

Preheat oven to 450°. For Caper Stuffing, combine cheese, garlic, capers, bread crumbs, lemon juice, salt, and pepper and mix well. To assemble, lightly coat fish in olive oil. Center small amount of stuffing on each fillet, roll fish around stuffing, and cut across the roll into 2" slices. On a large skewer, alternate a piece of tomato, a lemon quarter, and a slice of rolled fish. Repeat until skewer is almost full. Brush with olive oil, place in a baking dish, and add wine to cover bottom of pan. Bake approximately 10 minutes, check for doneness, and continue cooking if necessary. Serve with Lemon Sauce.

Crunchy Catfish with Lemon Parsley Sauce
Serves 4-5

4 large	catfish fillets
2 large	eggs, beaten
2 Tbs	water
1/2 cup	crushed buttery-flavored crackers
1 oz	freshly grated Parmesan cheese (¼ cup)
1 Tbs	Greek seasoning
2 Tbs	unsalted butter, melted
~	Lemon Parsley Sauce (see accompanying recipe)

Lemon Parsley Sauce

Yields 1 cup

3	green onions, chopped
2 Tbs	fresh lemon juice
½ cup	unsalted butter
1 Tbs	dried parsley
½ tsp	salt
½ tsp	pepper
~	Worcestershire sauce to taste
~	Tabasco Sauce to taste

Combine all ingredients and simmer briefly.

Preheat oven to 325°. Mix eggs and water. Combine crackers, cheese, and Greek seasoning. Dip fillets in egg mixture, then in seasoned cracker crumbs. Place in greased pan and drizzle melted butter over top. Bake for 30 minutes. Serve Lemon Parsley Sauce over cooked catfish.

Catfish Creole
Serves 6

Fish Facts

*When searching out fresh
fish and seafood, you should
follow your nose. While fish are
fish and do have an odor, that
odor should never be strong or
disagreeable.*

~

*Whole fish should look bright and
shiny, with clear eyes, red gills,
and a tail that is not dry. Fillets
and steaks should be firm and not
bruised or slimy.*

~

*Fresh fish should be cooked on the
day it is purchased.*

~

*One pound of whole fish will
serve one person. One 7-ounce
fillet or steak equals one serving.*

6	catfish fillets
¼ cup	unsalted butter
2 medium	green onions, chopped
2 cloves	garlic, minced
1	bay leaf, crushed
1 Tbs	fresh lemon juice
1 can	stewed tomatoes (16 oz), crushed
1 tsp	salt
½ tsp	freshly ground black pepper
¼ tsp	cayenne pepper
½ tsp	dried oregano
½ tsp	dried basil
¾ lb	vermicelli pasta, cooked, drained

Preheat oven to 325°. Pat catfish fillets dry with paper towel and place in baking dish. Sauté green onions and garlic in butter until tender. Add bay leaf, lemon juice, tomatoes, salt, pepper, cayenne, oregano, and basil. Cook until heated throughout. Pour sauce over catfish and bake, uncovered, until fish is flaky, 20 minutes. Divide pasta among six plates and place a fillet with sauce over each nest of pasta.

Rosemary Catfish Piquant
Serves 3-4

4	thin catfish fillets, in serving pieces
~	salt, pepper, all-purpose flour
2 Tbs	extra virgin olive oil
2 Tbs	white wine vinegar
1 Tbs	water
2 cloves	garlic, minced
¼ tsp	dried rosemary

Sprinkle fish with salt and pepper and dust with flour. Sauté in oil for 10 minutes per inch of thickness at the thickest part of the fillet. Turn once during cooking. The fish should be browned and flake easily. Transfer fish to a warm platter and keep warm. Add vinegar and water to pan drippings. When sizzling stops, add garlic and rosemary. Boil rapidly, stirring and scraping to release browned bits. Spoon sauce over fish and serve.

Baked Catfish in Orange Nutmeg Sauce
Serves 4

Orange Nutmeg Sauce:

²/₃ cup	fresh orange juice
1 Tbs	grated orange zest
1 tsp	freshly ground nutmeg
~	salt and black pepper to taste
~	cayenne pepper to taste
4	catfish fillets

Combine orange juice, zest, nutmeg, salt, pepper, and cayenne and set aside. Preheat oven to 450°. Lay fish fillets in greased baking dish and spoon over equal amounts of Orange Nutmeg Sauce. Bake, covered, 15 minutes. Uncover and bake 5 minutes longer.

Grilled Fish with Citrus-Sage Marinade
Serves 4

Citrus Sage Marinade:

12	fresh sage leaves, chopped (2 tsp dried)
1 Tbs	lemon zest
1 Tbs	orange zest
¼ cup	fresh lemon or lime juice
¼ cup	fresh orange juice
~	salt and freshly ground black pepper to taste
½ cup	extra virgin olive oil
4	swordfish or tuna fillets (8 oz)
10	fresh sage leaves for smoking (optional)
~	lemon, lime, orange slices for garnish
~	sage leaves for garnish

For marinade, combine sage, zests, juices, salt, and pepper and whisk in oil. For fish, score each fillet on both sides, place in glass dish, and pour Citrus Sage Marinade over. Marinate for at least 3 hours. Prepare grill and put a bundle of 10 fresh sage leaves on coals. Cook fish until flaky, 5 to 7 minutes per side. Baste fish with marinade while cooking. Garnish with sage leaves and fresh citrus slices before serving.

Add a Little Zest to Your Life

The zest is the thin, colored outer layer of the skin of an orange, lemon, or lime. When removing the zest, be careful not to include any of the bitter-flavored, spongy white pith that lies just underneath. There is a unique tool (called, interestingly enough, a "zester") designed specifically to remove the zest, but the fine side of a grater will do the job, too. A swivel-bladed vegetable peeler will also peel off the zest, which can then be finely minced in a food processor or by hand. Zest dries out quickly, so don't remove it until you're ready to use it.

Citrus Sage Marinade, with the addition of 3 minced garlic cloves, also makes a delicious complement for chicken and pork.

Baked Fish with Yogurt Horseradish Glaze
Serves 6

Yogurt Horseradish Glaze

Yields 1 cup

½ cup	plain yogurt
1 tsp	cornstarch
2 Tbs	prepared horseradish
4 tsp	dry mustard
¼ cup	freshly grated Parmesan cheese
2 Tbs	fresh lemon juice

Combine all ingredients.

6	catfish fillets
~	salt and pepper to taste
~	Yogurt Horseradish Glaze (see accompanying recipe)
1 ½ tsp	dried dill
2 Tbs	capers, drained
~	lemon slices for garnish

Preheat oven to 350°. Season fillets with salt and pepper. Coat both sides of fish with Yogurt Horseradish Glaze. Place fillets in glass baking dish, sprinkle with dill and capers, and bake until fish begins to flake, 10 to 12 minutes. Garnish with lemon slices and serve.

Red Snapper Royale
Serves 4-6

6	red snapper or fresh bass fillets
~	dry white wine
½	lemon, quartered
2 Tbs	chopped fresh basil (2 tsp dried), divided
2 ½ lbs	fresh spinach, chopped (2 pkgs frozen)
2 ½ Tbs	unsalted butter
2	shallots, finely chopped
2 Tbs	all-purpose flour
1 pt	half & half
3 Tbs	sun-dried or regular tomato paste
~	salt and freshly ground black pepper to taste
~	freshly grated Parmesan cheese

In a shallow pan over medium heat, poach fish fillets in wine to cover with lemon and 2 teaspoons basil. Remove fish from pan and break into large chunks, being careful to remove all bones. Set aside. Microwave spinach 6 minutes on HIGH. Squeeze all water out and set aside. Sauté shallots and 2 teaspoons fresh basil in butter over medium heat until tender, 5 minutes. Add flour and cook, stirring constantly, until light sand-colored. Blend in half & half and whisk until thickened. Remove from heat and whisk in tomato paste and 2 teaspoons basil. Add salt and freshly ground pepper to taste. Preheat oven to 350°. Spread spinach over bottom of large, greased baking dish, then layer fish pieces on spinach. Pour sauce over all and top with cheese. Bake until bubbly, 20 minutes.

Red Snapper Viennaise

Serves 4

Herbed Butter Sauce:

2 cups	shrimp stock or clam juice
³/₄ cup	white wine
1¹/₂ cups	heavy cream
2 Tbs	chopped fresh parsley
2 Tbs	chopped fresh tarragon
2 Tbs	chopped fresh dill
2 Tbs	chopped fresh chives
2 Tbs	unsalted butter
~	salt and white pepper to taste
2 cups	lentils
4	red snapper fillets
~	salt and white pepper to taste
¹/₄ cup	clarified unsalted butter

For sauce, heat stock and wine and reduce by half. Add cream and reduce by half again. Combine cream mixture with herbs in food processor. Blend for 5 minutes. Return to heat and bring to a simmer, then slowly add butter. Season with salt and pepper.

For fish, grind dried lentils in food processor to cornmeal-like consistency, 15 minutes. Place ground lentils on large plate. Season fish fillets with salt and white pepper, then dredge in ground lentils. Sauté fillets briefly in clarified butter over high heat, then reduce heat to avoid burning lentils. Continue cooking slowly until lentils and fish are done. To serve, ladle Herbed Butter Sauce around, not over, fish.

Grant Nooe, former executive chef, 400 East Capitol Restaurant, Jackson, MS

Clearing Up the Clarified Butter Question

Clarified butter can be cooked at higher temperatures than unsalted butter because the milk solids which cause burning have been removed. It will also keep longer without turning rancid than regular butter.

To clarify butter, melt unsalted butter slowly over low heat. Remove from heat and allow to stand 20 to 30 minutes. Using a spoon, remove foamy crust from surface. Do not pour or strain, but spoon the deep yellow liquid into a jar and store. Do not scrape bottom of pan— whey settles to bottom and is unusable.

Clarified butter can be refrigerated 2 to 3 weeks or frozen indefinitely.

Trout Meuniere with Pecans
Serves 4

Perfectly Cooked Fillets

~ fish fillets

~ salt, pepper

~ unsalted butter

~ water

Preheat oven to 500°. Pound fish fillets between sheets of wax paper to an even thickness (¼"). Place fish on buttered baking sheet and sprinkle with salt and pepper. Brush fish fillets with water. Bake in upper third of oven until opaque, 2 to 3 minutes—be careful not to overcook. Serve with your favorite sauce or simply garnished with lemon.

~

The general rule for length of cooking time is 10 minutes per 1 inch of thickness. This rule will vary, however, according to temperature and distance from source of heat. Cooked fish is perfectly done when the flesh loses its translucency and just begins to flake when tested.

¼ cup	vegetable oil
5 Tbs	unsalted butter, divided
4	trout or bass fillets
¼ cup	milk
~	salt and pepper to taste
½ cup	all-purpose flour, seasoned with salt and pepper
½ cup	pecan halves
2 Tbs	fresh lemon juice
2 Tbs	finely chopped fresh parsley

Melt 1 tablespoon butter with oil in large, heavy skillet. In another pan, combine milk, salt, and pepper. Coat trout in milk mixture and, without patting dry, dredge in seasoned flour. Sauté trout in oil and butter until golden on one side, 8 minutes. Turn and cook 8 minutes longer. Baste often during cooking. Remove trout to warm platter and sprinkle with salt and pepper. Empty and wipe out skillet, then add remaining 4 tablespoons butter. Sauté pecans in butter, shaking pan, until butter is golden brown. Add lemon juice and pour pecan sauce over trout. Sprinkle with fresh parsley.

Olive Grouper
Serves 2

1 tsp	capers, drained
½ tsp	dried dill
½ tsp	fennel seed
4	Greek olives, pitted, chopped
2 Tbs	fresh lemon juice
2	grouper fillets, wash, dried, halved
~	salt and pepper to taste
½ cup	all-purpose flour
¼ cup	extra virgin olive oil
½ cup	white wine

Combine capers, dill, fennel seed, olives, and lemon juice and set aside. Salt and pepper fish and dust with flour. Fry fish in oil 10 minutes for each inch of thickness at thickest part. Turn once during cooking. Place fish on warm platter in preheated oven. Add olive mixture to pan drippings, scraping to loosen browned bits. Add wine and reduce by half. Pour sauce over fish and serve immediately.

Broiled Peppered Swordfish

Serves 4

1 Tbs	soy sauce
1 Tbs	extra virgin olive oil
2 Tbs	fresh lemon juice
4	swordfish steaks
1 Tbs	black peppercorns, crushed
1 Tbs	green peppercorns, crushed
1 Tbs	red peppercorns, crushed
~	Green Onion Cream Sauce (see accompanying recipe)
¼ cup	chopped fresh chives or green onions
4	radishes, thinly sliced

Preheat broiler to 475°. Season steaks with soy, olive oil, and lemon juice. Combine peppercorns and sprinkle tops of swordfish steaks with mixture. Press pepper firmly into surface of fish. Place on broiler pan, peppered side up, and broil to desired degree of doneness, 4 to 6 minutes, depending on thickness. Just before serving, heat Green Onion Cream Sauce over medium-high heat. Reduce until thick enough to coat back of spoon, 2 minutes. Adjust seasonings. Spoon sauce onto serving plates and sprinkle chives and radishes over sauce. Position fish over sauce and serve immediately.

Green Onion
Cream Sauce

Yields 2 cups

1 cup	shrimp stock or clam juice
1 cup	white wine
1 ½ cups	heavy cream
1 bunch	green onions, tops only, chopped

Combine shellfish stock and wine and simmer over high heat until reduced to ½ cup, 10 minutes. Add cream and continue cooking until reduced to 1 cup, 10 minutes. Pour into food processor, add green onions, and steep 5 minutes. Puree until smooth, strain, and refrigerate.

Broiled Swordfish with Ginger Vinaigrette

Serves 6

2 Tbs	extra virgin olive oil
2 Tbs	fresh lemon juice
1 Tbs	chopped fresh thyme (½ tsp dried)
6	swordfish steaks
~	salt and pepper to taste
~	Ginger Vinaigrette (see accompanying recipe)

Combine oil, lemon juice, and thyme. Coat fish with lemon mixture and season with salt and pepper. Seal fish in plastic storage bag and marinate one hour. Preheat broiler. Place fish on oiled broiler rack 2 to 3 inches from heat and broil 5 to 7 minutes. Turn and cook another 3 minutes. Serve with warm Ginger Vinaigrette.

Ginger Vinaigrette

Yields 2 cups

2 Tbs	Dijon mustard
¼ cup	white wine vinegar
⅓ cup	vegetable oil
⅓ cup	extra virgin olive oil
½ cup	tomatoes, peeled, seeded, chopped
4 Tbs	chopped green onion
3 Tbs	grated fresh ginger
2 Tbs	chopped fresh parsley
~	salt and pepper to taste

Whisk all ingredients together until well blended. May be made ahead, if refrigerated.

Orange Roughy in Lemon Wine Sauce
Serves 4

Cornstarch vs. Arrowroot

Cornstarch can substitute for arrowroot, but twice as much cornstarch will be needed. Both cornstarch and arrowroot produce clear sauces, and both should be mixed into a cold liquid before being added to heated mixtures. Stir gently over medium heat to thicken. Cornstarch can impart a chalky taste when undercooked.

2 Tbs	chopped green onions
2 tsp	chopped fresh parsley
1 tsp	white wine Worcestershire sauce
½ tsp	lemon zest
½ cup	dry white wine
1 Tbs	fresh lemon juice
1 tsp	arrowroot
½ cup	buttermilk
4	orange roughy fillets
~	salt and pepper to taste
~	white wine for broiling
1 cup	seedless red grapes
1 Tbs	finely chopped almonds

Combine green onions, parsley, Worcestershire, lemon zest, wine, and lemon juice in a skillet. Bring to a boil and reduce to ½ cup. Combine arrowroot with buttermilk and add to sauce, stirring constantly until slightly thickened, then set aside. Preheat broiler. Salt and pepper fillets. Place fish in baking dish and add ⅛ inch white wine. Broil fish 3 to 5 minutes. Remove from broiler, pour sauce over fish, add grapes, and sprinkle with almonds. Broil until sauce bubbles and fish begins to flake, about 1 more minute.

Redfish Special
Serves 4

4	thin redfish fillets
1 tsp	lemon pepper seasoning
~	all-purpose flour
5 Tbs	unsalted butter
6 Tbs	fresh lemon juice
½ tsp	garlic salt
1 tsp	Worcestershire sauce

Sprinkle both sides of each redfish fillet with lemon pepper and dust with flour. Sauté fillets in 3 tablespoons butter for 5 minutes, turning once. Preheat a separate, oven-proof pan and add lemon juice, 2 tablespoons butter, and sautéed fish. Pour butter from sauté pan over fish and add garlic salt and Worcestershire. Broil 3 minutes without turning. Serve immediately.

Grilled Salmon with Tomato Cream Sauce

Serves 6

6	salmon steaks, 1" to 2" thick
~	celery salt to taste
~	freshly ground white pepper to taste
6 Tbs	unsalted butter
1 medium	onion, minced
2 cloves	garlic, pressed
3	fresh tomatoes, peeled, drained, seeded, diced
½ cup	dry white wine
1 Tbs	chopped fresh tarragon
½ pt	heavy cream
~	unsalted butter for basting
2 Tbs	unsalted butter, room temperature
2 Tbs	all-purpose flour
~	chopped fresh parsley for garnish

Rub salmon steaks with celery salt and pepper and refrigerate. Prepare grill. Gently sauté onion and garlic in 6 tablespoons butter until transparent. Add tomatoes, wine, and tarragon. Cook briefly to blend, then add cream. When mixture returns to simmer, cover and remove from heat. Grill salmon steaks, basting frequently with butter, until just translucent in center. Mix 2 tablespoons butter and 2 tablespoons flour into a smooth paste. Reheat sauce to simmer, being careful not to overcook. Stirring constantly, add butter-flour paste as needed until sauce is smooth and thickened. Serve sauce over salmon and sprinkle with chopped fresh parsley.

Nick Apostle, owner, Nick's and 400 East Capitol Restaurants, Jackson, MS

Fish Preparation Chart

FISH	BAKE	BROIL	POACH	GRILL OR SMOKE	PAN FRY	DEEP FRY
amberjack	•	√	•	√	•	•
bass, largemouth	√	√	√	√	√	√
bream	√	√	√	√	√	√
catfish, farm-raised	√	√	√	√	√	√
crappie	√	√	√	√	√	√
flounder	√	√	√	√	√	√
grouper	√	√	√	√	√	√
ling (lemon fish)	√	√	√	√	√	√
mackerel	•	•	•	√	•	•
mahi mahi	√	√	√	√	√	√
mullet	√	√	√	√	√	√
orange roughy	√	√	√	√	√	•
pompano	√	√	√	√	•	•
red snapper	√	√	√	√	√	√
redfish (red drum)	√	√	√	√	√	√
salmon	•	√	√	√	•	•
shark, mako	√	√	√	√	√	√
sole	√	√	√	√	√	√
triggerfish	√	√	√	√	√	√
trout, speckled (sea)	√	√	√	√	√	√
tuna	•	•	√	√	•	•

Creole Glazed Tuna with Tiger Shrimp
Serves 6

Creole Glaze

Yields 1 cup

½ cup	Cajun seasoning or Creole Seafood Seasoning (page 91)
½ cup	unsalted butter, melted
¼ cup	vegetable oil
2 Tbs	Creole mustard

Combine all ingredients.

2 cups	fine light white bread crumbs
4	jalapeño peppers, seeded, diced
½ cup	all-purpose flour
¼ tsp	salt
¼ tsp	white pepper
¼ tsp	garlic powder
⅛ cup	chopped parsley
~	Creole Glaze (see accompanying recipe)
18	Asian tiger shrimp, peeled
6	yellowfin tuna fillets

Combine bread crumbs, jalapeños, flour, salt, white pepper, garlic powder, and parsley in food processor. Coat shrimp with glaze, then crumb mixture. Brush tuna fillets with glaze and grill until flaky. Grill shrimp until golden brown and reglaze. For individual servings, place 3 shrimp on top of each tuna fillet.

Darryl Borden, chef, Bombay Café, Birmingham, AL

Shrimp Frederic
Serves 4

This savory herbed butter sauce works beautifully with catfish or redfish, as well. After cooking the fish in the sauce, run it under the broiler until golden.

8 Tbs	unsalted butter
1 Tbs	fresh lemon juice
1 tsp	dried parsley
1 tsp	dried chives
½ tsp	dried tarragon
½ tsp	dry mustard
¾ tsp	seasoned salt
⅛ tsp	cayenne pepper
⅛ tsp	garlic powder
1 lb	medium shrimp, uncooked, peeled
2 cups	cooked long grain rice

Melt butter in skillet and combine with lemon juice, parsley, chives, tarragon, mustard, seasoned salt, cayenne, and garlic powder. Cook shrimp in herbed butter over medium heat, uncovered, turning once, until shrimp are uniformly pink, 5 minutes. Serve on bed of hot rice.

Champagne Shrimp and Pasta

Serves 4

1 cup	sliced fresh mushrooms
1 Tbs	extra virgin olive oil
1 lb	medium shrimp, uncooked, peeled
1 1/2 cups	champagne
1/4 tsp	salt
2 Tbs	minced shallots
2	plum tomatoes, diced
1/2 pt	heavy cream, divided
~	salt and pepper to taste
1/2 lb	angel hair pasta, cooked
3 Tbs	chopped parsley

Sauté mushrooms in oil over medium-high heat until juices appear and evaporate. Remove mushrooms and set aside. In same pan, combine shrimp, champagne, and salt over high heat. When liquid just begins to boil, remove shrimp and set aside. Add shallots and tomatoes to cooking liquid and boil until liquid is reduced to 1/2 cup, 8 minutes. Blend in 3/4 cup heavy cream and boil until slightly thickened and reduced, 1 to 2 minutes. Add shrimp and mushrooms to sauce and heat thoroughly. Taste and adjust seasonings. Toss hot, cooked pasta with remaining 1/4 cup cream and parsley. To serve, spoon shrimp with sauce over pasta.

Shrimp Tips

Good shrimp are available year 'round.

~

Two pounds of heads-on shrimp are equivalent to one pound of headless shrimp. When recipes in this book call for shrimp, they are assuming the headless variety. It is better to buy heads-on shrimp when available for better flavor during cooking.

~

Fresh shrimp are easily peeled under cold running water over a colander. Deveining is usually unnecessary unless shrimp are extra large or if they are being used for a salad (the veins could be sandy). According to New Orleans food expert Jane Brock's mother, a native of the Crescent City, "A shrimp and an oyster eat the same thing. Do you try to clean an oyster?"

Attention Shrimp!

Serves 2

1 1/2 Tbs	Creole Seafood Seasoning (see accompanying recipe), or blackened fish seasoning
1 1/2 Tbs	paprika
1/2 cup	unsalted butter, melted
1 lb large	shrimp, unpeeled

Combine seasoning with paprika. Add half of spice mixture to butter and stir. Dip shrimp into butter mixture to coat and place in single layer in large foil-lined pan. Pour any remaining butter mixture over shrimp. Broil close to high heat until pink, about 5 minutes (watch closely to avoid overcooking). Sprinkle remaining half of spice mixture over shrimp and broil 30 seconds more. Present shrimp with spiced side up and serve pan drippings as dipping sauce for bread.

Creole Seafood Seasoning

Yields 1/2 cup

1 Tbs	sweet paprika
1 Tbs	salt
2 tsp	onion powder
2 tsp	garlic powder
1 tsp	cayenne pepper
1 tsp	white pepper
1 tsp	black pepper
2 tsp	dried thyme
2 tsp	dried oregano
2 tsp	dried basil

Thoroughly blend all ingredients.

Shrimp and Andouille Skewers with Shallot Mustard Sauce
Serves 4

Shallot Mustard Sauce
Yields ½ cup

1/4 cup	white vermouth
1 tsp	white wine vinegar
1 tsp	chopped shallots
½ cup	heavy cream
1 Tbs	diced red bell pepper, roasted
½ tsp	minced fresh tarragon (¼ tsp dried)
1 ½ tsp	Creole mustard
½ tsp	Dijon mustard
1 Tbs	unsalted butter
~	salt and cayenne pepper to taste

Combine vermouth, vinegar, and shallots in heavy saucepan and boil until reduced to 2 tablespoons. Add cream, bell pepper, and tarragon and boil until thickened and reduced to ⅓ cup. Reduce heat to medium-low, whisk in mustards, and cook 30 seconds. Whisk in butter, season with salt and cayenne, and keep warm.

16 jumbo	shrimp, uncooked, peeled, deveined, tails on
1 large	red bell pepper, seeded, in 1" squares
1 large	green bell pepper, seeded, in 1" squares
1 lb	andouille sausage, in ½" slices
4 large	skewers
⅓ cup	Creole Seafood Seasoning (page 91)
¼ cup	butter, melted
2 cups	cooked rice
~	Shallot Mustard Sauce (see accompanying recipe)

Prepare grill for high heat. On skewers, alternate shrimp, bell pepper pieces, and sausage. Sprinkle with Creole Seafood Seasoning and brush with melted butter. Arrange skewers on grill and cook until shrimp are just opaque, turning and basting occasionally, 7 minutes. Mound rice on one side of each plate and spoon Shallot Mustard Sauce onto the other. Slide shrimp, sausage, and peppers from skewers onto sauce and serve.

Shrimp Florentine
Serves 12

~	*vegetable cooking spray*
4 pkgs	frozen chopped spinach (40 oz total), thawed, drained
2 lbs	medium shrimp, cooked, peeled
½ cup	unsalted butter
1 medium	onion, chopped
½ cup	all-purpose flour
1 ½ pt	half & half
1 cup	dry white wine
~	salt and pepper to taste
2 tsp	paprika
8 oz	cheddar cheese, shredded

Preheat oven to 325°. Coat 9" x 13" dish with vegetable spray. Spread spinach over bottom of dish and layer shrimp over spinach. In a saucepan, sauté onions in butter until soft. Add flour, then gradually blend in half & half, stirring until thickened. Slowly stir in wine, then add salt, pepper, and paprika. Pour wine mixture over shrimp and sprinkle with cheese. Bake uncovered 30 minutes at 325 °. Allow to rest several minutes before serving.

Herbed Shrimp and Feta Casserole
Serves 12

~	vegetable cooking spray
2 large	eggs
1 cup	evaporated milk
1 cup	plain yogurt
8 oz	feta cheese, crumbled
⅓ lb	Swiss cheese, shredded
⅓ cup	fresh parsley, chopped
1 tsp	dried basil
1 tsp	dried oregano
4 cloves	garlic, minced
½ lb	angel hair pasta, cooked
1 jar	mild, chunky salsa (16 oz)
1 lb	medium shrimp, uncooked, peeled
½ lb	mozzarella cheese, shredded

Preheat oven to 350°. Coat bottom and sides of 8" x 12" baking dish with cooking spray. In separate bowl, blend eggs, milk, yogurt, feta and Swiss cheeses, parsley, basil, oregano, and garlic. Spread half of pasta over bottom of baking dish. Cover with salsa. Add half of shrimp. Spread remaining pasta over shrimp. Pour and spread egg mixture over pasta. Add remaining shrimp and top with mozzarella cheese. Bake 30 minutes. Remove from oven and let stand 10 minutes before serving.

Crabmeat Soufflé
Serves 6

8 large	eggs
1 cup	sour cream
1 tsp	salt
12 oz	fresh crabmeat, picked
6 oz	Swiss cheese, shredded
¼ cup	sliced black or green olives
3 medium	green onions, chopped
2 Tbs	unsalted butter, melted
~	fresh parsley and black or green olives for garnish

Preheat oven to 350°. In a bowl, beat eggs, sour cream, and salt until blended. Stir in crabmeat, cheese, olives, and green onions. Place in casserole or 6 ramekins. Drizzle with butter and bake 20 to 25 minutes. Garnish with fresh parsley and olives.

---

§ The Boss's Imperial Crabmeat
Serves 4

1 lb lump crabmeat, picked
1 Tbs Durkee's Sauce
2 Tbs mayonnaise
1 Tbs Worcestershire sauce
salt and pepper to taste
¼ tsp cayenne pepper
1 cup crushed potato chips
1 Tbs paprika
4 Tbs unsalted butter, melted

~

Preheat oven to 350°. Combine crabmeat, Durkee's, mayonnaise, Worcestershire, salt, pepper, and cayenne. Place crabmeat mixture in shells or ramekins lightly coated with mayonnaise. Combine potato chips and paprika and sprinkle over crabmeat mixture. Top with melted butter. Bake 12 to 15 minutes and serve at once.

"The Boss" was Dr. Reuel May, Jr.'s mother, a long-time member of the Junior League of Jackson. She served her Imperial Crabmeat at family dinners, ladies' luncheons, and many other occasions. She received the recipe from her mother, so it's been enjoyed by at least three generations, with many more to come, no doubt.

Seafood Stuffed Eggplant

Serves 6

3 medium	eggplants
³/4 cup	unsalted butter
1 ½ bunch	green onions, chopped
1 lb	medium shrimp, peeled
1 ½ tsp	dried basil
1 ½ tsp	dried oregano
2 Tbs	fresh lemon juice
2 Tbs	white wine
1 lb	fresh crabmeat, picked
~	salt and freshly ground black pepper to taste
½ cup	all-purpose flour
1 ½ cups	heavy cream
~	freshly grated Parmesan cheese

Preheat oven to 350°. Cut eggplants in half lengthwise and score flesh in a checkerboard pattern for easy removal after cooking. Bake eggplants until tender, 30 to 40 minutes. Sauté green onions, shrimp, basil, and oregano in butter until shrimp are just done, 3 to 5 minutes. Scoop out eggplant flesh, reserving shells. Combine eggplant with shrimp mixture and cook in sauce pan over medium heat until eggplant is soft. Add lemon juice and wine. Gently fold in crabmeat and season generously with salt and pepper. Whisk together flour and cream into a paste and gradually blend into eggplant mixture until desired consistency is reached (all flour/cream paste may not be needed). Stuff reserved eggplant shells with cooked mixture. Bake stuffed egg-plants at 350° until heated through, 30 minutes. Top with cheese halfway through cooking time.

Crawfish Tortellini Helen Mary
Serves 4

1 medium	onion, finely chopped
2 cloves	garlic, minced
½ cup	unsalted butter
1 lb	crawfish tails
½ cup	freshly grated Parmesan cheese
2 Tbs	chopped fresh parsley
1 pt	heavy cream
1 package	cheese or spinach tortellini (9 oz), cooked
~	Tabasco Sauce, cayenne pepper, and salt to taste

Sauté onion and garlic in butter. Add crawfish tails and continue to cook 5 minutes. Add cheese and parsley and gradually add enough cream to make a thick sauce. Fold tortellini into crawfish mixture. Season with Tabasco, cayenne, and salt (Parmesan cheese adds its own salty flavor, so use salt sparingly).

This versatile dish will be just as successful with shrimp or crabmeat standing in for the crawfish tails.

Creamy Crawfish Fettucini
Serves 6-8

1	bell pepper, chopped
2 medium	onions, chopped
2 cloves	garlic, minced
¾ cup	unsalted butter
¼ cup	all-purpose flour
1 cup	half & half
1	garlic cheese roll, cut into small pieces
6 drops	Tabasco Sauce
½ tsp	cayenne pepper
1 lb	frozen crawfish tails, thawed, liquid reserved
¾ lb	fettucine noodles, cooked
~	chopped fresh parsley for garnish

Sauté bell pepper, onions, and garlic in butter until onions are light brown. Gradually blend in flour. Add half & half and stir constantly over medium heat until mixture thickens. Add cheese pieces and continue to stir until cheese melts. Blend in Tabasco, cayenne, and crawfish with liquid. Pour over cooked fettucine noodles, and garnish with fresh parsley.

If substituting fresh crawfish tails or shrimp, add ¼ cup shellfish stock.

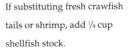

Seafood, Chicken, and Artichoke Casserole
Serves 10

White Sauce

Yields 3 cups

¾ cup unsalted butter, melted

¾ cup all-purpose flour

3 cups milk, heated

Over low heat, slowly blend flour with butter to form a thick roux. Then gradually stir in milk and continue stirring until sauce is creamy.

2 cans	artichoke hearts (28 oz total), drained
2 lbs	crabmeat, picked, or shrimp, cooked, peeled
4 whole	chicken breasts, boneless, cooked, chopped
1 ½ lbs	fresh mushrooms, sliced
2 Tbs	unsalted butter
3 cups	White Sauce (see accompanying recipe)
1 Tbs	Worcestershire sauce
~	salt and pepper to taste
½ cup	sherry
½ cup	freshly grated Parmesan cheese
~	paprika to taste
2 Tbs	chopped fresh parsley

Preheat oven to 375°. Arrange artichoke hearts in bottom of buttered casserole. Add crabmeat or shrimp and chicken. Sauté mushrooms in butter 2 minutes, drain, and add to casserole. Blend white sauce with Worcestershire, salt, pepper, and sherry and pour over casserole. Sprinkle top with cheese, paprika, and parsley. Bake, uncovered, 40 minutes.

Grilled Lobster Tails with Dilled Mayonnaise
Serves 4

Dilled Mayonnaise

Yields ½ cup

½ cup mayonnaise

¼ tsp dried dill

2-3 tsp fresh lemon juice

Blend mayonnaise and dill and thin with lemon juice to desired consistency. Heat, stirring occasionally, until warmed through.

4	lobster tails (6 oz each)
4 Tbs	unsalted butter, melted
2 tsp	fresh lemon juice
½ tsp	chili powder
~	Dilled Mayonnaise (see accompanying recipe)

With kitchen shears or sharp knife, cut through center of hard top shell and meat of lobster tails—do NOT cut through undershell. Spread tails open, butterfly style, to expose meat on top. Combine melted butter, lemon juice, and chili powder and brush over lobster meat. Place on grill, meaty side down. Grill over hot coals 5 minutes. Turn tails over, brush again with sauce, and continue grilling until meat is opaque, 5 to 10 minutes. Be careful not to overcook. Serve immediately with Dilled Mayonnaise.

Kitty Rueseler's Chicken Pie

Serves 12

2 chickens (3 lb each)
2 stalks celery with leaves
$^1/_4$ cup chopped fresh parsley
1 large onion, quartered
1 bay leaf

$^3/_4$ cup unsalted butter
$^3/_4$ cup all-purpose flour
6 cups stock reserved from chicken
salt and freshly ground pepper to taste

2 Tbs unsalted butter
$^1/_2$ lb mushrooms, sliced
2 stalks celery, chopped

pastry for double crust pie
2 carrots, chopped,
blanched (optional)
1 pkg frozen tiny green peas (10 oz), thawed, drained (optional)

~

Partially cover chickens with cold water (2 quarts).
Add celery, parsley, onion, and bay leaf. Simmer 1 $^1/_2$ hours.
Remove chicken from stock, separate meat from bone, keeping meat
in large pieces. Discard skin and return bones to stock.
Simmer stock 1 hour, then strain. Cool, skim fat, and reserve.

In a large saucepan over medium heat, cook together
butter and flour, stirring constantly, to make a light tan roux, 5 minutes.
Gradually whisk 6 cups reserved stock into roux.
Continue to cook, stirring, until thick and smooth.
Season generously with salt and pepper and remove from heat.
Sauté mushrooms and celery in butter.
Preheat oven to 400°.
Line each of two 9" x 13" casseroles, with $^1/_4$ of the pastry.
Bake for 5 to 10 minutes or until lightly browned.
Place chicken in casseroles and cover with mushrooms, celery, carrots, and peas.
Pour 1 $^1/_2$ cups gravy into each casserole and cover with remaining pastry crusts.
Bake until brown, about 20 minutes.
Serve any remaining gravy with chicken pie.

Cooked pie can be frozen.

The individual pie elements may be prepared a day in advance

and assembled for cooking just before serving.

§

Soon after World War II, Catherine McGowan Rueseler—known to her admirers as Kitty— packed up her new husband and the warm Southern traditions of her Georgia birthplace and transplanted them way up north to Cape Girardeau, Missouri. Following the example of her 86-year-old mother, Kitty loves to cook for her family (four children and seven grandchildren) and her friends (beyond number). She entertains with sparkling style, serving up lavish helpings of Southern hospitality and Southern food. Those folks up in Cape Girardeau just can't seem to get enough of either one.

Stuffed Chicken Breasts with Herbed Pasta
Serves 4

Quick Pesto

Yields 1 1/2 cups

¼ cup	extra virgin olive oil
¼ cup	unsalted butter, room temperature
¼ cup	freshly grated Parmesan cheese
¼ cup	finely ground walnuts
½ cup	minced fresh parsley
½ tsp	dried marjoram
½ tsp	dried basil
½ tsp	dried thyme
1 clove	garlic, minced

Combine all ingredients and refrigerate until needed.

Tomato sauce:

3 Tbs	extra virgin olive oil
3 cloves	garlic, minced
½ tsp	dried basil
2 Tbs	minced fresh parsley
2 cans	Italian stewed tomatoes (28 oz total), undrained, finely chopped
1	chicken bouillon cube
3 Tbs	vermouth

Chicken:

4	chicken breast halves, boneless, skinless
~	salt, pepper, garlic powder to taste
4 Tbs	Quick Pesto (see accompanying recipe)
~	all-purpose flour
1 Tbs	unsalted butter
2 Tbs	extra virgin olive oil

Herbed pasta:

1 pkg	fettucine (9 oz), cooked
2 Tbs	unsalted butter
2 Tbs	chopped fresh parsley
~	garlic powder to taste

For the tomato sauce, heat oil and sauté garlic. Blend in remaining tomato sauce ingredients and simmer 20 minutes. Pound chicken breasts to ¼" thickness. Season with salt, pepper, and garlic powder. Place 1 tablespoon pesto on each breast, roll up, and secure with toothpick. Dredge stuffed chicken breasts in flour and brown in butter and oil, 8 minutes. Cover and cook 6 more minutes until done. Prepare herbed pasta by tossing hot fettucine with butter, parsley, and garlic powder. Serve stuffed chicken breasts over herbed pasta and top with tomato sauce.

Sautéed Chicken Breasts with Mushroom Madeira Sauce

Serves 4

4	chicken breast halves, boneless, skinless
~	salt and freshly ground pepper to taste
1 Tbs	vegetable oil
1 Tbs	unsalted butter
1 medium	onion, finely chopped
1/2 lb	fresh mushrooms, sliced
1/8 tsp	dried thyme
1/4 cup	Madeira wine
1/4 cup	heavy cream
1/4 tsp	salt
1/4 tsp	pepper

Pat chicken breasts dry, sprinkle with salt and pepper, and cook in oil over medium-high heat until firm to the touch, 4 to 5 minutes per side. Remove chicken and keep warm. In same pan, combine butter, onion, mushrooms, and thyme and cook over medium heat, stirring occasionally, 5 minutes. Add Madeira and cook until almost all liquid is absorbed, 2 minutes. Stir in cream, salt, and pepper and continue cooking until sauce is slightly thickened, 3 to 5 minutes. Spoon sauce over chicken.

Artichoke-Stuffed Chicken Breasts

Serves 8

1 medium	onion, finely chopped
6	shallots, minced
3 Tbs	unsalted butter
1 can	artichoke hearts (14 oz), chopped
1 can	pitted black olives (6 oz), chopped
1/2 cup	slivered almonds, toasted
1 Tbs	minced fresh tarragon (1 tsp dried)
~	salt and pepper to taste
4 whole	boneless chicken breasts with skin
~	hollandaise sauce
1/2 cup	crème fraîche

Brown onion and shallots in butter. Add artichoke hearts, olives, almonds, tarragon, salt, and pepper. Loosen skin of chicken breasts, season with salt and pepper, and place artichoke mixture between skin and meat. Refrigerate until ready to bake. Bake uncovered in 350° oven 45 minutes. Serve cold or hot with a hollandaise sauce and a dollop of crème fraîche.

Lemon Roasted Chicken
Serves 4

If you don't have a trussing needle or kitchen twine handy, you can close up your chicken with toothpicks or with an ordinary sewing needle and black thread. Wooden clothespins rubbed with vegetable oil have also proven successful. This recipe responds to endless variation. Try rubbing the chicken with garlic, thyme, dill, rosemary, or any combination of your favorite herbs.

1 whole	young chicken (2 ½ lb), washed, dried
~	salt and pepper to taste
2 whole	lemons
~	sprigs of fresh rosemary, optional
~	*trussing needle and kitchen twine*

Preheat oven to 350°. Rub chicken with salt and pepper, inside and out. Roll lemons on counter to soften, then punch 20 holes in skin of each lemon. Place lemons and rosemary (if desired) inside chicken. Close neck and body cavities with string and trussing needle, being careful not to pull too tightly. Place chicken breast down in roasting pan and cook for 15 minutes. Carefully turn chicken—it will swell during cooking—but do not puncture or deflate. Roast 25 more minutes, then raise heat to 400° and cook for 15 minutes longer, or until meat thermometer reads 170°.

Sesame Chicken Kabobs
Serves 4

1 cup	vegetable oil
½ cup	soy sauce
½ cup	Chablis wine
½ cup	light corn syrup
2 Tbs	sesame seeds
¼ cup	fresh lemon juice
½ tsp	garlic powder
½ tsp	ground ginger
4	chicken breast halves, skinned, deboned, in 1 ½" pieces
1 small	green bell pepper, quartered
1 medium	onion, quartered
8 large	mushroom caps
8	cherry tomatoes

Combine vegetable oil, soy sauce, Chablis, corn syrup, sesame seeds, lemon juice, garlic powder, and ginger. Stir well. Add chicken and vegetables and chill for 2 hours. Drain chicken and reserve marinade. Alternate chicken and vegetable pieces on skewers, placing tomatoes on each end. Grill 6" from medium-hot coals 15 to 20 minutes, turning and basting often with marinade.

Grilled Lime Chicken

Serves 4

Lime Marinade:

¼ cup	extra virgin olive oil
½ cup	fresh lime juice
½ tsp	chili powder
½ tsp	ground turmeric
2 tsp	dried rosemary leaves, crushed
2 cloves	garlic, minced
~	salt and freshly ground black pepper to taste

4	chicken breast halves, boneless, skinless

¼ cup	fresh lime juice
3 Tbs	unsalted butter, melted
2 cups	cooked yellow rice

Prepare grill. For marinade, blend oil, lime juice, chili powder, turmeric, rosemary, garlic, salt, and pepper. Add chicken breasts and marinate until ready to cook, at least 2 hours. Grill marinated chicken on one side, 8 minutes. Turn, baste with marinade, and grill 8 more minutes. Turn once more, baste again, and cook 2 minutes longer. Remove chicken from grill. Combine remaining lime juice and butter, heat until warm, and drizzle over cooked rice. Top with chicken breasts.

Cinnamon Pepper Chicken

Serves 4

1	fryer, whole (4 lbs)
1 ½ tsp	salt
½ tsp	cayenne pepper
1 tsp	black pepper
1 tsp	cinnamon
1 tsp	allspice

Preheat oven to 325°. Clean chicken and season well, inside and out, with salt, peppers, cinnamon, and allspice. Bake, uncovered, 2 ½ to 3 hours, basting occasionally with pan juices.

Crunchy Pecan Chicken

Serves 4

1 cup	buttermilk biscuit mix
1/2 tsp	Creole seasoning
1/2 tsp	salt
1 tsp	paprika
1/2 cup	finely chopped pecans
4	chicken breast halves, boneless, skin on
1/2 cup	buttermilk
1/2 cup	unsalted butter, melted

Preheat oven to 350°. Combine biscuit mix, Creole seasoning, salt, paprika, and pecans. Dip chicken in buttermilk and coat with dry mixture. Place chicken in a greased 13" x 9" x 2" baking pan. Pour butter over chicken and bake uncovered for 1 hour.

Scarlet Chicken

Serves 4

4	chicken breast halves, boneless, skinless
~	salt and pepper to taste
3 Tbs	fresh lemon juice, divided
~	Hungarian paprika, generous amount to taste
~	*vegetable cooking spray*
1/4 lb	mushrooms, sliced
2 cloves	garlic, minced
1 Tbs	fresh lemon juice
2 tsp	soy sauce
1/2 cup	dry sherry
3	green onions, sliced

Pound chicken breasts to 1/2" thickness. Season with lemon juice, salt, pepper, and enough paprika to make the chicken red. Coat nonstick pan with cooking spray. Sear chicken breasts and cook for 2 to 3 minutes on each side, then remove chicken to serving plate. To sauté pan add mushrooms, garlic, lemon juice, soy sauce, and sherry. Cook for 5 minutes. Sprinkle green onions into pan and cook another 2 minutes. Pour sauce over chicken.

Southern Fried Chicken

Serves 4

1 fryer, in serving pieces
seasoned salt
pepper
all-purpose flour, seasoned with salt and pepper

vegetable shortening, melted for depth of $^1/_2$" to 1" in skillet
3 Tbs bacon drippings or unsalted butter

~

Salt and pepper chicken pieces very generously.
Place flour in paper sack, then toss seasoned chicken pieces
in flour in sack.

Heat shortening and bacon drippings
in heavy skillet over medium high heat until hot enough
to sizzle a drop of water.
Add chicken to skillet, being careful
not to crowd—cook in batches if necessary.
Cook covered about 15 minutes
or until "the brown creeps up the side of the chicken."
Remove cover, turn chicken, and continue to cook uncovered
until browned, about 15 minutes.

Drain uncovered on paper towels
to maintain crispness.

§

Black Magic

The only truly appropriate way to prepare Southern Fried Chicken is in an ominously black, unbelievably heavy, cast iron frying pan, handed down from your great-grandmother at the very least.

If you must buy a new one, you're more likely to find it at a hardware store than a gourmet shop.

Wash your new pan in hot water without soap. Dry it, then place it on the stove over low heat. Pour in a half-inch of vegetable oil and allow the pan to season for 30 to 40 minutes, coating the sides of the pan regularly with a pastry brush.

Pour out the oil, cool the pan, and wipe it with paper towels.

From this point on, you should never wash your pan again, although occasional scouring with a little salt is acceptable.

Regular use will produce the ominous blackness mentioned above, and you can hand the pan down to your great-grandchildren.

Baked Mustard-Thyme Chicken
Serves 4

~	extra virgin olive oil
4	chicken breasts, boneless
½ cup	sour cream
½ cup	Dijon mustard
1 Tbs	fresh lemon juice
~	salt and pepper to taste
8 sprigs	fresh thyme (½ tsp dried)

Preheat oven to 350°. Brush 4 sheets of aluminum foil with olive oil. Place 1 chicken breast on each sheet of foil. Blend sour cream, mustard, and lemon juice and brush mixture on both sides of each piece of chicken. Salt and pepper each piece and top with 2 thyme sprigs or lightly sprinkle with dried leaves. Fold foil around chicken breasts and seal well. Bake 30 to 45 minutes or until done.

Reese's Herb Microwave Chicken
Serves 4

1	chicken (3 lbs), in serving pieces, or 4 skinless breasts
1 ¼ tsp	garlic powder
1 ¼ tsp	paprika
¾ tsp	dried oregano
½ tsp	freshly ground pepper
2 Tbs	fresh lemon juice
1 cup	fresh mushrooms, sliced

Combine garlic powder, paprika, oregano, and pepper, and rub over chicken. Place chicken in baking dish, meaty side up. Drizzle with lemon juice and top with mushrooms. Cover with plastic wrap and microwave 20 minutes on HIGH, rotating once.

Chicken with Almond Butter

Serves 4

1/2 cup	ground almonds
2 Tbs	all-purpose flour
2 Tbs	unsalted butter, room temperature
1/2 tsp	salt
1/4 tsp	cayenne pepper
1/2 tsp	lemon zest
1 Tbs	fresh lemon juice
1/2 tsp	Worcestershire sauce
4	chicken breast halves, boneless, skinless
1/4 cup	slivered almonds

Blend almonds, flour, and butter until smooth. Add salt, cayenne, lemon zest, lemon juice, and Worcestershire and mix well. Pound chicken breasts slightly and spread generously with almond butter. Bake in a buttered baking dish at 425° for 15 minutes, turning once. Top with slivered almonds and broil for 30 seconds or until browned.

Chicken Terrine with Watercress Sauce

Serves 8

2 lbs	chicken breasts, boneless
1 medium	onion, finely chopped
2 large	egg yolks
2 cups	fresh bread crumbs
2/3 cup	heavy cream
1 bunch	watercress, finely chopped
1/4 tsp	freshly grated nutmeg
~	salt and freshly ground pepper to taste
~	pistachio nuts, coarsely chopped (optional)
~	Watercress Sauce (see accompanying recipe)

Preheat oven to 400°. Puree chicken in food processor to a smooth paste. Combine pureed chicken with onion, egg yolks, bread crumbs, cream, watercress, nutmeg, salt, and pepper. Spread half of chicken mixture in bottom of 6-cup loaf pan. Sprinkle 1/2" layer of chopped pistachios over chicken mixture, if desired. Press down gently, then add remaining chicken mixture. Cover with wax paper and close tightly. Place loaf pan inside larger pan and pour boiling water around. Bake 1 1/2 hours. Serve warm with Watercress Sauce.

Watercress Sauce

Yields 3 cups

6 Tbs	unsalted butter, divided
6 Tbs	all-purpose flour
3 cups	chicken stock
1/2 pt	heavy cream
~	salt and freshly ground pepper to taste
1/4 tsp	freshly grated nutmeg (1/8 tsp ground)
1 bunch	watercress, blanched, finely chopped

Melt 4 tablespoons butter over medium-high heat and whisk in flour. Add stock and continue to cook, stirring, 20 minutes. Blend in cream, nutmeg, and salt and pepper to taste and simmer 15 minutes. Strain sauce, add chopped watercress, and whisk in remaining 2 tablespoons butter.

Garlic Chicken with Apricot Sauce and Pasta
Serves 4

*The Prescription
for Perfect Pasta*

*"Al dente"—an Italian phrase
which means "to the tooth"—is
the key to perfect pasta.
It describes a texture which offers
a slight resistance when bitten
into, without being overdone
and mushy.*

~

*Bring salt and water to a boil.
Add pasta and return to a boil.
Cook uncovered until pasta is
done but still firm (al dente).
Fresh pasta, depending on its size,
can take 3 to 5 minutes to cook;
dried pasta, 7 to 10 minutes
(thicker dried pasta may need to
cook as long as 15 minutes).
While your pasta is cooking, stir
occasionally with a wooden spoon
or fork, lifting pasta to separate
strands. When the pasta is done,
drain it immediately in a colander
(you may want to rinse dried
pasta with hot water to remove
excess starch). If the pasta is not
to be served immediately, rinse it
with cold water to stop the
cooking process. Drain the pasta
and allow it to cool, then
generously oil your hands and
toss the pasta to coat.*

~

*Cooled pasta can be reheated,
or you can just mix it with a hot
sauce to warm it up. Pasta will
keep 1 or 2 days in the
refrigerator.*

4	chicken breast halves, boneless, skinless
1 Tbs	unsalted butter
~	salt and pepper to taste
2 cloves	garlic, pressed
4 tsp	balsamic vinegar
4 tsp	cider vinegar
4 tsp	white muscadine juice or white grape juice
1/4 tsp	honey
1/8 tsp	thyme
1/2 pt	heavy cream
2 Tbs	apricot preserves, puréed in food processor
1/2 lb	pasta, cooked
1/4 cup	sliced almonds, browned in butter
~	chopped chives for garnish

Cook chicken breasts in butter over medium-low heat 5 minutes on one side. Turn breasts and season with salt and pepper. Spread garlic over breasts and cover tightly. Turn heat to low and cook 3 minutes. Blend vinegars, muscadine juice, honey, and thyme. Pour mixture over chicken, cover, and cook 3 more minutes. Turn chicken and reduce liquid to a glaze. Remove chicken. Add cream, raise heat to high, and cook, stirring constantly, until sauce thickens. Blend in preserves. To serve, toss pasta with almonds and place on platter. Arrange chicken breasts and sauce on pasta and top with chopped chives.

Curried Chicken Breast with Cranberries

Serves 8

8	chicken breast halves, boneless, skinless
~	salt and pepper to taste
5 Tbs	unsalted butter, divided
3 Tbs	all-purpose flour
1 Tbs	curry powder
1/2 cup	chicken stock
1 1/4 cups	half & half
~	Cranberry Chutney (see accompanying recipe)
4 cups	cooked rice
8 slices	bacon, cooked, crumbled (optional)

Salt and pepper chicken, then sauté in 4 tablespoons butter until just firm, not browned. Remove from pan and reserve. Add 1 tablespoon butter to pan and blend in flour. Cook 3 minutes. Add curry powder and blend. Add chicken stock and stir until smooth. Add half & half and cook until thickened. Blend in Cranberry Chutney and stir well to combine. Return chicken to pan, cover, and cook over low heat until chicken is done, 15 minutes. Serve over rice and top with crumbled bacon, if desired.

Cranberry Chutney

Yields 2 1/2 cups

1 can	whole berry cranberry sauce (1 lb)
~	zest of 1 large lemon
1/2 cup	raisins
2 tsp	fresh ginger juice
1 tsp	dry mustard
1	green apple, peeled, chopped
1 large	onion, chopped
1/4	medium bell pepper, chopped
1/2 cup	cider vinegar
1/2 cup	dark brown sugar
1 tsp	salt
1 clove	garlic, pressed

In a saucepan, combine all ingredients. Simmer, stirring frequently, until thickened, 1 hour. Cool and store in refrigerator.

Grilled Chicken with Muscadine Hot Pepper Jelly Sauce

Serves 4

1 cup	Muscadine Hot Pepper Jelly (page 240) or sweet, hot pepper jelly
1 cup	dry white wine
1/4 cup	chopped fresh basil (1 Tbs dried)
4	chicken breast halves
~	salt and pepper to taste

Season chicken with salt and pepper. Prepare sauce by combining jelly, wine, and basil in saucepan over low heat. Divide sauce—1 cup for marinade and basting and 1 cup for serving. Marinate chicken for 30 minutes and grill, basting often. Serve with sauce.

Dijon Chicken in Phyllo
Serves 6-8

3	whole chicken breasts, boneless, skinless, in strips
~	salt and pepper to taste
¼ cup	unsalted butter
½ cup	Dijon mustard
1 pt	heavy cream
5 sheets	phyllo pastry
3/4 cup	unsalted butter, melted
¼ cup	toasted bread crumbs
1 large	egg
1 tsp	water

For fullest flavor, prepare the chicken and mustard combination the day before and refrigerate overnight. The phyllo roll can then be assembled early the next day, refrigerated, and baked and served that evening. You may find that two small rolls are easier to handle than one large one.

Salt and pepper chicken strips. Sauté chicken in butter 5 minutes. Transfer to platter and keep warm. Add mustard to sauté pan, scraping to release browned bits. Whisk cream into mustard and cook over low heat until sauce thickens and reduces by ¼. Stir in any juices from sautéed chicken that have accumulated on platter. Place chicken strips in bowl, strain mustard sauce over chicken, and toss to coat. On dish towel, lay out 1 sheet of phyllo. Working rapidly, brush phyllo with melted butter and top with 1 tablespoon bread crumbs. Continue layering buttered and crumbed phyllo sheets on top of each other until the final sheet, which should be buttered only. Arrange chicken strips on bottom ⅓ of long side of layered phyllo, keeping 2" border around chicken. Using dish towel to help, turn up bottom and sides and roll up jelly roll-style. Preheat oven to 450°. Place chicken roll on ungreased jelly roll pan. Beat egg with water and brush exposed surface of roll with egg mixture. Bake 12 to 15 minutes. Slice and serve.

Auby's Honey-Baked Turkey

Serves 10-12

1	uncooked turkey (12 to 15 lbs)
1 cup	Worcestershire sauce
1/2 cup	soy sauce
1 cup	honey
1 Tbs	freshly ground black pepper
3 Tbs	salt-free herb seasoning
8 Tbs	unsalted butter, room temperature
~	*cheesecloth*

Defrost turkey overnight. Wash turkey, removing neck and giblets. Preheat oven to 350° and place turkey in roasting pan, breast up. Mix Worcestershire and soy sauces and pour over turkey, working well into cavity and outside, adding more as turkey absorbs sauce. Pour any excess sauce into pan. Coat turkey liberally inside and out with honey. Mix pepper and seasoning and sprinkle over turkey inside and out. Coat breast of turkey with butter and cover with cheesecloth. Spoon sauce from pan over cloth. Cover pan with foil and place in oven. Reduce heat to 320°. Bake until meat thermometer reaches 180°, 2 to 3 hours, basting frequently with pan juices. Leg will move easily when done. During final 20 minutes of cooking, uncover pan, remove cheesecloth, and allow breast to brown. Watch carefully—honey burns easily.

If you prefer the flavor of smoked turkey—or if you want to save some cooking time—a frozen smoked turkey will do just fine in this recipe. Bake your thawed, smoked bird 8 minutes per pound. Baste frequently and do not brown.

Turkey While You Sleep!

Serves 10-12

1	uncooked turkey
1 tsp	salt
2 stalks	celery with leaves
1/2 cup	unsalted butter, melted
2 cups	boiling water

Sprinkle salt inside turkey cavity and insert celery stalks. Preheat oven to 450°. Place turkey on rack in roasting pan and rub with melted butter. Pour boiling water around turkey, cover pan tightly, and cook 2 hours for 14 pounds or less, 2 1/2 hours for more than 14 pounds. After cooking time, turn off heat, but DO NOT OPEN OVEN DOOR. Leave turkey in closed oven overnight (8 hours). Turkey will be ready to slice and refrigerate the next morning, with plenty of drippings for gravy.

This procedure results in a turkey that is extremely moist and so tender that it isn't really suitable for formal carving. The method is so easy, however, that you'll find yourself serving turkey all year 'round, not just during holidays.

Cornish Hens with Brown Rice Stuffing
Serves 4

1 cup	uncooked brown rice
2 ½ cups	chicken stock
1 small	onion, chopped
½	yellow bell pepper, chopped
½ cup	dried apricots, chopped
8 Tbs	unsalted butter
½ cup	toasted almonds, slivered or chopped
1 tsp	salt
¼ tsp	dried thyme
¼ tsp	dried marjoram
4	Cornish hens
~	salt and pepper to taste
4 slices	bacon

Bring chicken stock to a boil, add rice, and cover. Reduce heat and cook for 40 minutes or until stock is absorbed. Set aside. Preheat oven to 325°. Sauté onion, bell pepper, and apricots in butter. Mix with cooked rice, almonds, salt, thyme, and marjoram. Salt and pepper hens, inside and out. Stuff with rice mixture and place one bacon slice on top of each hen. Bake, uncovered, at 325° for 1 ½ to 2 hours, basting often with pan drippings. If not tender after 1 ½ hours, cover and steam for final 30 minutes.

Quail with Raspberry Vinegar
Serves 2

4	quail
10 Tbs	unsalted butter, divided (all may not be needed)
~	salt and pepper to taste
1 Tbs	chopped shallots
⅓ cup	raspberry vinegar
½ to 1 cup	chicken stock
~	fresh chopped tarragon for garnish

Remove backbone from quail and flatten, pressing down on breastbone. In a skillet, melt 3 tablespoons butter and brown birds on both sides. Season with salt and pepper and remove from pan. Add shallots to pan and deglaze with vinegar. Replace quail, add ½ cup stock, cover, and simmer until tender, 10 to 15 minutes. Remove quail. Either reduce liquid or add more stock to obtain ½ cup liquid. Bring to boil and whisk in butter, 1 tablespoon at a time, until desired consistency is attained. Adjust seasoning, add chopped tarragon, and serve over quail.

Deglazing
Demystified

After meat or other food has been cooked in a sauté pan or skillet, a great deal of flavor remains locked in the browned bits which stick to the pan's bottom during the cooking process.

Deglazing is a method of freeing that flavor by heating a small amount of liquid in the pan (usually wine or stock), then stirring and scraping to release those browned bits. The resulting mixture can then be incorporated into the recipe as the base for a sauce or gravy.

Smothered Quail

Serves 6

12 quail
1 tsp salt
2 tsp cayenne pepper
2 tsp freshly ground black pepper
1 tsp freshly ground white pepper
1 $^{1}/_{2}$ cups all-purpose flour
$^{1}/_{2}$ cup vegetable oil

3 medium yellow onions, chopped
2 medium bell peppers, chopped
2 stalks celery, chopped
$^{1}/_{3}$ cup sherry
1 cup chicken stock

1 bunch green onions, finely chopped
$^{1}/_{2}$ cup chopped fresh parsley
~
Preheat oven to 275°.
Combine salt and peppers and season quail with mixture, rubbing inside and out.
Dredge quail in flour and brown in hot oil in large iron skillet
over medium-high heat.
Remove quail to Dutch oven or large baking dish.

To skillet, add onions, bell peppers, and celery and sauté until almost tender.
Add sherry and chicken stock, scraping well to loosen browned bits.
Pour onion mixture over quail, cover, and bake about 1 $^{1}/_{2}$ hours
or until quail are very tender.

Stir in green onions and parsley and serve hot.

*This recipe can be prepared up to the baking point,
then refrigerated as long as one day.
Serve hot biscuits with the gravy.*

*"For as long as human
beings have walked the
lands of the South, they
have hunted animals for
food—and for almost
that long, they have
celebrated the success
of the hunt with
sumptuous spreads of
native food and drink.
In every Southern state,
all manner of special
occasions—coon
suppers, rabbit and
squirrel dinners, duck
and goose banquets,
venison feasts—are
widely enjoyed as
seasonal or annual
events."*

from Southern Food by John Egerton

HUNT BREAKFAST

Hot Tomato-Orange Juice
~
Café Mocha
~
Smothered Quail
~
"Sweetness" Biscuits
~
Blueberry Corn Muffins
~
Dollie's Tomato Pie
~
Baked Pears with Blue Cheese and Port

Fried Duck
Serves 8

8	duck breast fillets
~	milk
~	lemon pepper seasoning
~	all-purpose flour
~	vegetable oil

Cut breasts into finger-size strips and soak in enough milk to cover for 1/2 hour. Drain duck strips and coat liberally with lemon pepper seasoning. Roll in flour, drop into hot oil, and cook until just slightly pink, 4 to 5 minutes, depending on oil temperature.

Duck and Wild Rice Casserole
Serves 6-8

2 medium	ducks
1 pkg	crab boil
2 stalks	celery, chopped
2 medium	onions, quartered
~	salt and pepper to taste
1/2 cup	unsalted butter
1 medium	onion, chopped
1/4 cup	all-purpose flour
6 oz	sliced mushrooms
1 cup	chicken stock
1/2 cup	red wine
2 Tbs	chopped fresh parsley
1 1/2 cups	heavy cream or half & half
1 1/2 tsp	salt
1/4 tsp	pepper
~	Tabasco Sauce to taste
1 pkg	long grain and wild rice (6 oz), cooked
~	slivered almonds

Boil duck with crab boil, celery, onions, salt, and pepper in water to cover for 1 hour or until tender. Debone and coarsely chop duck meat; set aside. Preheat oven to 350°. Sauté onions in butter, then stir in flour, mushrooms, stock, and wine. Add duck , parsley, cream, salt, pepper, Tabasco, and cooked rice. Place in 2-quart casserole, sprinkle with almonds, and bake for 25 to 30 minutes.

CELEBRATION DINNER

Soft-Shell Crawfish in Praline Sauce

~

Salad with Asparagus and Creamy Garlic Dressing

~

Pork Tenderloin Stuffed with Apricots and Spinach

~

Roasted New Potatoes

~

Green Beans with Honey Cashew Sauce

~

Whole Wheat Crescents

~

Creme Brûlee with Blackberries

~

Wine

A story from the early part of this century describes an elegant Mississippi dinner party at which finger bowls were passed, each garnished with a slice of lemon.

One of the guests squeezed the lemon into his bowl, added sugar, and proceeded to drink what he assumed was lemonade.
The host of the dinner, rather than embarrass his guest, followed his example, as did the other members of the party.

The Governor's Mansion:
A Pictorial History
*by David G. Sansing
and Carroll Waller*

One of the tenets of Southern hospitality holds that, at all costs, no guest should ever be made to feel uncomfortable.

PHOTO:
*Charles and Lois Scott
find a cozy retreat in this
private side garden at their
Jackson home.*

Pork Roast with Red, Yellow, and Green Peppers
Serves 8

1 Tbs	vegetable oil
3 Tbs	unsalted butter
1 small	onion, finely chopped
1/2	green bell pepper, finely chopped
1/2 stalk	celery, finely chopped
1 Tbs	minced garlic
1 1/2 tsp	salt
2 tsp	black pepper
1 tsp	cayenne pepper
1 tsp	paprika
1 tsp	dried thyme
1/2 tsp	dry mustard
1	boneless pork loin roast (4 lbs)
1 each	red, yellow, orange, and green bell peppers, in 1" pieces
1/4 cup	extra virgin olive oil, or more
2 Tbs	balsamic vinegar, or to taste
~	salt and pepper to taste

For a variation, add tiny new potatoes during the last 30 minutes of cooking. Accompany with some good French bread and you have a classy company meal. Any leftovers (an unlikely prospect) will make great next-day sandwiches.

Sauté onion, green pepper, celery, and garlic in butter and oil. Add salt, black and cayenne peppers, paprika, thyme, and mustard. With pork roast fat side up, make several slits and stuff with vegetable mixture. Rub surface of roast with remaining vegetable mixture. Bake uncovered at 275° for 3 hours or until internal temperature reaches 160°, then raise heat to 425° and continue baking until brown on top, 15 minutes more. Sauté bell pepper pieces in olive oil and balsamic vinegar. Salt and pepper to taste and serve roast on large platter surrounded with sautéed peppers.

Mustard Pork Tenderloin

Serves 8

1	pork tenderloin (2 ½ lbs)
~	Creole mustard to coat pork
¼ cup	water
¼ cup	red wine
2 Tbs	unsalted butter
1 Tbs	chopped onion
2 Tbs	chopped green onion
1 clove	garlic, minced
⅓ cup	mayonnaise (homemade preferred)
2 Tbs	Creole mustard

Preheat oven to 350°. Completely cover tenderloin with thin coat of mustard. Place on rack in shallow baking pan and roast 20 minutes per pound or until internal temperature registers 160-165° on meat thermometer. To prepare mustard sauce, remove tenderloin and place baking pan with drippings on stove over medium-high heat. Pour in ¼ cup water and scrape to release browned bits. Add red wine, stir, and bring to boil. Reduce to glaze. Sauté onions, green onions, and garlic in butter and add to glaze. Let sauce cool briefly. Blend mayonnaise and mustard, then slowly add sauce, a bit at a time, until desired consistency is reached. Serve mustard sauce with sliced pork tenderloin.

Solving
the Pork Puzzle

Pigs are eating better than ever these days, which means we can, too. Because of modern feeding methods, trichinosis is rarely a problem in today's kitchens. Nevertheless, we should continue to take the normal precaution of thoroughly washing anything that contacts uncooked pork (especially our hands), and we should never taste raw pork. The parasite that causes trichinosis is destroyed at an internal temperature of 137°. However, at that temperature, the meat would be underdone for texture and taste. Always use a meat thermometer when cooking pork. An internal temperature of 150° to 165° produces juicy, tender results. 170° or higher produces overdone pork.

Peanut-Glazed Pork Roast

Serves 8

1	boneless rolled pork loin roast (2 ½ lbs), trimmed
1 clove	garlic, pressed
~	salt and pepper to taste
1 small	onion, sliced
~	Peanut Glaze (see accompanying recipe)
1 ½ tsp	cornstarch, mixed with ¼ cup cold water
1 tsp	fresh lemon juice

Preheat oven to 350°. Rub roast with garlic, salt, and pepper. Arrange onion slices over and around roast and seal tightly in foil. Bake 1 hour. After baking, unwrap roast; pour off and reserve juices. If juices have escaped to pan, deglaze and add to reserved juices from foil. Coat roast generously with prepared glaze mixture and roast, uncovered, for 1 additional hour. Remove roast from pan and keep warm. Degrease reserved juices and use to deglaze pan. Add cornstarch mixture, cook until thickened, and stir in lemon juice. Lightly coat slices of roast with sauce; serve additional sauce separately.

Peanut Glaze

Yields 1 cup

⅓ cup	peanuts, roasted
½ cup	sweetened orange marmalade
1 ½ Tbs	whole-grain mustard
½ tsp	prepared horseradish

Blend peanuts, marmalade, mustard, and horseradish in food processor until smooth.

Pork Tenderloin
Stuffed with Apricots and Spinach
Serves 4

1/2 lb	fresh spinach, washed, chopped
3 cloves	garlic, minced
3 Tbs	unsalted butter
1 cup	dried apricots, sliced
2 Tbs	chopped fresh rosemary (2 tsp dried)
~	salt and pepper to taste
1	pork tenderloin (2 lb), pounded to 3/4" thickness
2 Tbs	vegetable oil
1 cup	red wine
2 cups	beef stock

Preheat oven to 350°. Sauté spinach and garlic briefly in butter. Mix in apricots and rosemary and season with salt and pepper. Spread apricot stuffing over flattened tenderloin. Roll up and secure with kitchen twine. In Dutch oven on stove top, brown tenderloin in oil. Add wine to pot, transfer to preheated oven, and cook uncovered for 20 minutes per pound or until meat thermometer reaches 160-165°. Return pot to stove top and remove tenderloin. Add stock to pot and scrape to loosen browned bits. Cook until sauce is reduced and thickened. Slice tenderloin and serve with sauce.

Sweet and Spicy Pork Chops
Serves 2

2	pork chops, butterflied, 1/4" thick
1/4 cup	peanut oil
2 clove	garlic, minced
1/4 cup	sherry
1/4 cup	soy sauce
2 Tbs	brown sugar
1/2 tsp	crushed red pepper
1/4 lb	vermicelli or thin spaghetti, cooked, drained
1 tsp	toasted sesame seeds for garnish

Pound pork chops to 1/8" thickness. Brown in oil with garlic over medium heat. Pour off drippings. Combine sherry, soy sauce, brown sugar, and red pepper and pour over chops. Cover tightly and cook slowly 20 minutes, or until chops are tender. Place chops over cooked vermicelli, pour sauce over, and sprinkle with toasted sesame seeds to serve.

Dollie's Barbecued Ribs

Serves 8

8 slabs pork ribs (ask butcher for "3 ¹/₂-down")
garlic salt to taste
seasoned salt to taste

2 cans beer (24 oz total)
1 cup red wine
2 cups white vinegar
2 Tbs paprika
Tabasco Sauce to taste
2 Tbs pepper
2 medium onions, finely chopped

crushed ice

~

Trim ribs as uniformly as possible. Remove membrane
from concave side of ribs. Rub ribs with garlic salt and seasoning salt.
Prepare marinade and basting sauce by combining beer, wine, vinegar,
paprika, Tabasco, pepper, and onion. Place ribs in shallow pan, add sauce,
and cover with 8 scoops of ice (keeps ribs fresh and adds to liquid).
Marinate for 2 hours. Grill ribs slowly over low fire, turning and basting
regularly. Separate ribs and serve with T. C.'s Barbecue Sauce.

T. C.'s Barbecue Sauce

Yields 2 ¹/₂ qts

1 ¹/₂ cups vegetable oil
1 ¹/₂ cups white vinegar
2 cans tomato sauce (32 oz total)
2 bottles catsup (28 oz total)
1 cup unsalted butter
³/₄ cup Tabasco Sauce
1 box celery seed (1 ¹/₂ oz)
¹/₂ Tbs salt
3 cloves garlic, finely chopped
3 large onions, finely chopped
1 Tbs pepper

1 cup Worcestershire sauce
1 ¹/₂ cups fresh lemon juice

~

Combine oil, vinegar, tomato sauce, catsup, butter, Tabasco, celery seed,
salt, garlic, onions, and pepper. Mix well and bring to a boil.
Remove from heat and blend in Worcestershire and lemon juice.

§

With all due respect
to Kentucky mutton
and Texas beef, barbecue
in the Deep South
means pork, pure and
simple…and slow.

In these days of
fast food, barbecue is the
ultimate slow food,
requiring hours of
patient, low-temperature
cooking. Any good
barbecuer (even those in
Kentucky and Texas)
will agree that you can't
rush good barbecue.
Put a pig on the fire
and call in the neigh-
bors—as T. C. Buford
likes to do on
the 4th of July—and
you're set up for several
hours of swapping
gossip and spinning
stories, while absolutely
intoxicating fragrances
waft through the air.
By the time the porker is
ready for its debut,
tongues are tired and
appetites are sharpened
to an exquisitely fine
point.

In the South, barbecue
is as much a social
occasion as it is a food.
And Southerners,
hospitable to their very
soul, find it irresistible.

Tomato Gravy

Serves 8

*4 Tbs unsalted butter
or bacon drippings
4 Tbs all-purpose flour
2 cups milk, heated
salt and freshly ground
pepper to taste
1 clove garlic, minced
6 medium,
ripe tomatoes, peeled, cored,
cut into eighths,
or 1 can tomatoes (28 oz)*

~

*Melt butter or drippings
in skillet over medium-high
heat. Add flour and whisk
constantly until light
brown. Whisk in warm
milk and bring to a boil.
Season with salt and pepper
and add garlic. Reduce heat,
add tomatoes, and simmer
slowly until tomatoes are
soft and integrated into
gravy. Serve over hot
biscuits.*

Gravy 'n' Grits

*Tomato Gravy makes a rich addition
to breakfast or brunch, especially
when it's lavishly ladled over a
generous serving of that universal
Southern staple, grits. Grits are finely
ground, dried corn kernels, cooked
with water to a thick, porridge-like
consistency. Some historians say that
in 1607, when the first settlers arrived
in America to found the Jamestown
colony in Virginia, they were greeted
by Indians bearing grits.*

Meatloaf with Sun-dried Tomatoes and Herbs
Serves 6

Meatloaf:

1 medium	onion, finely chopped
1	bell pepper, finely chopped
1 Tbs	extra virgin olive oil
1 lb	ground round
2 oz	sun-dried tomatoes, rehydrated, drained, finely chopped
6 oz	provolone or mozzarella cheese, shredded
2 large	eggs, beaten
2 cloves	garlic, minced
1 slice	bread, softened in 1/8 cup milk, drained
2 tsp	dried basil
1 tsp	salt
1 tsp	dried oregano
1 tsp	dried thyme
1 tsp	freshly ground black pepper

Sun-dried Tomato Gravy:

1/4 cup	drippings from meatloaf
1 Tbs	all-purpose flour
1/2 pt	half & half
1/2 oz	sun-dried tomatoes, rehydrated, drained, finely chopped
1 Tbs	finely chopped green onion
1 Tbs	chopped fresh basil (1 tsp dried)
~	salt and pepper to taste

In microwave, soften onion and bell pepper in olive oil on HIGH, 2 minutes, and cool. Preheat oven to 350°. Combine onion, bell pepper, ground round, tomatoes, cheese, eggs, garlic, bread, basil, salt, oregano, thyme, and pepper. Press meatloaf mixture into lightly greased 5" x 9 1/2" loaf pan. Bake 1 hour, pouring off fat as necessary and reserving drippings for gravy, if desired. To make gravy, whisk drippings with flour over medium heat. Whisk in half & half and stir to thicken. Add tomatoes, green onion, basil, salt, and pepper and heat thoroughly. Serve gravy over sliced meatloaf.

Fillet of Beef Stuffed with Red Bell Peppers, Spinach, and Montrachet

Serves 6

1 ¼ lb	fresh spinach, stemmed
8 oz	goat cheese (Montrachet), crumbled
1 tsp	dried rosemary, crumbled
1 tsp	dried thyme
½ tsp	salt
½ tsp	freshly ground black pepper
1	fillet of beef (center plus tail), trimmed (3 lbs)
~	salt and pepper to taste
3 medium	red bell peppers, roasted, peeled, seeded, in quarters
~	*kitchen twine*
½ lb	bacon slices, blanched
2 Tbs	extra virgin olive oil
~	fresh chives for garnish

Set aside 8 large spinach leaves. Blanch remaining leaves until just wilted, 2 minutes. Drain, refresh under cold water, then drain again. Wrap spinach in towel, squeeze dry, and chop coarsely. Combine chopped spinach with cheese, rosemary, thyme, salt, and pepper. Place spinach mixture on wax paper and roll into 12"-long log. Wrap and refrigerate until firm. Butterfly beef fillet by cutting lengthwise down center, 2/3 of the way through. Open fillet flat, book-style. Pound butterflied fillet to ¾" thick. Season with salt and pepper. Arrange 8 reserved spinach leaves over cut side of beef, leaving 1" border. Layer with bell pepper pieces, skinned side up. Place spinach log on one side of fillet, then roll beef into tight cylinder, tucking tail end under. Tie with kitchen twine at 1" intervals. Preheat oven to 375°. Brown beef roll in oil on all sides, 10 minutes. Place beef on rack in roasting pan and arrange blanched bacon slices on top. Roast 35 minutes or until meat thermometer registers 125° for rare. Allow to rest 15 minutes after cooking. Discard bacon, slice beef, and serve garnished with fresh chives.

The Right Stuff
about
Roasting Peppers

When a recipe calls for hot or sweet peppers to be roasted, peeled, seeded, and chopped, here's the way to go about it. First, preheat your broiler. Place the peppers about 2 inches from the heat and roast them 2 to 3 minutes, turning regularly so that they blacken and blister on all sides. Put the blackened peppers into a paper bag, close it tightly, and allow the peppers to cool. The buildup of steam inside the bag will loosen the skins of the peppers so you can peel them off. After peeling, proceed to seed and chop according to recipe instructions. Incidentally, some cooks have been known to blacken their peppers with a blowtorch instead of a broiler. It seems a bit flamboyant, but to each his own.

Sautéed Pepper Steak

Serves 4

4	beef steaks (1/2" thick boneless strip, tenderloin, or rib-eye)
1 1/2 Tbs	black or green peppercorns, crushed
~	extra virgin olive oil to taste
~	Worcestershire sauce to taste
2 Tbs	extra virgin olive oil, divided
4 Tbs	unsalted butter, divided
3 medium	green onions, minced
1/4 cup	minced fresh parsley
1 Tbs	cornstarch
1 Tbs	Dijon mustard
1 cup	beef stock
~	Worcestershire sauce to taste
2 Tbs	fresh lemon juice
~	Cognac to taste

Trim steaks and pound to 1/4" thickness. Rub with pepper and sprinkle with olive oil and Worcestershire. Heat 1 tablespoon oil and 2 tablespoons butter in sauté pan. Sauté steaks, two at a time, 30 seconds on each side, and remove from pan. Add remaining oil and butter and sauté onions and parsley for 1 minute. Dissolve cornstarch and mustard in beef stock and add to pan. Stir in Worcestershire, lemon juice, and cognac. Return steaks to pan and coat with sauce. Serve immediately.

Tender Pot Roast with Herbs

Serves 8-10

To make a complete meal add potatoes, carrots and/or onions to the pot during the last hour of cooking.

1	boneless rump roast (5 lbs)
2 tsp	salt
1 tsp	pepper
3 Tbs	all-purpose flour
3 Tbs	vegetable oil
1	beef bouillon cube dissolved in 1/2 cup hot water
2	bay leaves
1/2 tsp	garlic salt
1/2 tsp	dried marjoram
1/4 tsp	dried basil
~	flour for gravy, optional

Preheat oven to 300°. Season roast with salt and pepper, dredge in flour, and brown in oil in Dutch oven. Pour off grease. Add bouillon, bay leaves, garlic salt, marjoram, and basil to beef. Cover tightly and cook until meat is tender, 3 to 3 1/2 hours. Remove meat to hot platter, discard bay leaves, and thicken cooking liquid with flour for gravy, if desired.

Stir-fried Beef with Vegetables

Serves 4-6

1	fillet of beef or pork (8 oz)
1 tsp	vermouth or sherry
1 tsp	cornstarch
2 tsp	soy sauce
8 Tbs	peanut oil, divided
3	Chinese mushrooms, soaked, sliced
1 cup	broccoli florets, blanched
1 cup	carrots, sliced, blanched
8 whole	water chestnuts, sliced
8 ears	baby corn
1/2 cup	bean sprouts
1 clove	garlic
1/2 cup	beef stock
2 1/2 cups	cooked rice

Slice meat very thinly across grain, then cut into julienne strips. Blend vermouth, cornstarch, and soy sauce. Pour mixture over meat and let stand 15 to 20 minutes at room temperature. Heat 4 tablespoons oil in wok over high heat. Stir-fry mushrooms, broccoli, carrots, water chestnuts, corn, and bean sprouts. Remove vegetables from wok. Heat remaining 4 tablespoons oil in wok. Burn garlic and discard. Add beef and cook until done but not overcooked. Return vegetables to wok, add stock, and stir-fry until thickened. Serve immediately over rice.

Peppered Chutney Beef Tenderloin
Serves 6-8

| ~ | Tangy Pineapple Marinade (see accompanying recipe) |
| 1 | beef tenderloin (4 lbs) |

2 tsp	freshly ground pepper
4 slices	bacon
1/3 cup	Major Grey chutney

Place tenderloin in plastic storage bag, pour in Tangy Pineapple Marinade, and seal securely. Refrigerate several hours or overnight, turning occasionally. When ready to cook, preheat oven to 425°. Drain tenderloin, reserving marinade. Rub beef with pepper. Place on rack in a shallow pan. Top with bacon and roast uncovered until meat thermometer registers 135°, 30 to 45 minutes. Baste twice with marinade during cooking. Remove bacon, spoon chutney over roast, and bake 10 minutes longer or until thermometer reaches 140°. Remove to serving platter and allow to rest 15 minutes before slicing. This recipe works equally well on the grill.

Tangy Pineapple Marinade
Yields 2 cups

3/4 cup	unsweetened pineapple juice
1/4 cup	steak sauce
1/3 cup	Worcestershire sauce
1/3 cup	port wine
1/4 cup	fresh lemon juice
1 tsp	pepper
1 tsp	lemon pepper seasoning
1 tsp	dry mustard

Stir together all ingredients.

Veal Scallops with Asparagus and Lime Sauce
Serves 4

1 tsp	saffron threads, divided
2 Tbs	all-purpose flour
~	salt and pepper to taste

| 12 | veal scallops |
| 2 Tbs | vegetable oil |

1 2/3 cups	dry white wine
1 tsp	lime zest
1 Tbs	fresh lime juice
4 Tbs	Crème Fraîche (see accompanying recipe) or heavy cream
12	green peppercorns

| 1 lb | fresh small asparagus, blanched |

REALLY REALLY REALLY REALLY REALLY GOOD!

Combine 1/2 teaspoon saffron with flour, salt, and pepper. Dust both sides of veal scallops with seasoned flour. Brown veal in oil on both sides, about 5 minutes total. Remove veal to serving platter and keep warm. Deglaze skillet with wine, then add lime zest, lime juice, and remaining 1/2 teaspoon saffron. Bring lime mixture to a boil and reduce to consistency of syrup. Stir in crème fraîche, bring to another boil, and stir in peppercorns. Surround veal scallops with asparagus and top with sauce.

Crème Fraîche
Yields 1 pint

| 2 cups | heavy cream |
| 4 tbs | buttermilk |

Mix cream and buttermilk in screwtop glass jar. Allow to stand at room temperature for 12 hours or until very thick, similar to sour cream. Refrigerate for 36 hours before using—can be stored in refrigerator as long as 10 days. Créme fraîche can be boiled without curdling and is a delicious alternative to whipped cream on fruit or desserts.

Veal Medallions
with Green Tomatoes and Mozzarella

Serves 4

1 lb	veal loin, trimmed
3	green (unripe) tomatoes
8 oz	fresh mozzarella cheese
1 cup	all-purpose flour for dredging
4 large	eggs
¼ cup	milk
3 cups	fresh breadcrumbs
2 Tbs	chopped fresh parsley
1 Tbs	chopped fresh chives
1 Tbs	chopped fresh basil
4 Tbs	finely grated Parmesan cheese
~	salt and freshly ground pepper to taste
~	extra virgin olive oil for frying
8 cups	mixed salad greens, washed, torn
1 small	red onion, thinly sliced
¼ cup	balsamic vinegar
¼ cup	peanut oil
~	salt and pepper to taste
2	lemons in wedges for garnish

Slice veal loin into 8 medallions ⅓" thick, then lightly pound each slice to 3" diameter. Slice tomatoes and mozzarella cheese into 8 slices each, equal in thickness to veal medallions. Place flour in shallow pan. Blend eggs and milk and pour into second pan. Combine breadcrumbs, parsley, chives, basil, and Parmesan cheese in third pan. Season meat, tomato, and mozzarella lightly with salt and pepper. Coat each slice of veal, tomato, and mozzarella thoroughly with flour, shaking off excess. Dip into egg wash and let excess drip off. Dredge in seasoned breadcrumbs. Coat the bottom of large sauté pan with olive oil and heat until nearly smoking, 325°. Sauté breaded slices 1 minute on each side and drain on paper towels. Toss salad greens with onion, vinegar, and peanut oil and season to taste with salt and pepper. Center mounds of salad on each of 4 large plates. Alternate slices of veal, tomato, and mozzarella (2 each per serving) around salad. Serve with lemon wedges.

Nick Apostle, owner, Nick's and 400 East Capitol Restaurants, Jackson, MS

Grilled Leg of Lamb in Mint Sauce
Serves 6-8

Mint Sauce
Yields 1 1/2 cups

1 cup	sugar
1/2 cup	sherry vinegar
1 Tbs	raspberry vinegar
5 Tbs	chopped fresh mint leaves
2 Tbs	hot pepper jelly

Combine sugar and vinegars and bring to a boil over medium-high heat. Reduce heat to medium and cook 5 minutes, stirring occasionally. Remove from heat, add chopped mint leaves, cover, and let stand 5 minutes. Add pepper jelly and serve warm with lamb.

1	leg of lamb (5 lbs), deboned and butterflied
2 cloves	garlic, thinly sliced
~	freshly ground black pepper to coat lamb
1/4 cup	extra virgin olive oil
1/2 cup	Mint Sauce (see accompanying recipe)

Prepare grill. On fat side of roast, make several small slits and stud with garlic slices. Coat completely with freshly ground pepper. Truss, fat side out, with kitchen string into a 3" thick rectangle and rub surface with olive oil. Place lamb over hot coals and sear both sides of meat until sealed. Cook for 10 minutes on each side or until meat thermometer reaches 140° for rare, 160° for medium rare. Three to 4 minutes before end of cooking, baste each side of lamb with Mint Sauce to form brown crust. Transfer lamb to platter, let rest, and baste again with Mint Sauce. Slice across grain into 1/4" slices. Serve with juices and additional Mint Sauce.

Herb-Baked Lamb Chops
Serves 4

4	lamb chops, 2" thick
~	all-purpose flour to coat chops
2 Tbs	unsalted butter
1/4 cup	wine vinegar
2 Tbs	extra virgin olive oil
1/4 cup	fresh lemon juice
3 Tbs	Worcestershire sauce
1/2 cup	water
1/2 tsp	dried oregano
1/2 tsp	dried thyme
2	bay leaves
2 Tbs	unsalted butter, melted
1/4 tsp	garlic salt
1/4 tsp	white pepper
2 medium	onions, sliced

Preheat oven to 325°. Flour chops and brown in 2 tablespoons butter. Combine vinegar, oil, lemon juice, Worcestershire, water, oregano, thyme, bay leaves, butter, garlic salt, and white pepper. Add lamb chops and sliced onions to vinegar mixture and bake, uncovered, 2 hours.

Broiled Lamb Chop

Serves 1

1	lamb chop
1 clove	garlic, pressed
~	salt and pepper
1 tsp	Dijon mustard
1 tsp	soy sauce
2 sprigs	fresh rosemary (¼ tsp dried)
½ tsp	unsalted butter (optional)

If this recipe sounds a little lonely for you, just multiply as many times as you like and call in the whole gang.

Rub chop with garlic and season with salt and pepper. Combine mustard, soy sauce, and rosemary. Add chop and marinate 1 hour. Top lamb chop with butter, if desired, and broil 3 to 5 minutes on each side, depending on thickness, being careful not to overcook.

Pasta Primavera with Roasted Red Peppers

Serves 6-8

3 Tbs	extra virgin olive oil
3 cloves	garlic, minced
4	green onions, finely chopped
½ lb	fettuccine noodles, cooked
1 cup	fresh snow peas, blanched
½ lb	fresh asparagus, blanched, in ½" pieces
2	red bell peppers, roasted, peeled, seeded, julienned
1	yellow bell pepper, roasted, peeled, seeded, julienned
3 Tbs	chopped fresh basil (2 tsp dried)
1 tsp	lemon pepper seasoning
2 oz	freshly grated Parmesan cheese (½ cup)
¼ cup	chopped fresh parsley
~	salt and pepper to taste

In a large skillet heat oil and add garlic and green onions, cooking over medium heat for 1 minute. Add fettuccine and all other ingredients, seasoning to taste. Heat until thoroughly warmed and serve.

Pasta Jambalaya
Serves 8

1 lb	angel hair pasta, cooked
4 Tbs	unsalted butter
1 lb	andouille or other smoked sausage, sliced in rounds
1 cup	chopped ham
¼ cup	all-purpose flour
1	bell pepper, chopped
2 medium	onions, chopped
3 stalks	celery, chopped
5 cloves	garlic, chopped
2 tsp	dried basil
2 tsp	dried oregano
1	bay leaf
1 can	Rotel tomatoes with chilies, drained, chopped (10 oz)
1 pt	oysters with their liquor
2 lbs	medium shrimp, peeled
2 tsp	unsalted butter
~	Creole seasoning, to taste
1 bunch	green onions, chopped
~	fresh parsley for garnish

Toss hot, cooked pasta with butter. Brown sausage, drain, and combine with pasta. In same skillet, brown ham, add flour, bell pepper, onions, celery, garlic, basil, oregano, and bay leaf and cook until vegetables are tender. Add tomatoes and stir to make gravy (thin with oyster liquor if necessary). Cook oysters with their liquor in microwave on HIGH for 1 ½ minutes or until they just curl. Drain oysters and add to pasta and sausage. Sauté shrimp in 2 teaspoons butter and add Creole seasoning to taste. Toss shrimp with pasta, then combine with gravy and green onions. Remove bay leaf, garnish with fresh parsley, and serve.

Southern Vegetable Pie

Serves 8

3 Tbs	extra virgin olive oil
1 large	red onion, thinly sliced
3 cloves	garlic, minced
3 medium	yellow squash, in ¼" slices
3 medium	zucchini, in ¼" slices
1	red bell pepper, seeded, in ¼"-wide strips
1	yellow bell pepper, seeded, in ¼"-wide strips
1	green bell pepper, seeded, in ¼"-wide strips
8 oz	fresh mushrooms, sliced
6 large	eggs
¼ cup	heavy cream
2 tsp	salt
2 tsp	freshly ground pepper
2 cups	stale French bread cubes (½")
8 oz	cream cheese, diced
10 oz	Swiss cheese, shredded (2 cups)

Preheat oven to 350°. In large skillet over medium-high heat, sauté onion, garlic, squash, zucchini, bell peppers, and mushrooms until crisp-tender, 15 to 20 minutes. Meanwhile, whisk eggs and cream together and season with salt and pepper. Stir in bread cubes and cheeses. Combine egg mixture with sautéed vegetables and stir until well combined. Pour into greased 10" springform pan, packing mixture tightly.

Place pan on baking sheet and bake until firm to the touch, puffed, and golden brown, 1 hour. If top browns too much, cover with aluminum foil. Serve hot, cold, or at room temperature.

PHOTO (left): Fountainhead, *on Glenway Drive in Jackson, is Mississippi's example of the architecture of Frank Lloyd Wright. Wright himself selected the site—deep in a ravine in the Woodland Hills section of the city—for its original owner, J. Willis Hughes. The house was built over a period of four years, using concrete, copper, and red cypress. Jackson architect Robert P. Adams and his wife, Mary, have renovated* Fountainhead *for their personal residence.*

PHOTO (overleaf):

Fresh Tomato Tart

Grilled Vegetable Kabobs

SIDE DISHES

Fresh Tomato Tart
Serves 8-10

~	basic pastry dough
8 oz	mozzarella cheese, shredded
2 Tbs	chopped fresh basil
4-5	ripe tomatoes, in ½" slices
½ tsp	salt
¼ tsp	pepper
1 Tbs	extra virgin olive oil
~	chopped fresh basil for garnish

Preheat oven to 400°. Line 10" loose-bottom tart pan with pastry dough. Spread bottom of pastry with cheese and sprinkle with basil. Cover with tomato slices, arranging to cover as evenly as possible. Sprinkle tomatoes with salt and pepper and drizzle with olive oil. Bake 30 to 40 minutes. Garnish with fresh chopped basil. Slice in wedges and serve warm or at room temperature.

If you don't already grow basil in your back yard, you will after you taste this recipe!

Basil is a member of the mint family, with a sweet and spicy flavor that lies somewhere between licorice and clove. It's a natural complement for tomatoes and the key ingredient for pesto sauce. Although normally a summer herb, basil can be grown on a sunny windowsill during the winter months. Some legends say that hanging basil in the doorways of a home will protect the family within.

Tomatoes Pinehurst
Serves 8

Presenting
the Pain-Free Path
to Perfectly Peeled
Tomatoes

Bring a large pot of water
to a boil. Add whole tomatoes and
boil for 15 seconds.
Drain the tomatoes immediately,
rinse them in cold water,
and just watch those skins go
slip-sliding away!

4 large	ripe tomatoes, peeled, halved
1 cup	Italian salad dressing
½ cup	unsalted butter, melted
1 packet	buttery flavored crackers (4 oz), crushed
1 jar	marinated artichoke hearts (6 oz), drained, sliced
~	fresh basil
~	freshly grated Parmesan cheese
8 tsp	unsalted butter

Pour Italian dressing over tomato halves and refrigerate 10 to 12 hours. When ready to cook, sauté cracker crumbs in melted butter. Preheat oven to 350°. Arrange artichoke slices over marinated tomato halves. Top with sautéed cracker crumbs and sprinkle with basil and cheese. Place 1 teaspoon butter on each tomato half and bake 20 minutes.

Parmesan Zucchini Slices
Serves 4-6

1 clove	garlic, sliced
3 Tbs	extra virgin olive oil
2 Tbs	unsalted butter
8 medium	zucchini, unpeeled, thinly sliced
¾ cup	grated Parmesan cheese
¼ tsp	dried basil
~	salt and pepper to taste
~	freshly grated Parmesan cheese for topping
~	chopped fresh parsley and chives for garnish

Preheat oven to 350°. Brown garlic in oil and butter in large heavy skillet. Discard garlic and add zucchini slices. Add ¾ cup cheese and basil and toss gently. Season with salt and pepper and transfer to lightly greased shallow baking dish. Sprinkle over with freshly grated cheese, cover, and bake at 350° for 10 minutes or until zucchini is tender but still crisp. Garnish with parsley and chives and serve immediately.

Tomatoes Lillian

Serves 8

VERY GOOD

4 large   firm ripe tomatoes, halved

1/2 cup	unsalted butter
1/2 cup	red pepper jelly
1 Tbs	curry powder
3 Tbs	bread crumbs

Preheat oven to 350°. Arrange tomatoes in baking pan. In saucepan, heat together butter, pepper jelly, curry powder, and bread crumbs until butter and jelly are melted. Pour jelly mixture over tomatoes. Bake until glaze has browned slightly.

Joe Middleton, executive chef, Nick's Restaurant; former executive chef, MS Governor's Mansion, Jackson, MS

Zucchini and Tomatoes in Basil Cream Sauce

Serves 4-6

Basil Cream Sauce:

3 Tbs	unsalted butter, melted
2 Tbs	all-purpose flour
1 cup	half & half
1/4 cup	chopped fresh basil (1 Tbs dried)
1 tsp	chicken bouillon granules
1/2 tsp	freshly ground black pepper
~	salt to taste

3 medium	zucchini, thinly sliced
8 small	ripe tomatoes, thinly sliced
1 medium	yellow onion, thinly sliced
~	salt and pepper to taste
1/2 cup	freshly grated Parmesan cheese, divided

To prepare cream sauce, cook butter and flour together over medium heat, stirring constantly, 2 minutes. Whisk in the half & half, basil, bouillon granules, salt, and pepper. Stir until thickened, 2 to 3 minutes. Remove from heat.

Preheat oven to 350°. Layer half the zucchini, tomatoes, and onion in greased 9 1/2" x 11" baking dish, seasoning each layer lightly with salt and pepper. Sprinkle half the cheese on top. Repeat layers, except for cheese. Spoon basil cream sauce over and top with remaining 1/4 cup cheese. Bake uncovered 45 minutes or until browned and bubbly.

§

Dollie's Tomato Pie

Serves 8

2 cans stewed tomatoes with green peppers and onions (29 oz total)
1/2 cup sugar
4 Tbs unsalted butter
1 Tbs vanilla extract
basic pastry dough , in strips

~

Combine tomatoes, sugar, butter, and vanilla and simmer until thickened, about 1 hour. Preheat oven to 350°. Pour tomato mixture into pie dish and arrange pastry strips on top in multiple layers. Bake until upper crust is crisp and lower pastry layers are like dumplings, 40 minutes.

Dollie's Tomato Pie is a permanent fixture for hunt breakfasts at plantation home Buford Hall in Glendora, MS. It will add an exuberant "Tallyho!" to any brunch menu.

Eggplant Casserole
Serves 4-6

1 medium	eggplant, peeled and cut into small pieces
2 large	eggs, lightly beaten
2 Tbs	unsalted butter
2 1/2 Tbs	chopped yellow onion
1/2 cup	saltine cracker crumbs
1/4 tsp	freshly ground black pepper
1/2 tsp	ground oregano
3 medium	tomatoes, unpeeled, in 3/8" slices
~	salt and pepper to taste
~	sugar to taste
6 oz	Swiss cheese, shredded

Preheat oven to 375°. Steam eggplant until tender but not mushy. Drain excess water and mash eggplant with a fork. Mix eggs, butter, onion, cracker crumbs, pepper, and oregano. Combine egg mixture with eggplant and blend thoroughly. Pour eggplant mixture into greased casserole. Layer tomato slices over eggplant and sprinkle with salt, pepper, and sugar. Top with cheese and bake, uncovered, for 25 minutes.

Eggplant Sticks
Serves 6

1 medium	eggplant
1 tsp	sugar dissolved in ice water for soaking
1 large	egg
1 tsp	prepared mustard
2 tsp	water
3/4 cup	plain cornmeal
3 Tbs	all-purpose flour
3 tsp	salt
1/4 tsp	black pepper
1/8 tsp	cayenne pepper
1 Tbs	fresh lemon juice

Peel and slice eggplant into finger-size pieces. Soak in sugared ice water 30 minutes and drain. Preheat oven to 425°. Whisk together egg, mustard, and water and set aside. Combine cornmeal, flour, salt, and peppers. Dip eggplant sticks in egg mixture, then roll in cornmeal mixture. Place sticks on oiled baking sheet and bake 10 to 15 minutes, turning once. Sprinkle with lemon juice and serve immediately.

Eggplant Pointers

A good eggplant should be heavy for its size and smooth-skinned, with no soft or brown spots. Eggplants become bitter with age and should be used within 1 to 2 days of purchase. To help eliminate the bitter taste of overripe eggplant, freely salt cut pieces and allow to rest 30 minutes. Rinse and pat dry before continuing recipe.

Children love these Eggplant Sticks dipped in catsup like French fries. Adults will probably prefer sweet-hot mustard or horseradish sauce.

Aunt Georgia's Squash Casserole

Serves 8-10

1 cup	water
2 tsp	salt, divided
1/8 tsp	sugar
6 medium	yellow squash, sliced
7 Tbs	unsalted butter, room temperature, divided
4 oz	cheddar cheese, shredded
1 carton	sour cream (8 oz)
5 medium	green onions, chopped
1/2 cup	Parmesan cheese
1 cup	bread crumbs

Preheat oven to 350°. Add 1 tsp salt and sugar to water and simmer squash over low heat, covered, 15 minutes. Drain squash and return to pan. Add 4 tablespoons butter and blend with squash. Stir in cheddar cheese, sour cream, green onions, 1 tsp salt, and Parmesan cheese. Pour squash mixture into greased casserole dish. Top with bread crumbs and dot with remaining butter. Bake 30 minutes.

Vidalia Onion Casserole

Serves 8

1/2 cup	unsalted butter, room temperature, divided
4 large	Vidalia or other sweet onions, sliced in rings
1 1/2 pkgs	buttery flavored crackers (6 oz or 50 crackers), crushed
8 oz	cheddar cheese, shredded
~	salt to taste
~	paprika to taste
3 large	eggs, beaten
1 cup	milk

Preheat oven to 350°. Sauté onion rings in 1/4 cup butter. Combine remaining butter with cracker crumbs. Reserve 1/4 of crumb mixture for topping and layer remaining crumbs into bottom of greased 9" x 13" casserole. Spread sautéed onion rings over crumb layer and sprinkle with cheese, salt, and paprika. Combine eggs and milk and pour over layers. Top with reserved crumb mixture and bake 35 to 40 minutes.

§ Squash Croquettes

Serves 8

4 medium yellow squash, in 1" pieces
1 medium onion, grated
2 cups fine light bread crumbs
1 cup fine cornbread crumbs
2 large eggs
1 1/2 tsp salt
1/2 tsp white pepper
2 tsp sugar
additional bread crumbs for coating
corn oil for deep frying

~

Cook squash in small amount of water until tender. Drain well and press out water. Mash squash thoroughly, mix in remaining ingredients, except for coating crumbs and oil, and chill.
Using large ice cream scoop, spoon out balls of chilled squash mixture. Coat squash balls in additional bread crumbs and fry in deep fat until light golden brown.

Old favorite at the Pioneer Cafeterias, Birmingham, AL

Onion Patties

Serves 10

¾ cup	all-purpose flour
2 tsp	baking powder
1 Tbs	sugar
¾ tsp	salt
¼ tsp	pepper
1 Tbs	plain cornmeal
¾ cup	milk
2 medium	onions, finely chopped
~	peanut oil for frying

Combine flour, baking powder, sugar, salt, pepper, and cornmeal. Add milk and mix well. Stir in onions. Drop small mounds of batter into shallow hot oil and fry 5 minutes on each side or until golden brown.

Potato and Onion Casserole

Serves 2

An easy, quick, and hearty side dish for grilled steak.

1 large	onion, peeled, cut into ¼" slices
1 large	baking potato, scrubbed, unpeeled, in ¼" slices
1 ½ Tbs	unsalted butter, melted
2 Tbs	water
¼ tsp	dried oregano
⅛ tsp	dried dill
1 Tbs	chopped fresh parsley
~	salt and pepper to taste

Cut onion slices in half. In microwave-safe dish, alternate and overlap potato and onion slices. Pour melted butter over slices. Add water, oregano, dill, parsley, salt, and pepper. Cover with plastic wrap, leaving one corner open to release steam. Microwave 13 minutes on HIGH. Remove dish from microwave, close vented corner, and allow to rest 5 minutes before serving.

Mashed Potatoes
with Green Onions and Parmesan

Serves 4

4 large	russet potatoes, peeled, in chunks
1/2 cup	milk
4 Tbs	unsalted butter, divided
2 bunches	green onions, chopped
1 1/2 cups	freshly grated Parmesan cheese
~	salt and freshly ground pepper to taste

Boil potatoes until tender. Drain well and mash until smooth. Blend in milk and 3 tablespoons butter. Sauté green onions in remaining tablespoon butter until wilted. Add sautéed onions and cheese to potatoes and mix gently. Season with salt and pepper to taste. Preheat oven to 350°. Transfer potatoes to a buttered casserole and bake for 10 to 15 minutes or until heated through. This recipe can be prepared to baking point and refrigerated until needed.

Golden Potato Bake

Serves 6

2 lbs	boiling potatoes, peeled, thinly sliced
1 tsp	salt
1 tsp	garlic powder
1/2 tsp	lemon pepper seasoning
1/4 tsp	cayenne pepper
3 Tbs	unsalted butter
6 oz	Swiss cheese, shredded
3/4 cup	chicken stock
~	fresh chopped parsley for garnish

Preheat oven to 425°. Spread half of potato slices in bottom of buttered baking dish. Sprinkle with half of salt, garlic salt, lemon pepper, and cayenne and dot with half of butter. Repeat with remaining potatoes, salts, pepper, and butter. Top with cheese and pour stock over all. Bake until golden and bubbly, about 40 minutes. Allow to stand 10 minutes, then garnish with fresh parsley.

§

Mattie B.'s Sweet Potato Pudding

Serves 8

4 cups grated raw sweet potatoes, sprinkled with lemon juice
3 cups milk
4 large eggs, beaten
1/2 cup unsalted butter, melted
2 cups sugar
1/2 cup brown sugar
1/2 cup powdered sugar
1 tsp ground cinnamon
1 tsp ground nutmeg
1/2 tsp ground allspice
1/2 tsp ground cloves
1 tsp vanilla extract

~

Preheat oven to 350°. Combine all ingredients in 13" x 9" pan and bake 1 hour.

A traditional accompaniment for the holiday bird. Can be assembled several days in advance.
W A R N I N G
This side dish could steal the show from the turkey at Thanksgiving!

~

Mattie B. has been cooking for the Cunningham family in Brooksville, Mississippi, for decades. Her Sweet Potato Pudding is famous in the area, and is welcomed as a gift during the holiday season.

Roasted New Potatoes with Herbs
Serves 4-6

Add that Deep South difference by substituting sweet potatoes, peeled and cut into chunks, for the new potatoes. If you prefer to straddle the Mason-Dixon Line, try a mixture of sweet and red potatoes.

¼ cup	extra virgin olive oil
8 large	cloves garlic, flattened
20	new potatoes, halved
1 Tbs	chopped fresh rosemary (1 ½ tsp dried)
1 ½ tsp	chopped fresh thyme (³/₄ tsp dried)
~	salt and coarsely ground pepper to taste
~	fresh rosemary for garnish

Combine olive oil and garlic and allow flavors to blend at least 1 hour. Preheat oven to 400°. Place potatoes in baking dish and sprinkle with rosemary, thyme, salt, and pepper. Pour oil and garlic over potatoes and toss well. Roast until potatoes are tender and crusty, stirring occasionally, for 45 minutes. Serve hot, garnished with fresh rosemary sprigs.

Brussels Sprouts in Chive Sauce
Serves 8-10

Chive Sauce:

4	shallots, chopped
¼ cup	dry white wine
4 tsp	chicken stock
1 ½ cups	heavy cream
5 sprigs	watercress
3 Tbs	cold water
1 Tbs	finely chopped fresh chives
6 ½ Tbs	unsalted butter, room temperature
1 Tbs	fresh lemon juice
~	salt and pepper to taste
2 lbs	fresh Brussels sprouts, steamed

Gently boil shallots and wine, uncovered, until nearly all wine has evaporated. Remove from heat. In another pan, mix stock and cream. Boil, uncovered, until mixture is rich and creamy. Remove from heat. In food processor, blend softened shallots, watercress, cold water, chives, and butter, 30 seconds. Add cream mixture and lemon juice and blend until smooth, 30 seconds more. Season with salt and pepper. Serve hot Chive Sauce over Brussels sprouts.

Joe Middleton, executive chef, Nick's Restaurant; former executive chef, MS Governor's Mansion, Jackson, MS

Carrots Marcelle

Serves 8

1 ½ cups	water
2 lbs	carrots, peeled, sliced
1	chicken bouillon cube
1 bunch	green onions, chopped
2 Tbs	unsalted butter, melted
8 oz	processed American cheese, cubed
1 carton	sour cream (8 oz)
¼ cup	milk
1 Tbs	seasoned bread crumbs
1 Tbs	chopped fresh parsley

Preheat oven to 350°. Bring water with carrots and bouillon cube to boil. Cook 15 to 20 minutes, or until carrots are crisp and tender. Drain and set aside. Sauté green onions in butter, then remove from heat and add cheese, sour cream, and milk. Blend until cheese is melted. Stir in sliced carrots and spoon mixture into greased 2-quart casserole. Sprinkle with bread crumbs and parsley and bake until heated through, 20 minutes.

Artichoke Hearts and Mushrooms

Serves 4

1 can	artichoke hearts (14 oz)
1 pkg	fresh mushrooms (8 oz), sliced
2 Tbs	unsalted butter
1 clove	garlic, minced
1 ½ tsp	cornstarch
¼ cup	sherry
1 tsp	fresh lemon juice
~	salt and pepper to taste
1 Tbs	chopped fresh parsley

Drain and quarter artichokes, reserving liquid. Sauté artichokes and sliced mushrooms in butter with garlic. Blend cornstarch with sherry, lemon juice, and reserved artichoke liquid. Heat liquid mixture, stirring constantly until smooth and clear. Add salt, pepper, and parsley. Combine liquid mixture with sautéed artichokes and mushrooms and heat gently before serving.

Baked Beets

Serves 4

1 bunch fresh beets, unwashed

~

Trim tops of beets to 3 inches. Gently brush off dirt and place beets on foil-lined cookie sheet. Leave the roots on and do not trim. Preheat oven to 375° and bake beets until easily pierced by a fork, 1 hour. Remove from oven, cool, and remove skins, tops, and roots. Beets may now be prepared any style: buttered, pickled, etc.

About Beets

Beets can be found in supermarkets the year around, and smaller ones are generally more tender than larger ones. Choose firm beets with smooth skins and crisp, bright greens (trim greens right away to prevent moisture loss). Beets may be sealed in a plastic bag and refrigerated up to three weeks.

Corn Soufflé with Creamed Onion Sauce
Serves 8

*"A special favorite
at our house was Beulah's
corn pudding.
I remember Mother's dinner
party for visitors from Chicago,
with Moses, my grandparents'
man of all work, serving.
The corn pudding was the subject
of great admiration.
Mother insisted that the guests
have more. Moses, in the
background, shook his head.
Mother could not see him.
The guests demurred, but she
finally persuaded them.
Moses, looking stricken,
passed a perfectly empty
serving dish to every one
at the table.
I can still hear the scrape
of the serving spoon as the guests
tried to capture at least one grain
of corn from the empty offering."*

Charlotte Capers,
*author, raconteur, and former director
of the Mississippi Department
of Archives and History*

3 Tbs	unsalted butter
1 medium	onion, finely chopped
3 ears	fresh corn, kernels and liquid scraped from cobs
4 large	eggs
1 tsp	cornstarch
1 cup	heavy cream
~	salt and pepper to taste

Creamed Onion Sauce

1 Tbs	unsalted butter
1 medium	onion, thinly sliced
$^2/_3$ cup	heavy cream
~	salt to taste
2 tsp	soy sauce
~	freshly ground black pepper to taste

For soufflé, sauté onion in butter until translucent. Add corn kernels with liquid and continue to sauté until soft. Remove from heat and cool. Process half the corn mixture with eggs, cornstarch, and heavy cream until smooth. Transfer processed corn mixture to mixing bowl, add salt, pepper, and remaining corn mixture, and fold to blend. Preheat oven to 350°. Fill buttered ramekins or large custard dish with corn mixture. Cover with non-stick parchment paper or buttered wax paper to prevent skin from forming. Bake in water bath 20 to 25 minutes.

For Creamed Onion Sauce, sauté onion in butter until golden brown. Add cream and reduce by half. Season with salt, soy sauce, and pepper. Remove from heat and set aside.

To serve, top soufflé with warm Creamed Onion Sauce.

Joe Middleton, executive chef, Nick's Restaurant; former executive chef, MS Governor's Mansion, Jackson, MS

Favorite Summer Vegetables
Serves 8

2 Tbs	bacon drippings
1 large	sweet onion, chopped
2 cups	sliced okra
1/2	red or yellow bell pepper, chopped
1 large	red tomato, diced
1 large	green tomato, diced
2 cups	shelled butter beans or butter peas, cooked, drained
2 tsp	fresh chopped rosemary (1/2 tsp dried)
~	salt and pepper to taste

In a large, heavy skillet, sauté onion in bacon drippings over medium heat for 2 to 3 minutes. Add okra and cook, stirring for 5 minutes. Add bell pepper, tomatoes, butter beans, and rosemary. Season with salt and pepper. Cook for 15 minutes, adding water if necessary. Serve hot.

Black-Eyed Peas with Sweet and Hot Peppers
Serves 8

1 lb	dried black-eyed peas, soaked overnight, drained
4 Tbs	unsalted butter, room temperature
4 Tbs	water
2 medium	onions, diced
2	red bell peppers, seeded, diced
2	green bell peppers, seeded, diced
2 cloves	garlic, minced
1 small	jalapeño chili, seeded, minced
1/2 tsp	cayenne pepper
~	salt and black pepper to taste

Cover peas with fresh water. Bring to a boil, cover, and lower heat. Simmer until tender, 30 minutes. Drain peas, reserving one cup liquid. Heat butter with water in saucepan. Add onions, bell peppers, garlic, and jalapeño and cook until softened. Season with cayenne, salt, and black pepper. Add cooked peas with reserved cooking liquid and simmer until heated completely.

§

Boiled Corn on Cob
Serves 6

4-5 qts water
1/4 tsp sugar
1 lemon wedge
6 ears corn,
fresh or frozen

~

Add sugar to water. Squeeze juice from lemon wedge into water and drop in wedge. Bring water to boil and add corn. For fresh corn, boil 8 to 10 minutes, depending on kernel size. Allow frozen corn to thaw partially before adding to boiling water. Boil frozen corn about 8 minutes.

Naturally, the fresher the corn, the better the flavor. We once heard of a farmer who took a portable gas cooker out to his cornfield so that he could boil ears of corn without even removing them from the stalk! Our procedure, however, does an excellent job of refreshing store-bought corn and giving it a nearly fresh-picked flavor. One additional note: Never, ever, put salt into the boiling water. It will toughen your corn.

Cauliflower Panache
Serves 6

The color contrast between cauliflower and broccoli makes a striking presentation when served in a clear glass baking dish.

1 large	cauliflower, in florets, cooked, drained
½ cup	freshly grated Parmesan cheese
1 large	bunch broccoli, stalks peeled, blanched
2 Tbs	unsalted butter
½ cup	sour cream
~	salt and pepper to taste
⅓ cup	bread crumbs

Place cauliflower in 1 ½-quart baking dish and sprinkle with cheese. Preheat oven to 350°. Chop broccoli coarsely and puree with butter and sour cream. Season with salt and pepper. Cover cauliflower with broccoli puree and sprinkle top with bread crumbs. Bake 20 minutes.

Broccoli with Tangy Sauce
Serves 4-6

The Beauty
of Blanching

To preserve the beautiful color, firm texture, and just-picked flavor of fresh vegetables, plunge them briefly into rapidly boiling water, then rinse them in cold water to stop the cooking process. The procedure is called blanching, and it can also loosen the skin of a vegetable for easier peeling. How long does the vegetable stay in the boiling water? Well, how long is a piece of string? The answer is: Long enough. Seriously, blanching time depends on the size and type of the vegetable and what you want to do with it—from 15 seconds for loosening the skin of a tomato to several minutes for cooking carrots to the crisp-tender stage. Test frequently until your desired effect is reached, then quickly rinse in cold water.

2 Tbs	unsalted butter
2 Tbs	extra virgin olive oil
1 ½ tsp	Worcestershire sauce
~	salt and pepper to taste
1 tsp	Dijon mustard
1 Tbs	cider vinegar
~	cayenne pepper to taste
1 bunch	broccoli, blanched

Combine all ingredients except broccoli and heat until butter melts. Pour sauce over cooked broccoli just before serving.

Grilled Vegetable Kabobs
Serves 8

2	yellow squash, in chunks
2	zucchini, in chunks
1 large	red onion, cut into wedges
2 large	bell peppers, blanched, in squares
16 large	mushroom caps
16	cherry tomatoes

Garden Herb Marinade:

¼ cup	fresh lemon juice
¾ cup	extra virgin olive oil
2 Tbs	wine vinegar
2 Tbs	minced fresh basil (1 Tbs dried)
1 Tbs	Dijon mustard
1	bay leaf, crumbled
½ tsp	dried thyme
½ tsp	dried marjoram
2 cloves	garlic, minced
2 Tbs	chopped fresh parsley
~	salt and pepper to taste

8	*wooden skewers (12"), soaked in water*

Sprinkle squash and zucchini with salt and allow to drain in colander 30 minutes. Blend all marinade ingredients and pour over squash, zucchini, onion wedges, bell peppers, mushrooms, and tomatoes. Refrigerate at least 2 hours or overnight. After preparing grill, drain vegetables, reserving marinade. Alternate vegetable pieces on skewers and grill until tender, basting frequently with reserved marinade, about 15 minutes.

Herb sauces, such as the Garden Herb Marinade in this recipe, add intriguing and exciting new flavor dimensions to grilled meats and vegetables. Here's another you might like to try:

Fresh Herb Grilling Sauce

Yields 2 cups

1 ½ cup	minced fresh herbs (basil, rosemary, parsley, oregano, etc.)
1 clove	garlic, minced
1 Tbs	fresh lemon juice
3 drops	Tabasco Sauce
½ tsp	salt
½ cup	extra virgin olive oil
~	freshly ground black pepper to taste

Thoroughly combine all ingredients and brush over vegetables or meat while grilling.

Grilled Asparagus
Serves 4-6

Dijon Vinaigrette

Yields 1 1/4 cups

3/4 cup extra virgin olive oil

6 Tbs fresh lemon juice

1 Tbs Dijon mustard

1 tsp salt

1 tsp freshly ground black
       pepper

2 cloves garlic, minced

Thoroughly blend all ingredients.

1 lb	fresh asparagus, trimmed, in 6" lengths
1/2 cup	Dijon Vinaigrette (see accompanying recipe)
~	fresh herbs for garnish

Preheat grill. Arrange asparagus in grill basket with tips toward outer edges of basket. Asparagus layer can be in doubled, if necessary. Brush asparagus with Dijon Vinaigrette. Grill 3 minutes, turn, and brush with more vinaigrette. Cook 3 more minutes or until asparagus is crisp-tender, being careful not to burn. Serve hot, at room temperature, or chilled. Fan on platter around grilled meat, sprinkled with fresh herbs.

Asparagus with Caper Dill Sauce
Serves 4-6

Blanching Tips

Never cover green vegetables while blanching—they release acids that will diminish their color.

~

Add cream of tartar when blanching white vegetables to prevent yellowing.

~

Never try to keep vegetables warm after blanching—they'll turn mushy and lose their color. Reheat them in their seasoning sauce or in butter. Store blanched vegetables in the refrigerator, covered, 2 to 3 days.

~

As an alternative to blanching, raw vegetables can be microwaved to the crisp-tender stage, following microwave directions. Always vent a small corner of the dish when microwaving green vegetables to prevent discoloration.

1 cup	sour cream or yogurt
1/4 cup	fresh lemon juice
1/4 cup	fresh dill, minced (1 Tbs dried)
1/4 cup	capers, drained
1/2 tsp	salt
1/2 tsp	freshly ground black pepper
1 lb	fresh asparagus or green beans, blanched

Blend all ingredients except asparagus or beans. Chill for at least 1 hour. Serve over blanched asparagus or green beans.

Green Beans with Honey Cashew Sauce

Serves 4

3 Tbs	unsalted butter
1/2 cup	coarsely chopped salted cashews
2 Tbs	honey
1 lb	fresh green beans, blanched, drained

Sauté cashews in butter over low heat, 5 minutes. Add honey and cook 1 minute longer, stirring constantly. Pour sauce over beans and toss until coated.

This sauce will happily lend its sweet crunch to numerous other vegetables, such as broccoli, Brussels sprouts, or carrots.

Green Beans and Red Bell Pepper in Balsamic Vinegar

Serves 6

2 Tbs	extra virgin olive oil
1 medium	red bell pepper, in 1/4" strips
2 cloves	garlic, finely minced
1 1/2 lbs	fresh green beans, blanched
1/4 cup	balsamic vinegar
~	salt and freshly ground black pepper to taste
~	freshly grated Parmesan cheese, optional

Sauté bell pepper in oil until tender. Add garlic, green beans, vinegar, salt, and pepper. Heat until beans are warmed. Serve hot, topped with freshly grated cheese, if desired.

Try applying this same procedure to fresh asparagus or broccoli.

Turnip Green Soufflé
Serves 8

1	ham hock
½ tsp	salt
2	hot red peppers (1 tsp dried red pepper flakes)
2 pkgs	frozen chopped turnip greens (20 oz total)
	or 1 ½ lbs fresh greens, washed, stemmed
1 large	yellow onion, chopped
¼ cup	unsalted butter
¼ cup	all-purpose flour
½ cup	half & half, heated
1 cup	reserved pot liquor from greens
4 oz	sharp cheddar cheese, shredded
½ tsp	salt
½ tsp	pepper
1 Tbs	prepared horseradish
3 large	eggs, separated
⅛ tsp	cream of tartar

Bring water to boil with ham hock, salt, and red pepper. Add greens and onion, lower heat, and cook 30 minutes to 1 hour. Drain greens and reserve 1 cup liquor. Remove ham hock and red peppers. Press as much water as possible out of greens. Puree greens in food processor. Preheat oven to 350°. Cook butter and flour together over medium heat, stirring constantly, 2 minutes. Stir in half & half and reserved pot liquor and whisk until thickened. Remove from heat and add cheese, salt, pepper, and horseradish, stirring until cheese melts. Add pureed turnip greens. Beat egg yolks until thick and lemon-colored and stir into turnip green mixture. Beat egg whites with cream of tartar until stiff peaks form. Fold egg whites into turnip green mixture. Spoon into greased soufflé dish and bake 45 minutes.

Sautéed Spinach
Serves 4

Add a bit of interest to Sautéed Spinach by dashing on a little heavy cream and grated Parmesan cheese during the last minute or two of cooking.

3 Tbs	unsalted butter
1 Tbs	extra virgin olive oil
1 clove	garlic, minced
1 lb	fresh spinach leaves, stemmed, washed, drained
~	salt and pepper to taste

Heat butter and oil over medium-high heat. Add garlic and spinach, reduce heat, and simmer, covered, 5 to 7 minutes. Season with salt and pepper and serve.

CONTEMPORARY COMFORT MEAL

Meatloaf with Sun-dried Tomatoes and Herbs

~

Mashed Potatoes with Green Onions and Parmesan

~

Black-Eyed Peas with Sweet and Hot Peppers

~

Turnip Green Soufflé

~

Sweet Potato Brioche

~

Tomato Jam

~

Muscadine Cobbler

~

Wine

"When I think of home,
I think of food like this.
We were raised on it.
Some people say it's too
rich or too sweet, but to
me it's just mighty good.
And I love the company
it attracts. Nothing
brings Southerners
together like a big
dinner."

Matalie Grant,
quoted in Southern Food
by John Egerton

"There's no telling
when she last had a
decent home-cooked
meal with honest
vegetables," said Miss
Tennyson Bullock.
"That goes a long way
toward explaining
everything."

from The Optimist's Daughter
by Eudora Welty

PHOTO:
*These folding doors provide
a peek into the kitchen at*
Fountainhead, *with its
copper-clad countertops and
meticulously efficient layout.
Frank Lloyd Wright's design
motif, cut by hand into the
kitchen doors, is repeated
on various surfaces throughout
the house.*

Andouille Sausage Cornbread Dressing
Serves 4-6

1 medium	yellow onion, chopped
2 large	stalks celery, chopped
2 Tbs	unsalted butter
3 cups	crumbled cornbread
3 small	biscuits, crumbled
¼ tsp	dried sage
¼ tsp	dried thyme
~	salt and freshly ground black pepper to taste
1 large	egg
2 cans	chicken stock (29 oz total)
½ lb	andouille or hot Italian sausage, cooked, thinly sliced or chopped

Preheat oven to 400°. Sauté onion and celery in butter until tender. Combine onion and celery mixture with cornbread, biscuits, sage, thyme, salt, pepper, egg, and chicken stock in greased casserole dish. Bake 45 minutes. Stir in sausage and cook 15 minutes longer.

LSU Banana Casserole
Serves 4

This recipe performs well as a side dish with pork, game or poultry or on its own as a dessert. Those who were in attendance declare that this recipe is the only good thing to come out of the Ole Miss-LSU football game in Baton Rouge on Halloween Night, 1961.

6	bananas, sliced lengthwise
½ cup	light brown sugar
½ cup	unsalted butter
½ cup	raisins
½ cup	chopped pecans
1 Tbs	brandy

Preheat oven to 350°. Line bottom of heavily buttered shallow casserole dish with half the bananas. Sprinkle with brown sugar and dot with butter. Layer over with half the raisins and half the pecans. Sprinkle with more brown sugar and dot with more butter. Repeat layers with remaining ingredients except brandy. Bake 30 minutes. Pour brandy over all and serve.

Stuffed Peppers

Serves 6

1 can	stewed tomatoes (14 ½ oz), drained, chopped, liquid reserved
1 cup	finely chopped ham
1 Tbs	bacon drippings
¼ cup	chopped celery
1 small	onion, chopped
1	8" skillet of cornbread, crumbled
1 tsp	salt
1 tsp	Worcestershire sauce
12 drops	Tabasco Sauce
~	sugar to taste, if needed
3 medium	bell peppers, halved and seeded

Preheat oven to 350°. Combine tomatoes, ham, bacon drippings, celery, onion, and crumbled cornbread. Moisten mixture with reserved tomato liquid. Season with salt, Worcestershire, and Tabasco (if flavor seems too acid, add sugar to balance). Generously fill bell pepper halves with cornbread mixture. Place stuffed peppers in pan with ½" water and bake until peppers are tender and stuffing is browned, 45 minutes to 1 hour.

Baked Swiss Grits

Serves 8

1 qt	milk
½ cup	unsalted butter, in pieces
1 cup	regular grits
1 tsp	salt
⅛ tsp	pepper
4 oz	Swiss cheese, shredded
1 ½ oz	grated Parmesan cheese (⅓ cup)

Preheat oven to 350°. Bring milk to a boil. Add butter pieces and stir to melt. Gradually blend in grits, stirring constantly. Remove grits from heat and add salt, pepper, and cheeses. Beat with portable electric mixer 5 minutes. Pour mixture into greased 1 ½-quart casserole and bake 1 hour.

Baked Oysters

Serves 6-8

2 pts oysters, drained
½ cup finely chopped fresh parsley
1 medium onion, finely chopped
1 Tbs Worcestershire sauce
salt and pepper to taste
2 Tbs fresh lemon juice
½ cup unsalted butter, melted
2 cups saltine cracker crumbs
¾ cup half & half
paprika to taste
~

Preheat oven to 350°. Layer half of oysters in bottom of greased baking dish. Sprinkle with half of parsley, onions, Worcestershire sauce, salt, pepper, lemon juice, butter, and cracker crumbs. Repeat layers, reserving ½ cup cracker crumbs. Just before baking, pour half & half over all and top with reserved crumbs. Sprinkle with paprika and bake, uncovered, 30 minutes.

Baked oysters are a traditional holiday treat for many families in coastal areas of the South.

Orange Wild Rice with Currants and Apples
Serves 6-8

1 cup	wild rice, cooked and drained
1 cup	brown rice, cooked and drained
1 cup	dried currants
4 Tbs	chopped fresh Italian parsley
2 Tbs	grated orange zest
1	Granny Smith apple, diced
2 Tbs	extra virgin olive oil
2 Tbs	freshly squeezed orange juice
~	salt and freshly ground pepper to taste
~	freshly grated Parmesan cheese
~	chopped fresh Italian parsley for garnish

Preheat oven to 350°. In mixing bowl, combine cooked rices. Gently toss currants, parsley, zest, apple, oil, orange juice, salt, and pepper with combined rices. Place mixture in casserole, cover with foil, and heat thoroughly 20 minutes. Sprinkle with cheese and garnish with Italian parsley.

Rice Casserole with Chili Peppers
Serves 6-8

1 medium	onion, chopped
1/2 cup	unsalted butter
4 cups	cooked rice
2 cups	sour cream
1 cup	cottage cheese
1 tsp	salt
1/4 tsp	black pepper
2 cans	green chili peppers (8 oz total), diced, divided
8 oz	sharp cheddar cheese, shredded

Preheat oven to 325°. Sauté chopped onion in butter. Combine sautéed onion with cooked rice, sour cream, cottage cheese, salt, and pepper. Reserve half of 1 can of green chilies and add remaining chilies to rice mixture. Place rice mixture in 2 1/2-quart casserole dish. Sprinkle with cheddar cheese and reserved chilies. Bake until hot, 20 minutes.

Fresh Basil and Tomato Pasta

Serves 4

½ lb	fettucine, cooked
½ jar	capers (1 ½ oz total), drained
¼ cup	chopped fresh basil
½ cup	extra virgin olive oil
1 ½ Tbs	wine vinegar
5	fresh tomatoes, peeled, seeded, chopped
~	salt and freshly ground pepper to taste

Thoroughly combine all ingredients and serve warm or cold.

Anchovy-Olive Pasta Sauce

Yields 4 cups

4 Tbs	extra virgin olive oil
1 can	anchovies in olive oil (2 oz), undrained
2 cloves	garlic, minced
1 medium	onion, finely chopped
1 can	chopped black olives (4 ¼ oz) , drained
20	green olives, sliced
2 Tbs	capers, drained
1 tsp	dried basil
2 tsp	Italian seasoning
½ tsp	freshly ground black pepper
1 can	tomatoes (16 oz)
1 can	tomato paste (6 oz)
¾ cup	water
½ cup	Marsala or other red wine
~	Tabasco Sauce to taste

A savory sauce for your favorite pasta and for pizza, as well. The anchovies are quite salty, so no additional salt should be needed. Freezes successfully.

Combine olive oil and anchovies. Cook over medium heat, stirring to puree anchovies, 3 to 5 minutes. Add garlic and onion and cook until tender, 5 minutes longer. Stir in remaining ingredients and simmer, uncovered, 15 minutes.

PHOTO (left): *The Epiphany Episcopal Church was originally built at Hermanville, Mississippi, in 1843. Today it rests on the grounds of the Mississippi Agriculture and Forestry Museum in Jackson.*

PHOTO (overleaf):

Sweet Potato Brioche with

Tomato Jam

Marbled Apricot Bread

Basil Biscuit with

Tomato Gravy

B R E A D S

Sweet Potato Brioche
Yields 1 large loaf

1 pkg	dry yeast
1 tsp	sugar
¼ cup	warm water (105°–115°)
5 large	eggs
1 cup	baked, pureed sweet potato
3 ½ cups	bread flour, unsifted
1 tsp	salt
2 Tbs	sugar
1 cup	unsalted butter, room temperature
1 large	egg, beaten

Dissolve yeast and sugar in warm water until bubbly. In a small bowl, beat five eggs and combine with pureed sweet potato. Place flour, salt, and sugar in food processor with plastic dough blade in place. With machine running, add sweet potato mixture and dissolved yeast. Process 20 to 30 seconds. Dough should be *sticky*—add more water if necessary. Hand-knead dough several times, then place in lightly oiled bowl. Incorporate butter into dough with back of large spoon. Cover with plastic wrap and allow to rise at room temperature until doubled in bulk, about 1 ½ hours. Punch down, cover, and let rise overnight in refrigerator. Shape dough, place in brioche mold or bundt pan, and allow to rise until doubled. Place metal baking sheet in oven while preheating to 400°. Brush dough with beaten egg and make several holes in dough with toothpick. Place pan on baking sheet and bake 10 minutes. Lower heat to 325° and continue baking 20 more minutes.

Use this light, rich bread to make sandwiches with blue cheese, chopped pecans, and brown sugar. Also try it toasted and served with tomato jam.

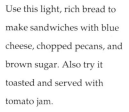

Best-Ever Potato Rolls
Yields 36

1 medium	potato, peeled, boiled, mashed
¼ cup	reserved potato water (105°–115°)
1 pkg	dry yeast
1 tsp	sugar
2 Tbs	vegetable shortening
1 cup	milk, warmed
¼ cup	sugar
1 ½ tsp	salt
4-5 cups	all-purpose flour
2 large	eggs, lightly beaten
~	unsalted butter, melted

If you'd like to freeze these rolls for later use, bake them just to the point when they begin to brown, then remove them from the oven and let them cool. Seal the rolls in plastic bags and store them in your freezer. When you're ready to use them, thaw the frozen rolls for 30 minutes, then bake at 350° for 10 to 12 minutes.

Dissolve yeast and 1 teaspoon sugar in warm potato water until bubbly. In large bowl, mix shortening and mashed potato until smooth. Blend warm milk with sugar and salt, add to potato mixture, and stir until smooth. Add 2 cups flour, one cup at a time, mixing well. Add eggs and mix again. Add yeast mixture and ½ to 1 cup additional flour. Cover and allow to rise 2 hours. Punch down and add about 2 cups flour to make workable dough. Turn out onto floured board and knead 8 to 10 minutes, adding up to 3 cups flour as needed. Dough will be sticky, but less flour makes lighter rolls. Roll out dough on floured surface to ¼" thickness and cut with 3" biscuit cutter. Brush each roll with melted butter and fold over, pressing edges together. Place rolls with edges touching on greased baking sheet. Cover and allow to rise 1 hour. Preheat oven to 350° and bake until lightly browned, 12 to 15 minutes.

Spoon Rolls
Yields 36

1 pkg	dry yeast
1 tsp	sugar
2 cups	warm water (105°–115°)
¾ cup	unsalted butter, melted
¼ cup	sugar
1 large	egg, beaten
4 cups	self-rising flour, unsifted

Dissolve yeast and 1 teaspoon sugar in warm water until bubbly. Blend melted butter with ¼ cup sugar. Add egg and beat. Stir in dissolved yeast, add flour, and mix well. Place in airtight bowl and refrigerate overnight. Preheat oven to 350°. Drop batter by teaspoonfuls into greased miniature muffin tins. Bake 15 minutes or until brown.

Yummy Rolls
Yields 100

3 pkgs	dry yeast
1 tsp	sugar
1/2 cup	warm water (105°–115°)
1 pt	milk, scalded
1/2 cup	vegetable shortening
1 tsp	salt
1/2 cup	sugar
3 large	eggs, beaten
6-8 cups	all-purpose flour
4 Tbs	unsalted butter, melted

Dissolve yeast and sugar in warm water until bubbly. Combine scalded milk with shortening, salt, and sugar and stir until shortening is melted and sugar dissolved. At this point, mixture should be cool enough to add beaten eggs. When mixture has cooled to lukewarm, stir in dissolved yeast. Add 3 cups flour and mix well. Continue adding additional flour until mixture just begins to pull away from bowl—if batter is too stiff, rolls will be heavy. Pour batter onto floured board—it should "puddle out," rather than stand on its own. Hand-knead 10 to 15 minutes. Wash mixing bowl, rinse with hot water, dry, and grease. Return dough to bowl, rubbing lightly with shortening and turning to coat. Cover dough with towel and allow to rise until doubled in bulk, 1 hour. Transfer dough to floured board and hand knead a few times. Cut dough into halves and roll out each half to 1/4" thickness. Cut with small round biscuit cutter and arrange on baking sheets 1/2" apart (recipe should make about 100 rolls—enough for 3 large baking sheets). Brush surface of each roll with melted butter. Fold in half and press edges together. Brush again with melted butter, cover with towel, and allow to rise until doubled in bulk, 1 hour. Preheat oven to 425°. Watch carefully as rolls bake, 1 pan at a time, about 5 minutes or until they turn light brown.

Flour Facts

Low-protein flours are best for use in quick breads, muffins, biscuits, pie crusts, and other recipes which employ chemical leavening (baking powder or baking soda).

Rolls, however, are the exception to this rule. Use low-protein flour for rolls, even though they are leavened with yeast.

~

High-protein flour (bread flour) is best for yeast-leavened breads that are kneaded.

~

To determine if flour is low- or high-protein, read the nutritional information on the package. Low-protein flour has 9 to 10 grams of protein per cup; high-protein has 14 to 15 grams per cup.

Country French Bread
Yields 2 loaves

1 pkg	dry yeast
1 Tbs	sugar
1 cup	warm water (105°–115°)
2 ½ cups	bread flour
1 tsp	salt
1 tsp	balsamic vinegar
¼ cup	extra virgin olive oil with 1 tsp salt, warmed

Because Country French Bread dough is very moist and does not hold its shape, French bread pans are a necessity.

Dissolve yeast and sugar in warm water until bubbly. Place flour and salt in food processor with metal blade in place and pulse to mix. Add dissolved yeast and vinegar and process 15 to 20 seconds. Turn dough out onto unfloured, lightly oiled board and hand-knead a few times. Place dough in warm, oiled bowl and turn to coat. Cover and allow to rise until doubled, 45 minutes to 1 hour. Punch dough down, cut into halves, and form each half into a cylinder. Place in 2 greased French bread pans and glaze with warm, salted oil. Allow to rise until doubled again, 30 to 45 minutes. Preheat oven to 425°. Bake 15 to 20 minutes.

Crusty French Bread
Yields 2 loaves

Flavor olive oil with herbs and use as a dip for this Crusty French Bread—a welcome change from butter or margarine.

1 pkg	dry yeast
1 tsp	sugar
1 cup	warm water (105°–115°)
2 cups	bread flour
1 cup	unbleached flour
1 tsp	salt
~	plain cornmeal for baking sheet
1 egg	beaten with ½ tsp salt for glaze

Dissolve yeast and sugar in warm water until bubbly, 5 minutes. Combine flours and salt in food processor with metal blade in place. With machine running, add dissolved yeast and mix 40 seconds. Transfer dough to oiled bowl and turn to coat. Cover with towel and allow to rise until doubled in bulk, 1 hour. Punch dough down, cover with plastic wrap, and refrigerate at least 8 hours. Four hours before serving, grease baking sheet and sprinkle with cornmeal. On lightly floured surface, roll out dough into two 12" rectangles, then roll up lengthwise, jelly-roll fashion, sealing ends and seams tightly. Place dough seam-side down on baking sheet. Cover with towel and allow to rise until doubled, 1 ½ to 2 hours. Preheat oven to 425°. Slash top of loaves with serrated knife at 2" intervals. Brush top of loaves with salted egg glaze and bake until deeply brown, 25 to 30 minutes. Cool on wire rack.

Herb Bread

Yields 1 large loaf

1 ½ cups	whole wheat flour
1 pkg	quick-rise dry yeast
¼ cup	non-fat dry milk
2 Tbs	sugar
½ tsp	ground nutmeg
1 Tbs	fresh sage (1 tsp dried)
1 tsp	celery seed or caraway seed
1 ½ tsp	salt
1 cup	hot water (120°–130°)
2 Tbs	vegetable shortening
1 large	egg, room temperature
1 ½ cups	bread flour
1 Tbs	unsalted butter, melted

Combine whole wheat flour, yeast, milk, sugar, nutmeg, sage, celery seed, and salt. Pour in hot water and add shortening and egg. Mix thoroughly. Gradually add additional flour, ¼ cup at a time, to make moderately soft dough. Knead until smooth with dough hook or by hand on lightly floured surface, 8 minutes. Place dough in lightly oiled bowl and turn to coat. Cover and allow to rise until doubled in bulk, 30 to 45 minutes. Punch down dough and turn out onto floured surface. Knead 30 seconds to press out bubbles that have formed throughout dough. Shape dough into round or rectangular loaf and place in greased pie plate or loaf pan. Cover with light cloth and allow to rise until almost doubled, 30 minutes. Twenty minutes before baking, preheat oven to 375°. Bake loaf 30 to 35 minutes or until done. Brush hot loaf with melted butter.

Rising to the Occasion: Tips on Using Yeast

When dissolving yeast, always add a small amount of sugar to the liquid to activate the yeast more quickly.

~

The temperature of the liquid in which the yeast is activated should be between 105° and 115°. Any cooler or warmer and the yeast will not work.

~

A pinch of ground spices added to the flour helps improve the yeast's activity.

~

Adding honey directly to the yeast mixture will kill the yeast.

~

Dissolve yeast in a clear glass bowl so that you are better able to see the bubbling action which should occur. If your yeast just lies there, discard it and start again.

~

Check to make sure the expiration date on your yeast package has not passed.

~

Adding a small amount of acid (vinegar or lemon juice) to your dough will produce a higher rise.

~

Quick-rising yeast may be used interchangeably with regular yeast (with adjustments to rising time). Quick-rise takes about half as long to leaven bread.

Rolled Herb Cheese Bread

Yields 2 loaves

5 ½ cups	bread flour
½ cup	sugar
2 tsp	salt
1 pkg	dry yeast
1 ½ cups	milk
4 Tbs	unsalted butter
2 large	eggs
8 oz	sharp cheddar cheese, coarsely shredded
8 oz	longhorn or colby cheese, coarsely shredded
5	green onions, finely chopped
1 tsp	dried basil
½ tsp	dried oregano
¼ tsp	dried thyme
1 large	egg beaten with 1 Tbs water
½ tsp	sesame seed

Combine 1 cup flour with sugar, salt, and yeast. Heat together milk and butter until warm (105°—115°). Add warm milk and 2 eggs to flour mixture. Blend with mixer at lowest speed to moisten, then beat at medium speed 3 minutes, scraping down sides of bowl. Gradually stir in enough additional flour to form stiff dough. Turn out onto floured surface and knead until smooth and elastic, 5 minutes. Place dough in oiled bowl, turning to coat. Cover with towel and allow to rise until doubled in bulk, 1 to 1 ½ hours. Punch dough down and divide in half. On a floured surface, roll out each half to 10" x 15" rectangle. Sprinkle half the cheeses, onions, and herbs on each half of dough, leaving 2" space at top and bottom and 1" space on sides. Carefully roll up dough, folding sides under and pinching along bottom seam to seal. Place each loaf in greased 9" x 5" bread pan. Roll up 2 or 3 cloth kitchen towels and gently place on top of each loaf to prevent bubble forming inside loaves during rising. Cover both loaves with another towel and allow to rise 45 minutes. Preheat oven to 375°. Brush surface of each loaf with egg/water mixture and sprinkle tops with sesame seeds. Place bread pans on cookie sheet and bake 35 to 45 minutes, checking for doneness. Remove loaves from pans and allow to cool on rack at least 1 hour before slicing.

Zippy Cheese Bread

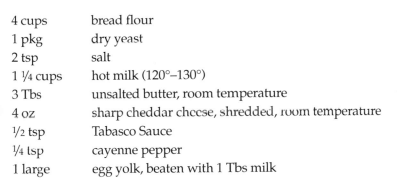

Yields 4 mini-loaves

4 cups	bread flour
1 pkg	dry yeast
2 tsp	salt
1 ¼ cups	hot milk (120°–130°)
3 Tbs	unsalted butter, room temperature
4 oz	sharp cheddar cheese, shredded, room temperature
½ tsp	Tabasco Sauce
¼ tsp	cayenne pepper
1 large	egg yolk, beaten with 1 Tbs milk

In mixing bowl, combine 2 cups flour, yeast, and salt. Pour in hot milk and mix well. Blend in butter and cheese and add Tabasco and cayenne. Stir in additional flour, ¼ cup at a time, until dough pulls away from sides of bowl to form a ball. Knead dough 10 minutes, sprinkling in flour if dough is too sticky. Place dough in large, oiled bowl, turning to coat. Cover tightly with plastic wrap, and allow to rise until doubled in bulk, 1 hour. Punch dough down, knead briefly, and turn out onto floured surface. Shape dough into 4 miniature loaves or 1 large loaf and place in greased pans. Cover loosely with wax paper and allow to double in bulk, 50 minutes. Preheat oven to 400°. Brush loaves with egg/milk mixture and bake 10 minutes. Reduce heat to 350° and bake miniature loaves 20 minutes longer; bake large loaf 25 to 30 minutes longer until golden brown (bread is done when a tap on the bottom of the loaf makes a hard, hollow sound). Cool loaves on wire rack.

Whole Wheat Crescents
Yields 24

1 pkg	dry yeast
¼ tsp	brown sugar
1 cup	warm water (105°–115°), divided
⅓ cup	almonds, blanched, toasted
2 cups	whole wheat flour, divided
3 Tbs	brown sugar
1 Tbs	salt
¼ cup	unsalted butter
½ cup	sour cream
2 large	eggs, room temperature
2 ¼ cups	bread flour

Dissolve yeast and ¼ teaspoon brown sugar in ½ cup warm water until bubbly. Finely grind almonds with 1 tablespoon whole wheat flour in food processor with plastic dough blade in place. Transfer to large bowl. Add remaining whole wheat flour, 3 tablespoons brown sugar, and salt. Melt butter in saucepan, add sour cream, and stir until warm (105°–115°). Add to flour mixture. Blend in remaining ½ cup warm water, eggs, and yeast mixture and stir vigorously with wooden spoon 3 minutes. Mix in enough bread flour, ½ cup at a time, to form soft dough. Knead until smooth, adding more flour if necessary, 5 to 6 minutes. Place dough in large, oiled bowl and turn to coat. Cover and allow to rise until doubled, 45 minutes. Gently punch dough down. Divide into 4 pieces and roll each piece into a 12" rope. Divide each rope into 6 pieces. Cover and allow to rest 10 minutes. Roll each piece of dough into a 6" rope and twist. Pinch ends together, forming a twisted oval. Place on greased baking sheet, cover loosely, and allow to rise until doubled, 30 minutes. Preheat oven to 375°. Bake twists until brown, 18 minutes.

Honey Wheat Berry Bread

Yields 1 loaf

1 pkg	dry yeast
1 tsp	sugar
¼ cup	warm water (105°–115°)
2 ½ cups	bread flour, divided
½ cup	wheat berries, soaked in water, drained
¼ cup	honey
1 ½ tsp	salt
1 tsp	ground cinnamon
⅛ tsp	ground cloves
½ cup	buttermilk
3 Tbs	vegetable oil
½ cup	seedless raisins or currants
1 tsp	cornstarch
¼ cup	hot water

Wet Your
Wheat Berries

Wheat berries are the whole, unprocessed wheat kernels. To use the berries in bread, they must be soaked in water to cover at least 2 hours. After soaking, drain the excess water. Berries will keep for about a week in the refrigerator.

Dissolve yeast and sugar in warm water until bubbly. In food processor with metal blade in place, finely grind ½ cup flour and wheat berries. Add remaining flour, honey, salt, cinnamon, and cloves. With machine running, add yeast mixture, buttermilk, and oil. Process until dough is smooth and elastic, 30 seconds. Add raisins and pulse to mix. Transfer dough to oiled mixing bowl and turn to coat with oil. Cover dough and allow to rise until doubled in bulk, 1 ½ hours. Punch down and shape dough. Place in greased loaf pan and allow to rise until doubled again, 45 minutes to 1 hour. Preheat oven to 375°. Dissolve cornstarch in hot water and brush lightly over surface of dough. Bake 15 minutes, brush again with cornstarch mixture and bake 15 to 20 minutes longer.

Lemon Butter Buns
Yields 20

Lemon Butter
Yields ¼ cup

¼ cup	unsalted butter, melted
1 ½ tsp	grated lemon zest
1 tsp	fresh lemon juice

Blend all ingredients.

1 pkg	dry yeast
1 tsp	sugar
½ cup	warm water (105°–115°)
¾ cup	warm milk (105°–115°)
½ cup	unsalted butter, melted
1 large	egg
1 large	egg yolk
1 Tbs	grated lemon zest
2 tsp	salt
4 cups	bread flour, divided
~	Lemon Butter (see accompanying recipe)

Dissolve yeast and sugar in warm water until bubbly. Combine warm milk, butter, egg, egg yolk, and lemon zest and add dissolved yeast. In food processor with plastic dough blade in place, combine salt and 3 cups of flour and pulse to blend. With machine running, add liquid mixture and process 20 seconds. Stop machine and add more flour, if needed, to form smooth, wet dough. Turn dough out onto floured surface and knead a few times. Place dough in large oiled bowl and turn to coat. Cover and allow to rise until doubled, 1 ¼ hours. Gently punch dough down and knead lightly until smooth. Divide into 20 equal pieces and roll each piece into a ball. Place rolls in greased 12" pan with sides just touching. Cover loosely and allow to rise until doubled, 20 minutes. Preheat oven to 375°. Gently brush rolls with Lemon Butter and bake until brown, 35 minutes.

Orange Bread

Yields 3 loaves

2 pkgs	dry yeast
1 tsp	sugar
1 cup	warm water (105°–115°)
¼ cup	unsalted butter
½ cup	sugar
1 tsp	salt
1 large	egg
¾ cup	fresh orange juice
3 Tbs	grated orange zest
5 ¼ cups	bread flour, divided

Dissolve yeast and 1 teaspoon sugar in warm water until bubbly. Mix in butter, sugar, salt, egg, orange juice, and zest. Add 2 cups flour and beat until smooth. Stir in enough additional flour to make a soft dough. Knead 8 to 10 minutes, until dough is smooth and does not stick to kneading surface or hands. Place dough in greased bowl, cover with cloth, and allow to rise until doubled in bulk, 1 to 1 ½ hours. Punch down and shape into 3 loaves. Place loaves in greased loaf pans and allow to rise 1 hour longer. Preheat oven to 400° and bake 25 to 30 minutes. Remove loaves from pans and cool on rack.

Sliced and toasted, Orange Bread is a natural match with orange marmalade for breakfast. You might also try shaping the dough into rolls—this recipe makes about 2 dozen.

Orange-Cinnamon Sweet Rolls
Yields 32

Orange Glaze
Yields 1/2 cup

1/3 cup   orange juice

1/4 cup   sugar

Combine orange juice and sugar, mixing well. Brush over rolls and bake 5 minutes longer.

Orange Cinnamon Icing
Yields 1/2 cup

1/4 cup   orange juice

1/2 tsp   vanilla extract

1/4 tsp   cinnamon

3/4 cup   powdered sugar, sifted

Combine orange juice, vanilla, cinnamon, and powdered sugar. Mix until smooth and drizzle over hot rolls.

Rolls:

2 pkgs	dry yeast
1 tsp	sugar
1/4 cup	warm water (105°–115°)
1/2 cup	unsalted butter
1 cup	milk, scalded
1 Tbs	grated orange zest
1/2 cup	sugar
1 tsp	vanilla extract
4 1/2 cups	all-purpose flour, unsifted

Filling:

1/2 cup	unsalted butter, room temperature
1 cup	powdered sugar
1 tsp	vanilla extract
1 tsp	cinnamon
1 cup	chopped pecans, toasted
~	Orange Glaze or Orange Cinnamon Icing (see accompanying recipes)

Dissolve yeast and 1 teaspoon sugar in warm water until bubbly. Place butter in large bowl of electric mixer, pour in hot milk, and stir until lukewarm (105°–115°). Add zest, dissolved yeast, 1/2 cup sugar, and vanilla. Beat well, then gradually add just enough additional flour to make soft dough. Cover and allow to rise until doubled in bulk. Prepare filling by combining butter, powdered sugar, vanilla, and cinnamon. Mix thoroughly, stir in pecans, and set aside. Punch dough down and turn out onto floured surface. Roll dough into 24" x 12" rectangle. Spread lower half of long side with filling. Fold top half of dough over filling and pinch edges to seal. Cut crosswise into 1" strips and twist each strip into a circle, tucking end under to make a pinwheel. Cover and allow to rise until doubled in bulk, 1 hour. Preheat oven to 350°. Bake rolls 15 to 20 minutes or until golden. Glaze or ice as desired.

"My mother and my
grandmother Mamie
fixed fried chicken
and huge steaming
casseroles, and chocolate
cake and meringue pie,
and while we digested
this feast…my mother
played, on the grand
piano, some of the
old hymns:
Faith of Our Fathers,
Bringing in the Sheaves,
Living with Jesus,
Abide with Me."

from Terrains of the Heart
by Willie Morris

DINNER ON THE GROUNDS

Southern Fried Chicken

~

Spiced Peach Salad

~

Old Fashioned Potato Salad

~

Aunt Georgia's Squash Casserole

~

Mattie B.'s Sweet Potato Pudding

~

Mum's No-Roll Biscuits with Muscadine Hot Pepper Jelly

~

Mama's Lemon Meringue Pie

~

Minnie Miller's Pecan Pie

~

Milk Chocolate Cake with Old-Fashioned Glazed Icing

~

Watermelon

PHOTO:
*The window of Epiphany
Episcopal Church looks out upon
arrangements for a traditional
dinner on the ground.*

Whole Wheat Cake Doughnuts with Caramel Glaze

Yields 24

Caramel Glaze

Yields ²/₃ cup

⅓ cup	evaporated milk
2 Tbs	brown sugar
1 ½ cups	powdered sugar
1 tsp	vanilla

To prepare glaze, combine evaporated milk and brown sugar and cook over medium heat, stirring constantly, until mixture begins to boil. Pour milk mixture into mixing bowl and add powdered sugar and vanilla. Beat until creamy, about 2 minutes.

If you have one, an electric wok is just the thing for cooking doughnuts. It requires less oil, and the thermostat assures proper temperature.

1 cup	buttermilk
¼ cup	unsalted butter, melted
2 large	eggs
1 tsp	vanilla extract
3 ¼ cups	all-purpose flour
1 cup	whole wheat flour
1 cup	sugar
2 tsp	baking powder
½ tsp	baking soda
½ tsp	ground nutmeg
1 tsp	ground cinnamon
¼ tsp	salt
~	vegetable oil for frying
~	Caramel Glaze (see accompanying recipe)

Blend together buttermilk, butter, eggs, and vanilla, beating well. Combine flours, sugar, baking powder, baking soda, nutmeg, cinnamon, and salt. Gradually add dry ingredients to buttermilk mixture, mixing well. Turn dough out onto heavily floured surface. Roll out to ½" thickness and cut with floured 2 ½" doughnut cutter. In a heavy saucepan heat 3 inches oil to 375°. Carefully drop in 3 or 4 doughnuts at a time. Cook until golden brown, 3 to 4 minutes per side. Drain on paper towels. Dip warm doughnuts in caramel glaze.

Oven French Toast

Serves 4

Thick slices of stale French bread can substitute for the white bread in this recipe, but let the French bread soak in the orange zest/egg mixture overnight.

¼ cup	unsalted butter
⅓ cup	sugar
¼ tsp	cinnamon
1 tsp	grated orange zest
²/₃ cup	orange juice
4 large	eggs, beaten well
8 slices	white bread
~	powdered sugar for garnish

Preheat oven to 325°. Melt butter in rectangular baking pan. Combine sugar, cinnamon, and orange zest and sprinkle evenly over butter. Stir together orange juice and eggs. Dip bread slices in orange zest/egg mixture and arrange in a single layer on baking pan. Bake until browned, 25 minutes, and garnish with powdered sugar.

Morning Glory Muffins
Yields 36-48

3 cups	all-purpose flour
1 ½ cups	whole wheat flour
1 cup	unprocessed bran
1 cup	quick-cooking oats
1 cup	chopped walnuts or pecans
1 cup	raisins
2 ½ cups	firmly packed light brown sugar
1 ½ Tbs	baking soda
1 ½ Tbs	cinnamon
½ tsp	salt
2 cups	vegetable oil
5 medium	carrots, grated
3 medium	Granny Smith apples, grated
6 large	eggs, beaten
2 Tbs	vanilla extract

Preheat oven to 350°. Combine flours, bran, oats, nuts, raisins, and brown sugar. Add soda, cinnamon, and salt and mix well. Blend in oil, carrots, apples, eggs, and vanilla. Fill oiled muffin cups ⅔ full with batter and bake 30 to 35 minutes.

Cornbread Muffins for Two
Serves 2

4 scant tsp	vegetable oil for muffin cups
½ cup	plain white cornmeal
1 Tbs	all-purpose flour, unsifted
¼ tsp	sugar
½ tsp	salt
2 tsp	baking powder
¼ tsp	onion powder (optional)
2 Tbs	beaten egg
1 Tbs	vegetable oil
½ cup	milk, or more
~	Tabasco Sauce to taste

Preheat oven to 425°. In 6-cup muffin tin, place 1 scant teaspoon oil in each of 4 cups. Partially fill remaining cups with water and heat muffin tin in oven. Whisk together cornmeal, flour, sugar, salt, baking powder, and onion powder. Blend egg, oil, milk, and Tabasco and add all at once to dry mixture. Mix thoroughly and pour into hot oiled muffin cups, filling each cup ⅔ full. Place muffin tin on center rack in oven and bake 12 to 15 minutes.

Blueberry Corn Muffins
Yields 12

1 cup	plain cornmeal
1 cup	all-purpose flour
1/2 cup	sugar
2 1/2 tsp	baking powder
1/4 tsp	salt
1 cup	buttermilk
6 Tbs	unsalted butter, melted
1 large	egg, lightly beaten
1 2/3 cup	blueberries, fresh or frozen, drained
1/2 tsp	grated lemon zest

Preheat oven to 400°. Line 12 muffin cups with paper liners. Sift cornmeal, flour, sugar, baking powder, and salt into mixing bowl. Make a well in center of dry ingredients and pour in buttermilk, melted butter, and egg. Stir just until combined. Fold in blueberries and lemon zest, fill lined muffin cups, and bake 20 to 25 minutes.

Blueberry Corn Muffins are a buttery new twist on the traditionally sweet corn muffin—try them with butter or Lemon Curd (page 181) and you'll never turn back.

Zesty Lemon Muffins
Yields 12

1 3/4 cups	all-purpose flour
3/4 cup	sugar
1 Tbs	grated lemon zest
1 tsp	baking powder
3/4 tsp	baking soda
1/4 tsp	salt
1 container	lemon yogurt (8 oz)
6 Tbs	unsalted butter, melted
1 large	egg, room temperature
1 Tbs	fresh lemon juice
~	Lemon Glaze (see accompanying recipe)

Lemon Glaze

Yields 1/2 cup

1/3 cup	fresh lemon juice
1/4 cup	sugar
2 tsp	grated lemon zest

Cook juice, sugar, and zest in small, non-aluminum pan over low heat until sugar is dissolved.

Preheat oven to 400°. Blend flour, sugar, zest, baking powder, baking soda, and salt in large bowl, making well in center. In a separate bowl, whisk together yogurt, butter, egg, and lemon juice. Pour yogurt mixture into well in dry ingredients and stir until just blended—batter will be lumpy. Spoon into greased muffin tins and bake until golden brown, 20 minutes. Remove baked muffins from tins, pierce 6 to 8 holes in each, and coat tops generously with hot Lemon Glaze.

Orange Poppy Seed Mini-Muffins

Yields 36

1 ⅓ cups	all-purpose flour
1 cup	sugar
½ cup	sour cream
⅓ cup	unsalted butter, room temperature
1 large	egg
2 Tbs	grated orange zest
2 Tbs	orange juice
1 Tbs	poppy seeds
½ tsp	salt
½ tsp	baking soda

Orange Butter Spread:

½ cup	unsalted butter, room temperature
1 pkg	cream cheese, room temperature (3 oz)
¼ cup	powdered sugar
1 Tbs	grated orange zest

During the holidays (or anytime you feel the need for a little holiday spirit), add ½ cup fresh cranberries to the batter. These muffins can be baked in advance, cooled, sealed in a plastic bag, and stored in the refrigerator for two days or in the freezer for two weeks. They reheat beautifully in the microwave (45 seconds on HIGH for frozen muffins).

Preheat oven to 400°. Thoroughly combine all muffin ingredients and beat with electric mixer at low speed until moistened, 1 minute. Spoon batter into greased or lined muffin cups. Bake 10 to 15 minutes. Prepare Orange Butter Spread by thoroughly blending all ingredients. Spread over warm muffins.

Banana Muffins

Yields 18

½ cup	unsalted butter, room temperature
1 cup	sugar
2 large	eggs, separated
3	ripe bananas, mashed
½ tsp	vanilla extract
½ tsp	fresh lemon juice
1 ½ cups	sifted all-purpose flour
1 tsp	soda
1 ½ Tbs	hot water

Preheat oven to 400°. Cream together butter and sugar. Add egg yolks and beat well. Blend in bananas, vanilla, and lemon juice. Mix in flour and soda, then add hot water. Beat egg whites and fold into batter. Spoon batter into greased muffin tins, bake 20 minutes, and cool on rack.

Peach Muffins

Yields 12

½ cup	unsalted butter
¾ cup	sugar
1 large	egg, lightly beaten
1 tsp	vanilla extract
½ cup	sour cream
1 ½ cups	all-purpose flour
1 ½ tsp	baking powder
1 cup	pecans, coarsely chopped
1 cup	peaches, frozen, coarsely chopped while frozen

Preheat oven to 400°. Cream butter, add sugar and egg, and mix until combined. Stir in vanilla and sour cream, but do not beat. Combine flour and baking powder and blend into sour cream mixture. Fold in peaches and pecans and stir to moisten. Grease bottoms only of miniature or full-size muffin cups. Fill cups ⅔ full with batter and bake 20 minutes.

Marbled Apricot Bread

Yields 1 loaf

Cream Cheese Filling

Yields 1 cup

⅓ cup	sugar
6 oz	cream cheese, room temperature
1 large	egg, room temperature

Blend sugar, cream cheese, and egg in food processor.

1 cup	dried apricots, in thin strips
½ cup	golden raisins
4 Tbs	unsalted butter, room temperature
½ cup	sugar
½ cup	firmly packed light brown sugar
1 large	egg, room temperature
2 cups	all-purpose flour
2 tsp	baking powder
½ tsp	baking soda
½ tsp	salt
¾ cup	orange juice
½ cup	chopped walnuts
~	Cream Cheese Filling (see accompanying recipe)

Preheat oven to 350°. Combine apricots and raisins and cover with boiling water. Allow to stand 30 minutes, then drain. In a separate bowl, cream together butter, sugar, and brown sugar. Beat in egg. In a separate bowl, sift together flour, baking powder, baking soda, and salt. Add flour mixture alternately with orange juice to butter mixture. Stir in apricots, raisins, and walnuts. Pour ⅔ of batter into greased and floured 9" x 5" loaf pan. Spread Cream Cheese Filling over, then top with remaining batter. Using a knife, swirl filling through batter for marbled effect. Bake until golden, 50 to 60 minutes.

Blueberry Buttermilk Biscuits

Yields 15

2 cups	all-purpose flour
1 Tbs	baking powder
¼ tsp	baking soda
1 tsp	salt
½ cup	sugar
⅓ cup	vegetable shortening
1 large	egg, beaten
¾ cup	buttermilk
½ cup	blueberries, fresh or frozen, drained
3 Tbs	unsalted butter, melted
3 Tbs	sugar
¼ tsp	ground cinnamon
⅛ tsp	ground nutmeg

Preheat oven to 400°. Combine flour, baking powder, baking soda, salt, and sugar in medium bowl. Cut in shortening until mixture resembles coarse meal. Combine egg and buttermilk and stir into flour mixture until moistened. Blend in blueberries. Turn out dough onto lightly floured surface and knead 4 or 5 times. Roll or pat dough to ½" thickness and cut with 2 ½" biscuit cutter. Place biscuits on lightly greased baking sheet and bake 15 minutes or until golden brown. Thoroughly combine melted butter, sugar, cinnamon, and nutmeg and brush on warm biscuits.

§

Mum's No-Roll Biscuits

Yields 12

2 cups low-protein
self-rising flour
¼ cup vegetable shortening
⅔ cup buttermilk
2 Tbs unsalted butter,
melted

~

Preheat oven to 450°.
Blend flour and shortening
to coarse consistency
(hands work best).
Overmixing produces
tough biscuits.
Add buttermilk all at once
and mix with fork until
dough sticks together.
Dough should be wet and
sticky—do not overwork.
Flour hands and pat out
biscuits. Do not roll or cut.
Dip each side of biscuits in
hot butter. Bake until
golden brown, 10 minutes.

Our mothers always told us
that real Southerners never roll or cut
their biscuits—they pat them out with
their hands. Why? Because Southern
cooks know that over-rolling the
dough will produce tough biscuits,
and cutting the dough can pinch the
top and bottom surfaces together,
sealing the edges and preventing a
proper rise. The perfect Southern
biscuit is like the perfect little cloud in
a clear blue Southern sky—tender,
light, and fluffy. The only reason we
put butter on them is to keep them
from floating off the plate.

Basil Biscuits
Yields 7

⅔ cup	freshly grated Parmesan cheese, divided
2 cups	all-purpose flour
2 tsp	baking powder
½ tsp	baking soda
8 Tbs	unsalted butter, chilled, divided
⅓ cup	finely chopped fresh basil (1 Tbs dried)
¾ cup	unflavored yogurt

Preheat oven to 400°. Combine all but 2 tablespoons cheese with flour, baking powder, and baking soda. Add 7 tablespoons butter and rub with fingers until mixture resembles coarse crumbs. Stir in basil. Add yogurt and mix until dough clings together in lumps. Pat dough into ball and knead 10 times or until dough holds together. Gently form dough into 7" log and cut across into 7 equal pieces (for a rounded biscuit, roll each piece into a ball). Set 1 biscuit in center of buttered cake pan, then evenly space remaining biscuits around center. Melt remaining 1 tablespoon butter and brush over tops of biscuits. Sprinkle with reserved 2 tablespoons cheese. Bake until biscuits are golden brown, 20 minutes. Serve hot.

"Sweetness" Biscuits
Yields 18

Walter "Sweetness" Payton, retired Chicago Bears running back and alumnus of Jackson State University in Jackson, Mississippi, holds the National Football League record for career rushing yardage. This is his mother's recipe.

2 cups	low protein, self-rising flour
⅓ cup	vegetable shortening
1 cup	milk

Preheat oven to 400°. Make a well in flour and work shortening in by hand. Gradually add milk to mixture to make dough. Roll out dough on floured surface, being careful not to incorporate too much flour and not to work dough too much. Cut out biscuits and bake 8 to 10 minutes on greased baking sheet until well browned.

Hush Puppies
Serves 8

2 cups self-rising cornmeal
1 cup self-rising flour
1 tsp baking powder
2 green onions, finely chopped
1 small bell pepper, finely chopped
1 rib celery, finely chopped
1 small onion, finely chopped
1 jalapeño pepper, finely chopped
1 large egg
1 tsp salt
½ tsp black pepper
½ tsp garlic powder
¾ cup milk
vegetable oil for frying

~

Combine all ingredients.
Mix well and drop by teaspoonfuls into medium-hot oil.
When bottom turns golden brown,
turn and brown other side.

§

We'll tell this story
once more for those who
may have missed it.
During the early
frontier days in the
South, a group of
hunters were sitting
around a campfire
preparing a standard
trail meal of cornbread,
beans, and bacon.
Their hunting dogs,
hoping to share in the
feast, crouched nearby,
howling desperately.
In an attempt to achieve
some peace and quiet,
one of the hunters fried a
bit of cornbread batter in
bacon fat and tossed it
toward the dogs with
this command:
"Hush, puppy!"
The rest, as they say,
is Southern culinary
history.

Lagniappe Spoonbread
Serves 6

This batter can be prepared early in the day and set aside until baking time. To make Fancy Spoonbread, gently stir in ½ pound of cooked and drained finely ground round steak just before baking. Add salad and dessert, and a complete meal is born.

3 cups	milk, divided
1 cup	plain cornmeal
2 rounded Tbs	vegetable shortening
1 tsp	salt
1 tsp	baking powder
4 large	egg yolks, beaten
4 large	egg whites, stiffly beaten

Preheat oven to 375°. Pour 1 cup milk over cornmeal in medium-sized bowl. Scald remaining 2 cups milk over medium heat. When milk begins to boil, add cornmeal mixture and cook 10 minutes, stirring constantly, until mixture becomes very thick. Add shortening, salt, and baking powder. Remove from heat, add beaten egg yolks, and fold in beaten egg whites. Pour batter into greased 1 ½-quart casserole and bake 50 minutes. Serve immediately with gravy or plenty of butter.

Winifred Green Cheney's Southern Hospitality Cookbook;
courtesy Oxmoor House, P.O. Box 2463, Birmingham, AL 35202. Copyright 1976

Cornbread Cutouts
Yields 30

1 cup	buttermilk
1 tsp	baking soda
1 cup	all-purpose flour
1 cup	yellow cornmeal
1 tsp	salt
1 tsp	dried basil
2 large	eggs
2 Tbs	bacon drippings or unsalted butter, melted

Cornbread Cutouts can be reheated at a low temperature or crisply toasted before serving. They are the designated accompaniment for the grilled pork tenderloin appetizer on page 13.

Position rack in lower third of oven and preheat to 450°. Grease a 10" x 15" shallow baking pan or cookie sheet. Mix buttermilk and soda. Combine flour, cornmeal, salt, and basil in food processor and mix well. With processor running, pour in buttermilk, then add eggs and melted bacon drippings or butter, blending until just combined. Pour batter into prepared pan, smoothing top. Bake until bread shrinks away from sides of pan and springs back when touched, 10 to 14 minutes. Remove and cool. With a biscuit or cookie cutter, cut bread into desired shapes. Be creative!

Cornmeal Pizza Crust

Yields 4 10" crusts

2 pkgs	dry yeast
½ tsp	sugar
1 ¼ cups	warm water (105°-115°)
2 ½ cups	all-purpose flour, divided
1 tsp	salt
1 cup	plain yellow cornmeal
1 Tbs	corn oil

Combine yeast, sugar, and water and allow to stand until bubbly, 5 minutes. In bowl of food processor, with plastic dough blade in place, add 2 cups flour, salt, and cornmeal. With machine running, add yeast mixture and process 15 to 20 seconds. Add corn oil and process 15 to 20 seconds. Remove dough from processor and hand knead a few times, adding small amounts of flour if too sticky. Dough should be smooth but not dry. Place dough in oiled bowl and turn to coat. Cover and allow to rise until doubled in bulk, 1 hour. Punch down dough, then allow to rise 1 more hour. Preheat oven to 500°. Divide dough into 4 equal balls. Press 1 ball of dough into 10" pizza pan. Bake in lowest oven rack until brown, 5 to 10 minutes. If not using right away, seal remaining dough balls in plastic bags and store in freezer.

PHOTO (left): *The Fortenberry-Parkman farmhouse was originally built in 1860 in rural Jefferson Davis County, Mississippi. The house has been relocated to the grounds of the Mississippi Agriculture and Forestry Museum, where it has been restored to look as it did during the 1920s.*

PHOTO (overleaf):

Blueberry Lemon Tart

Watermelon Sorbet

Pepper Custard Pie

DESSERTS

Blueberry Lemon Tart
Serves 8

Nut Crust:

5 oz	finely chopped almonds
1/2 cup	unsalted butter, room temperature
2 Tbs	sugar
1 1/2 cups	all-purpose flour
1/4 tsp	salt
1 large	egg
1/2 tsp	almond extract

Filling:

2 pints	fresh blueberries, washed, drained
~	sugar to taste
~	Lemon Curd (see accompanying recipe)
3/4 cup	red currant jelly, melted

Blend almonds, butter, sugar, flour, and salt in food processor until well combined. Add egg and almond extract and pulse until well mixed. Press mixture into buttered tart pan with removable bottom. Chill at least 30 minutes. Preheat oven to 350° and bake crust until golden brown, 20 to 30 minutes. Allow to cool. Combine blueberries with sugar and set aside. To assemble, spread Lemon Curd over crust. Arrange blueberries over Lemon Curd, then lightly brush melted currant jelly over berries. Blackberries, peaches, or other favorite fruit may be substituted for blueberries.

Lemon Curd

Yields 3 cups

2 tsp	grated lemon zest
1 1/2 cups	sugar
5 large	egg yolks
1/2 cup	fresh lemon juice
1/8 tsp	salt
1/2 cup	unsalted butter, melted

Combine zest and sugar in food processor. Pulse to mince zest, then process until zest is as fine as sugar. Add egg yolks, lemon juice, and salt and process 10 seconds. With machine running, pour in melted butter. Transfer mixture to double boiler and cook over low heat until thickened. Cool and refrigerate.

Vanishing Blueberry Pie

Serves 8

Pie:

1 cup	sour cream
2 Tbs	all-purpose flour
3/4 cup	sugar
1 tsp	vanilla extract
1/4 tsp	salt
1 large	egg, beaten
2 1/2 cups	fresh blueberries, washed, drained
~	pastry for 9" pie shell, unbaked

Topping:

3 Tbs	all-purpose flour
3 Tbs	unsalted butter, room temperature
3 Tbs	chopped pecans or walnuts

Preheat oven to 400°. For the pie, blend sour cream, flour, sugar, vanilla, salt, and egg until smooth. Fold in blueberries. Pour filling into pastry shell and bake 25 minutes. Make the topping by thoroughly combining flour, butter, and nuts. Sprinkle topping over pie and bake 10 additional minutes. Chill before serving.

Apple Custard Tart

Serves 8

~	pastry for 9" pie shell, unbaked
2	apples, peeled
1 1/2 tsp	cinnamon
2 Tbs	sugar
2 Tbs	unsalted butter
3 large	eggs
1 1/2 cups	milk
1/3 cup	sugar
1 Tbs	cornstarch
1 tsp	vanilla extract

Preheat oven to 425°. Place pastry in 9" tart pan. Slice apples into pastry shell. Sprinkle with cinnamon and 2 tablespoons sugar, then dot with butter. Place tart in oven and bake for 5 minutes. Mix eggs, milk, 1/3 cup sugar, cornstarch, and vanilla. Remove tart from oven and carefully pour in custard mixture. Reduce heat to 350° and return tart to oven. Bake until custard is set, about 40 to 45 minutes.

Streusel-Topped Pear Pie

Serves 8-10

~	pastry for 9" pie shell, unbaked

Filling:

4 1/2 cups	fresh ripe pears, peeled, cored, sliced
1/2 cup	sugar
1/4 cup	all-purpose flour
2 Tbs	fresh lemon juice
1/4 tsp	salt

Topping:

1 cup	all-purpose flour
1/2 tsp	salt
1/2 cup	light brown sugar
1 tsp	cinnamon
1/4 tsp	nutmeg
1/4 tsp	cloves
1/2 cup	unsalted butter, room temperature
2 oz	cheddar cheese, shredded
~	vanilla ice cream

Preheat oven to 375°. Toss pears with sugar, flour, lemon juice, and salt. Spoon mixture into unbaked pie shell. For the topping, combine flour, salt, brown sugar, cinnamon, nutmeg, and cloves. Cut in butter and cheese until crumbly. Spread topping over filling and bake, uncovered, 30 to 40 minutes. Then cover with foil and bake 10 to 20 minutes longer. Serve with vanilla ice cream.

§

Mama's Lemon Meringue Pie

Serves 6

pastry for 9" pie shell, baked
1 cup milk
3/4 cup sugar
1/4 tsp salt
1 tsp grated lemon zest
5 Tbs cornstarch
1/2 cup cold water
2 large eggs, separated
1 Tbs unsalted butter
7 Tbs fresh lemon juice, divided
4 Tbs sugar

~

Heat milk, sugar, salt, and zest in top of double boiler until hot to touch. Blend cornstarch with water and add to milk mixture. Cook, stirring constantly, until thick, then remove from heat. Individually add well-beaten egg yolks, butter, and 6 tablespoons lemon juice, mixing well after each addition. Pour mixture into baked pie shell and preheat oven to 325°. For the meringue, beat egg whites until frothy. Gradually add sugar and continue beating just until egg whites hold their shape in peaks. Fold in remaining 1 tablespoon lemon juice. Heap meringue on top of pie and brown 15 minutes.

Muscadine Cobbler

Serves 10-12

Muscadines

The muscadine is a thick-skinned purple grape found mainly in the Southeastern United States. In fact, it may have been the first grape from which wine was made in America. Muscadines are only in season during the late summer.

Filling:

2 ½ lbs	muscadines
¼ cup	all-purpose flour
1 ½ cups	sugar (more or less)
2 Tbs	fresh lemon juice

Cobbler:

~	basic pastry dough for 2-crust pie, unbaked
1 qt	prepared muscadine pie filling, thawed, if frozen
2 Tbs	unsalted butter
~	vanilla ice cream

Due to the seasonal nature of muscadines, it's probably best to make the filling for this cobbler in bulk and freeze it in 1-quart portions until needed. When using frozen muscadine filling, you may want to add lemon juice for freshness or sugar for sweetness. If muscadines are not available, scuppernong grapes will substitute.

To prepare filling, wash muscadines and squeeze pulp from hulls, reserving hulls for later use. Heat pulp with juice over low heat until seeds begin to separate, 45 minutes. Remove seeds by pressing pulp through colander, saving pulp and juice and discarding seeds. Combine pulp and juice with reserved muscadine hulls and cook over low heat, covered, until hulls are tender, 30 to 40 minutes. Blend in flour and about 1 ½ cups sugar (amount of sugar will vary according to sweetness of muscadines—taste and add sugar as needed). Continue cooking until pie filling consistency is reached, then add fresh lemon juice.

Preheat oven to 400°. Roll out ½ pastry dough to ⅛" thickness. To assemble cobbler, place bottom pastry crust in 13" x 9" baking pan. Place filling in bottom crust and dot with butter. Roll out remaining pastry to ⅛" thickness and cut into strips. Arrange in lattice pattern on top. Sprinkle with granulated sugar and bake 10 minutes at 400°. Reduce heat to 350° and bake 25 to 30 minutes longer. Serve hot, with a sizeable scoop of vanilla ice cream.

Pumpkin Cream Cheese Pie
Serves 8

~ basic pastry for 9" deep-dish pie shell, unbaked

Cream cheese layer:

1 pkg	cream cheese (8 oz), room temperature
¼ cup	sugar
½ tsp	vanilla extract
1 large	egg

Pumpkin layer:

1 can	pumpkin puree (16 oz)
½ cup	sugar
1 tsp	cinnamon
¼ tsp	ginger
¼ tsp	nutmeg
⅛ tsp	salt
2 large	eggs, lightly beaten
1 cup	evaporated milk

Preheat oven to 350°. For the cream cheese layer, combine cream cheese, sugar, and vanilla and blend in egg. Spread cream cheese mixture over unbaked pie shell. For the pumpkin layer, combine pumpkin, sugar, cinnamon, ginger, nutmeg, and salt. Blend in beaten eggs and evaporated milk and pour over cream cheese layer. Bake until firm, 60 minutes or longer.

Basic Pastry Dough

Yields two 9-inch or 1 double crust

2 cups	all-purpose flour
1 tsp	salt
1 tsp	sugar (optional)
3/4 cup	unsalted butter, chilled, diced
1/4 cup	vegetable shortening, chilled
4 Tbs	ice water (or more, if needed)

In food processor, combine flour and salt (plus sugar, if needed for sweet crust). Pulse to sift. Add butter and pulse 5 or 6 times. Add shortening, turn machine on, and immediately add 4 tablespoons water. Stop machine, then pulse 2 or 3 times. Remove cover and test dough with fingers—it should feel like small lumps that hold together when pressed. If too dry, pulse in additional water in droplets, being careful not to overprocess the dough mixture. Turn dough out onto lightly floured work surface. Knead dough one time only with heels of hands, pushing dough away—do not overwork. Form dough into cake, wrap in plastic, and refrigerate at least 2 hours before rolling out into 2 pie crusts.

Pepper Custard Pie
Serves 8

Crust:

1 package	plain dark chocolate wafers (9 oz), crushed
1/3 cup	sugar
1/2 cup	unsalted butter, melted

The Scalding Truth

To scald milk or cream,
heat it in a sauce pan to a point
just below boiling, or until
bubbles begin forming at the sides
of the pan. Scalding milk
prevents souring.

White chocolate filling:

8 oz	white chocolate, finely chopped
3/4 cup	heavy cream, scalded

Pepper Jelly Custard Filling:

4 large	egg yolks
2 Tbs	sugar
1/8 tsp	salt
1 pkg	unflavored gelatin
1 cup	milk, scalded
1/2 cup	green hot pepper jelly

Final assembly:

1/2 pt	heavy cream
1 1/2 Tbs	powdered sugar
1/8 tsp	salt
1/2 oz	semi-sweet chocolate, shaved

To make crust, preheat oven to 325°. Mix crushed wafers, sugar, and butter. Press into 9" pie pan, bake 8 minutes, and cool. For the white chocolate filling, place chopped white chocolate in heat-proof bowl. Pour hot cream over white chocolate and beat until melted. Allow to cool, stirring occasionally. When evenly cooled, beat to consistency of soft whipped cream and reserve. For the Pepper Jelly Custard Filling, beat egg yolks with sugar and salt. Dissolve gelatin in hot milk and whisk into egg yolks. Cook mixture until thickened, whisking constantly over low heat, being careful not to boil. Cool slightly, then add hot pepper jelly and stir until dissolved. Cover custard mixture with plastic wrap and cool to a consistency similar to white chocolate mixture. To assemble pie, fold custard mixture and white chocolate mixture together. Pour into prepared pie shell and chill. Combine heavy cream with powdered sugar and salt and whip until stiff. Spread whipped cream over chilled pie and sprinkle with chocolate shavings.

Weidmann's Black Bottom Pie

Serves 8

Crust:
20 ginger snaps, crushed to fine crumbs
5 Tbs unsalted butter, melted

Chocolate layer:
2 cups milk, scalded
4 large egg yolks, well beaten
1/2 cup sugar
1 1/2 Tbs cornstarch
1 1/2 squares unsweetened chocolate, softened
1 tsp vanilla extract

Bourbon layer:
1 Tbs gelatin
2 Tbs cold water
2 Tbs bourbon
4 large egg whites
1/4 tsp cream of tartar
1/2 cup sugar
sweetened whipped cream
unsweetened chocolate shavings

~

Preheat oven to 325°.
Prepare the crust by combining cookie crumbs with enough butter to make crumbs hold together—all butter may not be needed. Press crumb mixture into 9"-deep pie dish, bake 10 minutes, and allow to cool.

For chocolate layer, mix small amount of scalded milk into egg yolks, then stir yolks into remaining milk. Blend sugar and cornstarch in double boiler and add yolk mixture. Cook over medium heat, stirring often, until custard coats back of spoon, 20 minutes. Remove from heat. Combine 1 cup custard with softened chocolate (reserve remaining custard). Add 1 teaspoon vanilla, pour mixture into prepared crust, and chill.

Prepare bourbon layer by dissolving gelatin in cold water. Add gelatin to reserved custard, stir until dissolved, and allow to cool. Stir in bourbon. Beat egg whites with cream of tartar until frothy, then slowly beat in sugar until stiff. Fold beaten egg whites into cooled custard, then carefully spoon mixture over chocolate layer in pie crust. Chill until set. Serve topped with sweetened whipped cream and shavings of unsweetened chocolate.

§

In Southern Food, John Egerton quotes Marjorie Kinnan Rawlings on Black Bottom Pie: "I think this is the most delicious pie I have ever eaten…a pie so delicate, so luscious, that I hope to be propped up on my dying bed and fed a generous portion. Then I think that I should refuse outright to die, for life would be too good to relinquish." Egerton himself writes, "The well-defined layers of whipped cream, rum custard, chocolate custard, and crumb crust make a spectacular pie—to look at, and to taste."

The recipe at left, which replaces rum with bourbon, was adapted from the version served at the nationally known Weidmann's Restaurant in Meridian, Mississippi.

Mocha Meringue Ice Cream Pie

Serves 8-10

Chocolate
Caramel Sauce

Yields 4 cups

1 box	light brown sugar
	[1 lb]
3 cups	cold water
5 Tbs	cornstarch
½ cup	chocolate syrup
4 Tbs	unsalted butter

Combine brown sugar, water, and cornstarch. Stir over low heat until completely dissolved and thoroughly mixed. Add chocolate syrup and butter, raise heat to medium, and cook, stirring constantly, until thickened. If additional thickening is needed, stir in 1 teaspoon cornstarch blended with 1 teaspoon cold water. Keep refrigerated.

3 large	egg whites, room temperature
½ tsp	baking powder
¾ cup	sugar
⅛ tsp	salt
1 cup	chocolate wafer crumbs
½ cup	finely chopped pecans
1 tsp	vanilla extract
1 qt	coffee ice cream, softened
½ pt	heavy cream
½ cup	powdered sugar
~	chocolate curls or chopped toffee bars for garnish
~	Chocolate Caramel Sauce (see accompanying recipe)

Preheat oven to 350°. Beat egg whites until frothy. Add baking powder, beating slightly. Gradually add sugar and salt and continue beating until stiff and glossy. Fold in crumbs, pecans, and vanilla. Spoon meringue into buttered 10" pie pan. Use spoon to shape meringue into pie shell, swirling sides high. Bake 30 minutes at 350°, then cool. Spread ice cream evenly over meringue crust. Cover and freeze overnight. Beat heavy cream with powdered sugar until light and fluffy, then spread over pie. Garnish with chocolate curls or chopped toffee bars and freeze until firm. Allow pie to stand at room temperature 10 minutes before slicing. Serve slices topped with Chocolate Caramel Sauce.

German Chocolate Macaroon Pie
Serves 8

Pie:

5 large	egg whites, room temperature
1/8 tsp	salt
1 cup	sugar
1 tsp	baking powder
6 oz	German's sweet chocolate, grated, divided
1 1/4 cups	graham cracker crumbs
2/3 cup	chopped pecans, toasted
1 tsp	vanilla extract

Topping:

1 tsp	vanilla extract
1/2 tsp	water
2 tsp	instant coffee
1/4 cup	powdered sugar
1/2 pt	heavy cream

Preheat oven to 350°. Beat egg whites with salt in large bowl until soft peaks form. Combine sugar and baking powder and gradually beat into egg whites, then continue beating 2 minutes longer. Reserve 2 tablespoons grated chocolate for garnish, then carefully fold in remaining grated chocolate, graham cracker crumbs, pecans, and vanilla. Spoon into buttered pie pan and bake until brown, 30 to 35 minutes, then cool thoroughly. For the topping, add vanilla and water to instant coffee and stir to dissolve. Blend coffee mixture and powdered sugar into cream and chill several hours or overnight. To assemble, whip cream until stiff and spread over pie. Sprinkle with reserved grated chocolate and chill until ready to serve.

§

Minnie Miller's Mississippi Pecan Pie
Serves 8

pastry for 9" pie shell, unbaked
1 cup sugar
1/4 cup unsalted butter, room temperature
3/4 cup light corn syrup
4 large eggs
2 tsp vanilla extract
1 1/4 cup pecan halves (more if desired)

~

Preheat oven to 400°. Cream butter and sugar. Beat in eggs all at once, then stir in syrup. Add vanilla and pecans and mix thoroughly. Pour filling into pie shell. Bake 5 minutes at 400°, then reduce heat to 325°, and continue baking until done, 45 minutes.

If you dare fiddle with such a monument to Southern culinary culture, try flavoring the filling with a bit of cinnamon or 2 tablespoons of sour cream.

~

Minnie Miller was the cook at the Mississippi Governor's Mansion for 15 years. She had a fresh piece of her award-winning pecan pie ready for Governor William Winter on every day of his administration.

Peanut Butter Mousse Pie

Serves 8

Libby's Chocolate Sauce

Yields 2 cups

1 cup	sugar
5 Tbs	cocoa, sifted
3 Tbs	all-purpose flour
1 cup	milk
4 Tbs	unsalted butter
1 tsp	vanilla extract

Combine sugar, cocoa, and flour in sauce pan. Stir until well-blended. Stir in milk and add butter. Cook over low heat until thickened, then remove from heat and stir in 1 teaspoon vanilla. Pour into storage containers and allow to cool before refrigerating.

On some occasions, you might prefer to omit the crust and serve Peanut Butter Mousse in a pool of Libby's Chocolate Sauce, garnished with chopped peanuts.

Crust:

1 ½ cups	graham cracker crumbs or chocolate wafer crumbs
⅓ cup	chopped peanuts
3 Tbs	sugar
⅓ cup	unsalted butter, melted

Filling:

½ cup	unsalted butter
¾ cup	sugar
3 large	eggs, separated
1 tsp	vanilla extract or nut-flavored liqueur
¾ lb	smooth peanut butter, heated
2 ½ cups	heavy cream, whipped
~	Libby's Chocolate Sauce (see accompanying recipe)

To make the crust, preheat oven to 350°. Mix graham cracker crumbs, peanuts, sugar, and melted butter. Press mixture into greased 10" springform pan. Bake 10 minutes, then set aside. For the filling, cream butter until fluffy. Gradually add sugar, then egg yolks and vanilla or liqueur. Fold in warm peanut butter. Clean metal bowl and beater with vinegar and salt to remove all residue, then wipe dry. Beat egg whites until stiff and fold into peanut butter mixture. Add whipped cream. Spoon mousse into prepared springform pan and freeze. Remove pie from freezer 30 to 60 minutes before serving. Drizzle Libby's Chocolate Sauce over top and slice.

Almond Tart

Serves 8

~	pastry for 9" pie shell, unbaked
½ cup	heavy cream
⅓ cup	sugar
1 tsp	grated orange zest
¼ tsp	almond extract
1 cup	sliced almonds
~	whipped cream for garnish
~	raspberry preserves (optional)

Preheat oven to 400°. Place pastry in 9" tart pan with removable bottom. Line pastry with double thickness of foil and bake 8 minutes. Remove foil and bake until golden, 4 minutes more. Cool on wire rack. For the filling, combine cream, sugar, orange zest, and almond extract. Stir to dissolve sugar, then blend in almonds. Spoon filling mixture into cooled pastry and bake in 400° oven until golden, 20 to 25 minutes. Cool and top with circle of whipped cream. Drizzle with preserves around the edge.

Schaum Torte

Serves 12

6 large	egg whites, room temperature
1 tsp	cream of tartar
2 cups	sugar
1 tsp	white vinegar
~	heavy cream for topping
~	sliced fresh strawberries for garnish

Preheat oven to 300°. Beat egg whites with cream of tartar until frothy. While continuing to beat, gradually add sugar, by tablespoons, and then add vinegar. Spoon egg white mixture into springform pan. Reduce heat to 250°, place pan in oven, and bake 1 hour—do not allow to brown. Remove from oven and cool. Beat heavy cream until stiff. Spread cooled torte with whipped cream and garnish with sliced strawberries.

We think you'll find that eggs separate more easily when they are still cold from the refrigerator. Then you can allow the whites to come to room temperature before you begin to prepare this flamboyant dessert.

Peaches and Cream Short Cake
Serves 8

Cake layer:

½ cup	unsalted butter, room temperature
½ cup	sugar
1 large	egg
1 ½ cups	all-purpose flour
1 ½ tsp	baking powder
½ tsp	vanilla extract
½ tsp	almond extract
4 cups	sliced fresh peaches

Cream layer:

2 cartons	sour cream (16 oz total)
2 large	egg yolks
½ cup	sugar
½ tsp	nutmeg
½ tsp	vanilla extract
½ tsp	almond extract

Topping:

1 ½ cups	heavy cream
¼ cup	powdered sugar
~	fresh peach slices for garnish

For the cake layer, cream butter with ½ cup sugar. Add egg, beating well. Combine flour and baking powder and add to creamed mixture, mixing just until blended. Stir in vanilla and almond extract and pat mixture into greased 9" springform pan. Arrange peach slices on top. Prepare the cream layer by combining sour cream, egg yolks, ½ cup sugar, nutmeg, vanilla, and almond extract. Pour sour cream mixture over peaches. Bake at 350° for 1 hour or until edges are lightly browned. Cool on rack, then cover and chill. To serve, remove cake from springform pan to serving plate. Beat heavy cream until foamy, gradually adding powdered sugar. Beat until soft peaks form. Spoon or pipe whipped cream over top of cake and garnish with fresh peach slices.

Miss Chris's 15-Layer Lemon Cake
Serves 15-20

Icing:
10 large eggs, well beaten
1 1/2 cups sugar
1 cup unsalted butter
1 cup fresh lemon juice
zest of 4 lemons

Cake:
3 cups all-purpose cake flour
3 tsp baking soda
1/2 tsp salt
1 cup unsalted butter, room temperature
2 heaping cups sugar
5 large eggs
1 cup milk, cold

non-stick vegetable spray
~

First, make the icing by blending beaten eggs with sugar.
Cook mixture in double boiler over medium heat until sugar dissolves, 2 to 3 minutes. Add butter, lemon juice, and zest and cook, whisking constantly, 5 minutes. Refrigerate icing 1 to 2 hours until cold, then store in freezer.
If icing begins to freeze, return to refrigerator.
Icing should, however, be very cold.

For the cake, preheat oven to 350°.
Double-sift together flour, baking soda, and salt.
With an electric mixer, cream together butter and sugar.
Add eggs one at a time, blending well after each addition.
Add half the flour mixture and blend well. Stir in cold milk and mix well.
Add remaining flour mixture and mix until very smooth.
Grease and flour four 9" cakepans
and also spray each lightly with vegetable spray.
Put 2 heaping tablespoons cake mix into each pan and smooth out with spoon.
Bake, watching closely, until layers brown around edges, 3 to 5 minutes.
Remove from oven and quickly turn warm layer out onto cake plate.

Ice cake layer with 2 1/2 tablespoons cold icing.
Repeat with remaining 3 layers, working very quickly.
Return icing to freezer and put assembled cake in refrigerator.
Re-grease, re-flour and re-spray pans and repeat baking, icing, and layering procedure for 15 layers.

When assembly is complete, ice top and sides of cake.
Cover and refrigerate at least 1 day—preferably 3 to 4 days—before serving.

§

The late Mrs. Ed Henson, known as "Miss F," ran a boarding house for teachers in Philadelphia, Mississippi. Miss F baked her 6-layer Lemon Cake as a reward for deserving students as well as for church socials and other community gatherings. Miss Chris (Christine Warren) carries on the tradition with her 15-layer version of this remarkable concoction.

The success of this production depends on your technique. Work as quickly as possible and keep the icing very, very cold. If one of your cake layers should break during assembly, discard it and forge ahead. You'll have fewer layers, but then, who's counting?

Carrot Cake
with Lemon Cream Cheese Frosting
Serves 12-15

Lemon Cream Cheese Frosting

Yields 2 cups

1 pkg	cream cheese (8 oz), room temperature
¼ cup	unsalted butter, room temperature
2 cups	powdered sugar
1 ½ tsp	vanilla extract
1 Tbs	grated lemon zest

Cream together cream cheese and butter until fluffy. Add powdered sugar and beat until well blended. Beat in vanilla and lemon zest.

The whole-wheat flour in this recipe adds a new dimension to the taste and texture of carrot cake, and it gets even better after a mellowing period. Refrigerate up to a week or freeze without frosting.

1 ¼ cups	vegetable oil
1 cup	firmly packed light brown sugar
1 cup	granulated sugar
4 large	eggs
1 cup	all-purpose flour
1 cup	whole-wheat flour (less 2 Tbs)
1 tsp	salt
2 tsp	baking soda
2 tsp	baking powder
2 tsp	ground cinnamon
3 cups	finely shredded raw carrots, packed
1 can	crushed pineapple (8 ½ oz), drained
½ cup	finely chopped pecans
~	Lemon Cream Cheese Frosting (see accompanying recipe)

Preheat oven to 350°. In large bowl, blend together oil and sugars. Add eggs one at a time, beating until blended. In separate bowl, sift together flours, salt, soda, baking powder, and cinnamon. Add flour mixture, ⅓ at a time, to oil mixture, beating just enough to blend. Fold carrots, then pineapple, into batter and stir in nuts. Pour batter into 2 greased and floured 9" round cake pans. Bake 35 to 40 minutes or until toothpick inserted in center comes out clean. Cool cakes in pans on rack 10 minutes, then turn cakes out onto rack and cool completely. Spread Lemon Cream Cheese Frosting over first cake layer. Top with second layer and spread icing over top of cake. Allow to rest one day for best flavor.

Nippersink Spice Cake
Serves 10-12

Cake:

1 ½ cups	sugar
1 cup	vegetable oil
½ cup	buttermilk
1 heaping cup	mashed prunes
1 tsp	cinnamon
1 tsp	allspice
1 tsp	nutmeg
1 tsp	vanilla extract
1 tsp	baking soda
3 large	eggs, lightly beaten
1 cup	chopped pecans

Buttermilk Glaze:

½ cup	buttermilk
½ tsp	baking soda
1 cup	sugar
1 ½ cups	unsalted butter, melted
~	sweetened whipped cream for garnish

The Nippersink Lodge, located at Mentone, Alabama, near the DeSoto and Alpine Camps for children, is a favorite retreat for parents and grandparents of campers.

In spite of this flourless treat's traditional name, bakers should expect a consistency more reminiscent of bread pudding than cake.

Preheat oven to 300°. Combine sugar, oil, buttermilk, prunes, cinnamon, allspice, nutmeg, vanilla, and soda. Blend in eggs and pecans. Pour batter into greased and floured 9" x 13" pan and bake 1 hour. For the glaze, mix buttermilk and soda and add sugar. Combine with melted butter, bring to boil, and remove from heat. Serve cake with heated glaze poured over individual squares. Garnish with sweetened whipped cream.

Hot Milk Cake with Caramel Icing

Serves 10-12

Cake:

4 large	eggs
2 cups	sugar
2 cups	all-purpose flour
2 tsp	baking powder
¼ tsp	salt
1 cup	milk
½ cup	unsalted butter
1 tsp	vanilla extract

Icing:

2 ½ cups	sugar, divided
1 cup	heavy cream
⅛ tsp	salt
5 ⅓ Tbs	unsalted butter
1 tsp	vanilla extract

Preheat oven to 350°. Butter and flour a 13" x 9" cake pan. Beat eggs until thick, then gradually add sugar. Sift together flour, baking powder, and salt and slowly blend in egg mixture. Combine milk and butter in saucepan over medium heat. When milk mixture reaches boiling point, stir rapidly into egg mixture and add vanilla. Pour batter into prepared pan and bake 30 to 35 minutes, or until toothpick inserted into center comes out clean. Allow cake to cool.

To prepare icing, combine 2 cups sugar, cream, and salt in heavy saucepan. Mix well and bring to a boil, then reduce heat to low. In a cast iron skillet over medium-high heat, caramelize remaining ½ cup sugar by shaking skillet (don't stir) until sugar is light brown and transparent. Add caramelized sugar to cream mixture, increase heat, and cook to soft ball stage (236°). Test for doneness by dropping a few drops of mixture into cup of cold water. When soft ball forms, remove mixture from heat and stir in butter. Return to heat and cook again to 236°. Remove from heat, cool 5 to 10 minutes, and add vanilla. Let icing thicken, then beat by hand to spreadable consistency and spread over cooled cake.

Chocolate and Cream Layer Cake

Serves 12-15

Cake:

1 cup	cocoa
2 cups	boiling water
1 cup	unsalted butter, room temperature
2 ½ cups	sugar
4 large	eggs
1 ½ tsp	vanilla extract
2 ¾ cups	all-purpose flour
2 tsp	baking soda
½ tsp	baking powder
½ tsp	salt

Filling:

½ pt	heavy cream
1 tsp	vanilla extract
¼ cup	powdered sugar

~	Chocolate Cream Frosting (see accompanying recipe)
~	pecan halves for garnish

Preheat oven to 350°. Combine cocoa and boiling water, stir until smooth, and set aside to cool. Combine butter, sugar, eggs, and vanilla and beat at high speed until light and fluffy, 5 minutes. Combine flour, soda, baking powder, and salt. Beating at low speed, add flour mixture and cocoa mixture in alternate additions to butter mixture, beginning and ending with flour mixture—be careful not to overbeat. Pour batter into 3 greased and floured 9" pans. Bake 25 to 30 minutes. Cool cakes in pans 10 minutes, then remove from pans and cool completely. For the filling, beat heavy cream and vanilla until foamy, gradually adding powdered sugar. Continue beating until peaks hold their shape. To assemble cake, spread filling between layers and frost with Chocolate Cream Frosting. Garnish with pecan halves and refrigerate for at least 4 hours.

*Chocolate
Cream Frosting*

Yields 3 cups

1 pkg	semi-sweet chocolate chips (6 oz)
½ cup	half & half
¾ cup	unsalted butter
2 ½ cups	sifted powdered sugar

Combine chocolate chips, half & half, and butter. Stir over medium heat until chocolate melts. Remove from heat and add powdered sugar, mixing well. Set sauce pan in ice and beat until frosting holds shape and loses gloss (add drops of half & half, if necessary, to achieve spreading consistency).

For highest volume whipped cream, chill bowl and beaters as well as the cream.

Milk Chocolate Cake
with Old-Fashioned Glazed Icing

Serves 15-20

Old-Fashioned
Glazed Icing

Yields 2 cups

4 Tbs	unsalted butter
1 cup	sugar
¾ cup	milk
1 tsp	vanilla extract

Boil butter, sugar, and milk to soft-ball stage (234°-240°). Remove from stove, allow to cool, and add vanilla. Beat until thickened and fully cooled (for a thicker icing, increase sugar to 1 ½ cups).

½ cup	unsalted butter
1 ½ cups	sugar
2 large	eggs
1 square	unsweetened chocolate, melted
1 tsp	vanilla extract
2 cups	all-purpose flour, sifted with pinch of salt
1 cup	buttermilk
1 tsp	soda dissolved in 1 Tbs vinegar
~	Old-Fashioned Glazed Icing (see accompanying recipe)

Preheat oven to 350°. Butter and flour 13" x 9" baking pan. Cream butter and sugar until light. Add eggs one at a time, beating after each addition. Blend in melted chocolate and vanilla. Add flour alternately with buttermilk and stir in soda and vinegar. Spread batter in pan and smooth top. Bake 25 to 30 minutes. Spread warm cake with Old-Fashioned Glazed Icing and serve.

Glazed Raspberry-Chocolate Cakes

Yields 24 squares

Cake:

6 ½ oz	semi-sweet chocolate
1 oz	unsweetened chocolate
15 Tbs	unsalted butter, room temperature
½ cup	seedless raspberry jam
2 Tbs	raspberry vinegar
1 Tbs	orange liqueur
6 large	eggs, separated
1 cup	superfine sugar, divided
½ cup	cake flour, sifted

Serious Chocolate Glaze:

5 oz	semi-sweet chocolate, chopped
¼ cup	heavy cream, heated
2 Tbs	unsalted butter, room temperature

~	fresh raspberries for garnish
~	white chocolate shavings for garnish

Preheat oven to 350°. Butter and flour 9" x 13" baking pan. Melt chocolates in double boiler over hot water. Add butter and stir until smooth, then remove from heat. Combine jam, vinegar, and orange liqueur. Beat egg yolks with ½ cup sugar until mixture is light in color and forms ribbon from beater. Stir chocolate into egg yolks, then add raspberry mixture. Beat egg whites until frothy. Slowly add remaining ½ cup sugar and beat to soft peaks. Fold cake flour into chocolate mixture. Gently fold in egg whites. Spread batter in pan and smooth top. Bake 25 minutes or until toothpick inserted in center comes out clean. Cool completely, remove cake from pan, cover, and chill. For the glaze, melt chocolate in top of double boiler over simmering water, stirring until smooth. Remove from heat and whisk in hot cream and butter. Cover and refrigerate until ready to use. Before serving, warm glaze in double boiler, whisking to a fluid consistency, then allow to stand until just cool to touch. Cut cake into serving pieces and drizzle glaze over tops. Decorate with fresh raspberries and white chocolate shavings.

The cake and the glaze may be prepared separately a day ahead of time, then assembled for serving. The cakes may also be baked in midget muffin tins. Granulated sugar can substitute for superfine sugar if you whirl it in the food processor for 15 to 30 seconds.

Bourbon-Chocolate Tipsy Cake

Serves 12

2 cups	sifted all-purpose flour
1 tsp	baking soda
¼ tsp	salt
¼ cup	dry instant coffee or espresso
~	boiling water
~	cold water
½ cup	bourbon
1 cup	unsalted butter, room temperature
1 ½ tsp	vanilla extract
2 cups	sugar
3 large	eggs
3 oz	unsweetened chocolate, melted
2 oz	German's sweet chocolate, melted
~	butter and powdered cocoa to coat pan
2 Tbs	bourbon
~	powdered sugar
~	sweetened whipped cream, for garnish
~	fresh strawberries, for garnish (optional)

This is a not-too-sweet cake for adults. It makes a welcome dessert at tailgate parties, and it's terrific as a special occasion gift, baked in a small bundt pan.

Preheat oven to 325°. Sift together flour, baking soda, and salt. In 2-cup glass measure, dissolve coffee in small amount of boiling water. Add cold water to 1 ½-cup line and stir in ½ cup bourbon. Cream butter in large bowl of electric mixer. Add vanilla and sugar and beat to mix well. Add eggs, one at a time, beating until smooth after each addition. Add melted chocolates and beat until smooth. Shift mixer to low speed and add sifted dry ingredients in three additions, alternating with liquid mixture in two additions. Butter 9" bundt pan and dust with powdered cocoa. Pour in batter and bake 1 hour 15 minutes or until a toothpick inserted in middle of cake comes out clean and dry. Cool cake in pan 15 minutes, then remove to rack and sprinkle with remaining 2 tablespoons bourbon. To serve, dust with powdered sugar and garnish with sweetened whipped cream and fresh strawberries, if desired.

Over the generations, we Southerners have learned to savor the pleasures of life when they appear. Perhaps that's why we put so much stock in the sweet treat at the end of a meal, whether it's a simple bowl of homemade peach ice cream or an elaborately decorated chocolate layer cake. Dessert is like the "happily ever after" that closes out a favorite fairy tale or the promise of the Pearly Gates at the end of a fire-and-brimstone sermon.

DESSERT BUFFET

Molasses Snaps

~

Apricot Bars

~

Granny's Walnut Bourbon Balls

~

Hot Milk Cake with Caramel Icing

~

Blueberry Lemon Tart

~

Almond Tart

~

Miss Chris's 15-Layer Lemon Cake

~

Bourbon-Chocolate Tipsy Cake

~

Watermelon-Wine Punch

PHOTO:
The old pie safe now protects the good china at the Agriculture and Forestry Museum's farmhouse.

Short'nin' Bread

Yields 24

1 cup powdered sugar,
sifted
2 cups unsalted butter,
melted
3 cups cake flour, sifted

~

*Preheat oven to 325°.
Mix all ingredients
and press into ungreased
9" x 9" pan.
Roll top surface smooth
with straight-sided
water glass.
Bake until golden
brown, 30 minutes.
Cut into squares and
serve warm.*

*This shortbread makes
an easy, sweet treat anytime,
but it really shines when it's
topped with strawberries
or raspberries and
a generous dollop of freshly
whipped cream.
We also highly recommend
Short'nin' Bread served with
Chocolate Paté.*

Chocolate Paté

Serves 25–35

Paté:

1 ½ cups	half & half
4 oz	semi-sweet chocolate, coarsely chopped
4 oz	white chocolate, coarsely chopped
4 large	eggs, slightly beaten
2 Tbs	brandy
1 pkg	almond paste (3 ½ oz)

Glaze:

1 cup	semi-sweet chocolate chips
¼ cup	unsalted butter
2 Tbs	corn syrup
~	sliced almonds for garnish

Preheat oven to 350°. Combine half & half, semi-sweet chocolate, and white chocolate over low heat and cook, stirring constantly, until chocolates are melted and mixture is smooth. Cool slightly and gradually stir in eggs and brandy. Pour into 8 ½" x 4 ½" x 2 ½" loaf pan lined with foil with 2" overhang. Place loaf pan in second pan and add 1 inch of very hot water. Bake until knife inserted halfway between edge and center comes out clean, 45 to 50 minutes. When done, remove loaf pan from water. While paté is baking, roll out almond paste between 2 sheets of wax paper to 8" x 4" rectangle. When paté is done, remove wax paper and immediately place almond paste over paté. Cool 1 hour, then cover and refrigerate at least 8 hours but not longer than 24 hours. Prepare chocolate glaze by combining chocolate, butter, and syrup over low heat and stirring constantly until chocolate is melted. Cool. Remove paté from pan by inverting onto serving plate. Carefully remove foil and spread glaze evenly over sides and top of paté. Decorate with almond slices in flower design.

*Mary Leigh Furrh and Jo Barksdale, reprinted from their book
Great Desserts of the South, Pelican Publishing Company, Gretna, LA*

Chocolate Marquise

Serves 10-12

Chocolate mousse:

8 oz	semi-sweet chocolate
1 cup	powdered sugar
¾ cup	unsalted butter, room temperature
5 large	eggs, separated
¾ cup	cocoa
⅛ tsp	salt
1 pinch	cream of tartar
½ pt	heavy cream

Hazelnut Custard Sauce:

4 large	egg yolks
½ cup	sugar
1 ⅔ cups	milk, scalded
1 tsp	vanilla extract
~	hazelnut liqueur to taste
~	chopped hazelnuts for garnish

Melt chocolate in double boiler. Add sugar, mix well, then blend in butter by tablespoons. Remove from heat and add egg yolks one at a time. Sift cocoa into mixture, beating continuously, then allow to cool. Beat egg whites with salt and cream of tartar until stiff peaks form. Stir ⅓ of egg whites into chocolate mixture, then fold in remaining egg whites. Whip cream to soft peaks and fold into mixture. Line loaf pan with plastic wrap, fill with mousse mixture, and chill overnight. To prepare custard sauce, beat egg yolks and sugar until pale. Gradually beat hot milk into eggs. Being very careful not to overheat, cook mixture over low heat, stirring continuously, until sauce coats back of spoon. Remove from heat and stir in vanilla and liqueur. To serve, unmold mousse and remove plastic wrap. Slice and serve surrounded by custard sauce and sprinkled with chopped hazelnuts.

How Do You Melt Chocolate? Carefully...Very Carefully.

Chocolate scorches easily. And the flavor of scorched chocolate is an acquired taste— one which has been acquired by absolutely nobody that we know of. Consequently, a kinder, gentler approach is appropriate. Never try to melt chocolate over direct heat. Instead, heat it slowly in a double boiler, turning off the heat as soon as the water in the lower pot reaches boiling. An important note: Be very careful not to let any water get into your melted chocolate. Chocolate can be melted along with a liquid, but introducing a single drop of moisture to chocolate which has already been melted will cause clumping. You can, however, correct the curse of the clump by adding vegetable oil (1 tablespoon oil to 6 ounces chocolate), and remelting slowly. Kindly. Gently.

Chocolate Charlotte with Strawberries
Serves 8-10

Chocolate layer:

8 oz	German's sweet chocolate
3 Tbs	water
4 large	eggs, separated
3 Tbs	sugar
½ tsp	vanilla extract
28	ladyfingers, split

Strawberry layer:

1 pt	sliced strawberries
2 Tbs	sugar

Topping:

1 pt	heavy cream
¼ cup	sugar
1 tsp	vanilla extract
~	fresh whole strawberries for garnish

Begin chocolate layer by heating chocolate with water in top of double boiler. Beat egg yolks with sugar and slowly add egg mixture to melting chocolate, whisking continuously until mixture begins to thicken. Remove from heat and cool. Beat egg whites until stiff and fold into cooled chocolate mixture, then add vanilla. Line bottom and sides of charlotte mold or springform pan with ladyfingers. Pour in half of chocolate mixture. Layer with ladyfingers and top with remaining chocolate mixture. Refrigerate until firm. For the strawberry layer, mix strawberries with sugar and spoon over chilled chocolate layer. Cover with plastic wrap and refrigerate. Two hours before serving, prepare topping by whipping cream with sugar and vanilla. Spread topping over charlotte and refrigerate until serving time. Garnish with fresh whole strawberries.

Creme Brulée with Blackberries

Serves 8

8 Tbs	sugar
10 large	egg yolks
1 qt	heavy cream
½ cup	milk
5 Tbs	vanilla extract (2 fl oz)
1 cup	fresh blackberries, or frozen, thawed, drained
1 ½ cups	light brown sugar
~	blackberries, mint sprigs, or edible flowers for garnish

Preheat oven to 300°. In food processor with machine running, pulverize sugar. Add egg yolks and blend briefly, then transfer mixture to bowl and set aside. In sauce pan, combine cream and milk and heat gently until warm but not scalded. Whisk cream mixture into egg yolk mixture, ½ cup at a time, until thoroughly blended. Stir in vanilla. Divide blackberries evenly among 8 ramekins. Add custard mixture to 1 ½" depth in each ramekin. Place ramekins in baking pan with 1" hot water. Bake 45 minutes or until knife inserted in center comes out clean. Refrigerate overnight. Preheat broiler. Sift a thin layer of brown sugar over each custard, covering surface completely. Place ramekins under broiler for just a few seconds to caramelize sugar—watch very carefully. This procedure may be done as early as 4 hours prior to serving. Allow to cool, then serve immediately or refrigerate up to four hours. Present ramekins on doily-covered dessert plates and garnish with two blackberries, a sprig of mint, or edible flowers.

A Rose is a Rose is a Snack

Henry Ward Beecher once wrote that "Flowers are the sweetest things that God ever made and forgot to put a soul into." True enough, but flowers are not always sweet. They can be peppery, like nasturtiums; or onion-flavored, like chive blossoms; or perfumey, like the rose. There are a surprising number of edible flowers that will not only add beauty to your culinary presentations but flavor as well.

~

Flowers can be tightly wrapped and stored in the refrigerator up to a week. Just be sure to stay away from flowers that have been sprayed with pesticides, like those from a florist's shop. A selected list of edible flowers, in addition to the ones we've already mentioned, would include pansies, violas, peach blossoms, plum blossoms, squash blossoms, chrysanthemums, daisies, geraniums, jasmine, marigolds, and violets.

Peach Soufflé Pauline

Serves 15

10 large	eggs, separated
2 ¼ cups	sugar, divided
3 pkgs	plain gelatin
¼ cup	fresh lemon juice
½ cup	amaretto
4 cups	pureed peaches, fresh or frozen
1 pt	heavy cream
⅛ tsp	salt
½ cup	toasted almonds, finely chopped
~	sweetened whipped cream

Beat egg yolks with 1 ¼ cups sugar. Soften gelatin in lemon juice. Add amaretto and heat until dissolved. Pour gelatin mixture into beaten eggs and cook over low heat until mixture coats back of spoon—be very careful not to boil. Add peaches and cook until mixture begins to thicken, then remove from heat and chill. Beat egg whites until foamy, then gradually beat in ¾ cup sugar until peaks are firm but not dry. Fold egg whites into chilled peach mixture. Beat cream with salt until similar in consistency to peach mixture, then fold whipped cream and peach mixture together. Fix collar of oiled wax paper around rim of soufflé dish. Pour soufflé mixture into dish and chill overnight. Remove collar, cover sides of soufflé with toasted almonds, and decorate top with sweetened whipped cream.

Honey Mousse with Blackberry Sauce

Serves 6

Blackberry Sauce

Yields 1 ½ cups

12 oz	fresh or frozen unsweetened blackberries
¼ cup	powdered sugar

Defrost and drain blackberries, if frozen. Puree berries in food processor and add powdered sugar. Continue processing until smooth, then strain. Sauce will keep in refrigerator up to 5 days.

½ pt	heavy cream
6 large	egg yolks
½ cup	honey
1 tsp	vanilla extract
~	Blackberry Sauce (see accompanying recipe)
~	fresh mint sprigs and blackberries for garnish

Whip cream until stiff. Using electric mixer bowl, beat egg yolks until frothy. Add honey and vanilla and beat until light, thick, and pale, 5 to 10 minutes. Fold whipped cream into honey mixture. Pour into 8" x 4" baking dish and freeze 6 hours or until serving time. Mousse can be kept tightly covered and frozen up to 2 weeks. Do not thaw before serving. To serve, spoon thin layer of Blackberry Sauce in center of each dessert plate, then tip plate to cover completely. Cut mousse into 1" slices and place one slice in center of each plate. Garnish with fresh mint sprigs and fresh blackberries. Serve immediately.

Praline Soufflé with Caramel Sauce

Serves 8

1/2 pt	heavy cream
5 Tbs	all-purpose flour
1/2 cup	dark brown sugar
4 large	egg yolks
1/2 cup	ground toasted pecans
6 large	egg whites
1 pinch	cream of tartar
1/8 tsp	salt
2 Tbs	sugar
~	Caramel Sauce (see accompanying recipe)

Preheat oven to 350°. In small saucepan, combine cream, flour, and brown sugar. Bring to boil, whisking constantly. Remove from heat and cool slightly. Blend in egg yolks and pecans and set aside. Beat egg whites with cream of tartar and salt until soft peaks form. While beating, gradually add sugar and continue to beat until stiff peaks form. Fold egg whites into pecan mixture and spoon into 8 chilled, buttered, sugared ramekins. Bake 15 minutes and serve warm with Caramel Sauce.

Joe Middleton, executive chef, Nick's Restaurant; former executive chef, MS Governor's Mansion, Jackson, MS

Caramel Sauce

Yields 1 1/4 cups

1/2 cup	dark brown sugar
1/8 cup	white sugar
1/4 cup	white corn syrup
1/2 cup	heavy cream

Combine all ingredients. Bring mixture to boil, stirring constantly. Remove from heat.

Molasses Flan

Serves 8

~	Molasses Bourbon Caramel (see accompanying recipe)
2 cups	milk
2	vanilla beans
1/2 cup	light molasses
3 large	eggs
3 large	egg yolks

Preheat oven to 325°. Bring milk and vanilla beans to boil in heavy saucepan, then remove vanilla beans. In separate bowl, whisk together molasses, eggs, and egg yolks. Gradually whisk in hot milk. Ladle custard into ramekins prepared with Molasses Bourbon Caramel. Place ramekins in large baking pan and add enough boiling water to come halfway up sides of ramekins. Bake until knife blade inserted in center of custards comes out clean, about 1 hour. Cool, cover, and refrigerate until well chilled, 4 hours or overnight. To serve, loosen custards from ramekins with sharp knife and unmold onto dessert plates.

Molasses Bourbon Caramel

Yields 1 cup

2/3 cup	sugar
1/4 cup	light molasses
2 Tbs	bourbon
3 Tbs	water

Cook sugar, molasses, bourbon, and water over low heat, stirring until sugar dissolves. Increase heat to medium-high and boil without stirring until syrup turns deep caramel color. Immediately pour caramel into eight 2/3-cup ramekins. Swirl to coat bottom and sides, then cool.

Apricot Bread Pudding

Serves 6

¾ cup	sugar
4 large	eggs
1 qt	milk
1 Tbs	vanilla extract
12 dried	apricots, in very small pieces
4 large	slices stale, firm, white bread, buttered
~	cinnamon and sugar to taste
~	Hazelnut Custard Sauce (page 203)

For some Southern families, bread pudding is a Christmas Eve tradition, served in large, wide goblets.

Preheat oven to 350°. Beat sugar and eggs together in large bowl. Add milk, vanilla, and apricots and mix well. Transfer to greased 1 ½-quart soufflé dish. Add bread to milk mixture and push down until soaked through. Sprinkle top generously with cinnamon and sugar. Place soufflé dish in pan and add hot water to reach halfway up sides of dish. Bake about 1 hour 15 minutes or until knife blade inserted into center comes out clean. Cover with foil if top is browning too quickly. The pudding should have a custard-like consistency—be careful not to overbake. Allow to cool briefly before serving. Serve warm with Hazelnut Custard Sauce, if desired.

Baked Pears with Blue Cheese and Port

Serves 4

4	Bosc or Bartlett pears, peeled, halved, cored
½ cup	port wine
½ cup	honey
4 Tbs	blue cheese

Preheat oven to 350°. Bake pears with port and honey, uncovered, basting with pan juices, 30 minutes or until tender. Place a generous 1 ½ teaspoon blue cheese in center of each pear. Heat in oven 1 minute or until cheese is partially melted.

Brown Sugar Peaches with Rum

Serves 8

3 lbs	ripe peaches, peeled, sliced, sprinkled with lemon juice
¼ cup	dark brown sugar
¼ cup	dark rum
1 cup	heavy cream
1 cup	sour cream

Sprinkle peaches with brown sugar and rum and toss lightly. Cover mixture securely with plastic wrap and refrigerate 4 hours or more. Whip heavy cream to soft peak stage and fold into sour cream. Refrigerate until ready to use. To serve, place peaches in glass bowl and top with cream mixture.

Rose Hill Strawberries

Serves 8

1 carton	sour cream (8 oz)
¼ cup	maple syrup
3 pts	whole strawberries, washed and hulled
2 ½ Tbs	firmly packed brown sugar

Combine sour cream and maple syrup, cover, and : ate at least 1 hour. Arrange strawberries in 8 dessert bowls. Sprink¨ brown sugar evenly over strawberries and chill. Pour sour crear ˭ over strawberries and serve.

Mother Pryor's Peach Ice Cream

Yields 1 gallon

4 cups	fresh peaches (mashed before measuring)
3 ½ cups	sugar
¼ cup	fresh lemon juice
1 pt	heavy cream
¼ tsp	salt
~	milk

Mix together peaches, sugar, and lemon juice. Slowly blend in cream and add salt. Place mixture in ice cream freezer, add appropriate amount of milk for freezer, and process according to manufacturer's instructions.

Aunt Sis's
Ambrosia
Serves 8

20 navel oranges,
peeled, sectioned
2 cups shredded coconut
1 ½ cups fresh pineapple
chunks
3 oz maraschino cherries
with juice
1 cup sugar

~

Combine all ingredients
and toss lightly.

cient Greeks and
ia meant
₍ous."
. ǝ dish,
ch grandiose

ıplicated
, and
tınal

serve it
ith the meal.
And during the Christmas season
in the South, the already groaning
holiday table would still be
incomplete without a decorative
glass bowl of ambrosia.

¹/₂ cup unsalted butter
¹/₂ cup light corn syrup
¹/₂ cup sugar
8 oz chopped pecans
¹/₂ cup all-purpose flour
ice cream
Blackberry Sauce
(page 206)
~
Preheat oven to 350°.
Over medium heat,
stir together butter,
syrup, sugar, and pecans
until mixture is warm
and butter is melted.
Blend in flour.
On lightly greased
cookie sheet, place
1 tablespoon of mixture
for each cookie, making
only 3 cookies at a time.
Bake 10 minutes,
then cool 15 seconds.
Working quickly,
remove cookie carefully
and mold inside teacup
to form cookie cup.
For each cookie cup,
allow another cookie to
lie flat, forming saucer.
Just before serving,
fill cups with ice cream
and top with
Blackberry Sauce.

Frozen Cream Cups with Chocolate Sauce
Serves 8

1 pkg	cream cheese (8 oz), room temperature
1 cup	powdered sugar, sifted
1 pt	heavy cream
1 tsp	vanilla extract
~	Libby's Chocolate Sauce (page 190)
~	sliced fresh strawberries and kiwi for garnish

Beat cream cheese until smooth. Blend in sugar, then heavy cream and vanilla. Pour mixture into muffin tins lined with paper liners and freeze. To serve, spoon bed of Libby's Chocolate Sauce onto dessert plate. Remove paper liner from frozen cream cup and place cup on chocolate sauce. Garnish with strawberries and kiwi.

Frozen Eggnog Cream
Serves 6

1 cup	vanilla wafer crumbs
3 Tbs	unsalted butter, melted
2 large	eggs, separated
2 Tbs	bourbon
5 Tbs	sugar, divided
¹/₂ pt	heavy cream
~	red and green maraschino cherries for garnish

Combine vanilla wafer crumbs and butter and press into bottom of loaf pan. Beat egg yolks until thick, add 2 tablespoons sugar, and beat again. Add bourbon and beat 2 minutes longer. Beat egg whites until stiff, adding 2 tablespoons sugar, one at a time. Beat heavy cream, adding 1 tablespoon sugar. Combine egg yolks, egg whites, and whipped cream. Pour mixture into prepared loaf pan and freeze (mixture will not freeze solid). To serve, scoop eggnog with vanilla wafer crumbs into dessert dishes and garnish with cherries.

Southern Strawberry Sorbet

Serves 6

4 cups	fresh strawberries, hulled
2 cups	sugar
2 cups	buttermilk

Puree strawberries and sugar in food processor. Add buttermilk and blend well. Pour mixture into 9" x 12" baking dish and freeze 1 hour (center will still be mushy). Transfer mixture to processor and whip. Return to freezer for at least 4 more hours.

Watermelon Sorbet

Serves 6-8

3 quarts	1/2" watermelon cubes, seeded
3 Tbs	sugar
1 Tbs	fresh lemon juice
~	fresh mint leaves for garnish

Sprinkle watermelon cubes with sugar and lemon juice. Place in plastic storage bags and freeze at least 4 hours or overnight. In food processor, puree frozen watermelon, 2 cups at a time, until fluffy. Spoon sorbet into parfait glasses and garnish with fresh mint.

Orange Ginger Sorbet

Serves 8

4 cups	fresh orange juice
1 tsp	orange zest
1/2 tsp	fresh ginger juice
1 1/4 cups	sugar
1/2 cup	fresh lemon juice
3 Tbs	peach schnapps
~	fresh mint sprigs for garnish

In a non-aluminum pan over medium heat, bring orange juice, zest, ginger juice, sugar, and lemon juice to a boil, stirring frequently. Pour mixture into bowl and stir in peach schnapps. Cool to room temperature and freeze in ice cream maker according to manufacturer's instructions. To serve, spoon into chilled mint julep cups and garnish with fresh mint.

§

Mr. Sam's Pineapple Sherbet

Serves 12

1 can crushed pineapple (20 oz)
1/2 cup fresh lemon juice, reserving hulls
1 tsp lemon zest
1 cup boiling water
1 1/4 cups sugar
1 jar maraschino cherries (6 oz) , in small pieces
2 Tbs cherry juice
2 large egg whites, stiffly beaten
2/3 cup half & half

~

Pour pineapple into ice cream freezer container. Fit strainer over top of container and place lemon hulls in strainer. Pour boiling water over hulls onto pineapple, then discard hulls. Add lemon juice, zest, sugar, and cherries. Stir until sugar is dissolved. Add cherry juice to desired color. When mixture has cooled, stir in half & half and fold in beaten egg whites. Freeze according to manufacturer's instructions.

Flying in the face of old Southern tradition, Mr. Sam was not only the patriarch but also the cook in his family. He whipped up this signature treat every 4th of July.

PHOTO (left): *Ancient cedar trees and Spanish moss frame an inviting picnic spot*

in an urban meadow at the intersection of Beasley and Hanging Moss Roads in

Jackson, Mississippi.

PHOTO (overleaf):

Miss Kate's Frozen Tea

Cornmeal Pizza with Green and Red Tomatoes and Sausage

Smoked Turkey Sandwiches with Chutney and Alfalfa Sprouts

F U N   F O O D

Cornmeal Pizza
with Green and Red Tomatoes and Sausage
Serves 4

½ lb	bulk sausage, mild or hot, in 1" balls, flattened
3	cloves garlic
8 oz	provolone cheese, in cubes, chilled
1	Cornmeal Pizza Crust, baked (page 177)
1 large	green tomato, peeled, thinly sliced
1 large	red tomato, peeled, thinly sliced
2 Tbs	coarsely chopped fresh basil (2 tsp dried)
~	salt to taste
~	hot red pepper flakes to taste

If you can't find good quality tomatoes (they seem to be getting rarer and rarer these days), drained canned plum tomatoes make an acceptable substitute. Italian sausage can take the place of the bulk sausage—just remove the casing and prepare as directed.

Cook sausage balls over medium heat until done but not dry, 7 minutes. Drain. With food processor running, drop in garlic, then cheese, and process until cheese is finely chopped. Preheat oven to 450°. Spread cheese mixture over baked pizza crust. Arrange tomato slices and sausage balls on top of cheese. Lightly sprinkle with basil, salt, and red pepper flakes. Bake in pizza pan on middle rack of oven until bubbly, 15 to 20 minutes.

Cold Roast Tenderloin of Beef with Horseradish Mousse

Serves 8

Horseradish Mousse

Serves 8

1 envelope	unflavored gelatin
½ cup	water
6 oz	prepared horseradish
1 tsp	Dijon mustard
½ pt	heavy cream
1 cup	sour cream
½ tsp	salt
2 Tbs	green peppercorns, drained, lightly crushed
2 Tbs	very finely chopped green onion tops for garnish

Stir gelatin into water and allow to stand until softened, 5 minutes. Drain horseradish thoroughly and squeeze dry in towel. Blend together mustard and cream in medium saucepan. Bring to simmer over medium heat. Remove from heat and whisk in softened gelatin. In separate bowl, gradually whisk mustard mixture into sour cream until well incorporated. Stir in horseradish, salt, and peppercorns. Pour mousse mixture into oiled 4-cup mold or soufflé dish. Cover loosely with plastic wrap and refrigerate six hours or until set, but not more than 1 day. Unmold onto serving plate and sprinkle with chopped green onion tops.

1 fillet	beef tenderloin (3 lbs), trimmed, patted dry
~	salt and pepper
6 Tbs	vegetable oil
1 medium	onion, chopped
1 large	carrot, chopped
1 medium	stalk celery, chopped
2	bay leaves
10 slices	bacon, blanched, drained
~	Horseradish Mousse (see accompanying recipe) or Sweet Red Pepper and Zucchini Relish (page 246)
~	curly endive for garnish
~	red bell pepper, sliced into thin rings for garnish
~	pumpernickel and rye bread slices for serving

Preheat oven to 350°. Season beef with salt and pepper. In large, heavy skillet, brown beef well in oil over medium-high heat. Transfer meat to roasting pan rack. Thoroughly combine onion, carrot, and celery and pat vegetable mixture onto top and sides of meat. Crumble bay leaves over all. Arrange blanched bacon slices over top and extending down sides of meat. Roast the meat to desired degree of doneness, 45 minutes for medium rare (meat thermometer should read 140°-145°). Discard vegetables and bacon and allow beef to cool completely. Cover and refrigerate until firm. Slice beef diagonally in ¼" slices. To serve, place Horseradish Mousse in center of serving platter. Surround with border of endive and arrange meat in overlapping slices around endive. Garnish with red pepper slices. Serve with pumpernickel and rye bread slices.

Nick Apostle, owner, Nick's and 400 East Capitol Restaurants, Jackson, MS

Roast Beef Po-Boys

Serves 6

1	boneless rump roast (3 lbs), trimmed of all fat
~	seasoned salt
~	garlic powder
~	pepper
4 Tbs	all-purpose flour, divided
4 Tbs	unsalted butter, divided
2 large	yellow onions, chopped
3 cloves	garlic, minced
2 cans	beef stock (21 oz total)
½ cup	dry red wine
~	salt and freshly ground pepper to taste
~	Worcestershire sauce to taste
~	New Orleans French bread
½ head	green cabbage, shredded
~	mayonnaise
~	Creole mustard

Season meat with seasoned salt, garlic powder, and pepper. Coat surface of meat with 2 tablespoons flour. In Dutch oven, brown meat on all sides in 1 tablespoon butter over medium heat. Remove meat and add 1 tablespoon butter to Dutch oven. Sauté onions until tender, then add garlic and cook 1 to 2 minutes. Remove and reserve onions. Add remaining 2 tablespoons butter and 2 tablespoons flour and cook, stirring constantly, until medium-brown. Add beef stock, increase heat to medium-high, and whisk until gravy thickens. Return meat and sautéed onions to Dutch oven. Add wine, salt, pepper, and Worcestershire. Cook on low until very tender, 5 hours. To serve, remove meat and slice, discarding gristle or fat. Skim grease from gravy and adjust seasoning. If gravy needs thinning, add beef stock. Bathe meat slices in gravy and serve on hot, split French bread dressed with cabbage, mayonnaise, and mustard.

A Pike's Peak end or sirloin tip roast or a venison roast will work just fine in this recipe, as long as it's well trimmed. And, if you prefer, you can do the cooking in a crock pot or in a roasting pan in the oven. You might also consider adding a tablespoon of chopped fresh rosemary for extra flavor.

Just remember to provide plenty of napkins!

Twice-Spiced Corned Beef Sandwiches
Serves 8

1	packaged spiced corned beef brisket (3-4 lbs)
¼ cup	peppercorns
2 cloves	garlic, pressed
¼ cup	whole cloves
2 Tbs	vegetable oil
4 Tbs	light brown sugar
3 Tbs	vinegar
3 Tbs	dry mustard
~	rye bread slices

If already-spiced corned beef is not available, double the cloves and peppercorns in this recipe and add two bay leaves. We like to serve it with hot, sweet mustard.

Place corned beef in pot with water to cover. Add peppercorns, garlic, cloves, oil, brown sugar, vinegar, and mustard. Bring to boil, then lower heat and simmer until tender, 1 hour. Remove from heat, cool, then cover and refrigerate at least 24 hours. Remove beef from liquid, dry thoroughly, and trim off fat. Slice and serve on rye bread slices for sandwiches.

Reuben Bread
Serves 6

1 package	dry yeast
1 cup	warm water (105°-115°)
1 Tbs	sugar, divided
3 ¼ cups	bread flour
1 tsp	salt
1 Tbs	unsalted butter, room temperature
⅓ cup	Thousand Island dressing
6 oz	corned beef, thinly sliced
4 oz	Swiss cheese, sliced or shredded
1 can	sauerkraut (8 oz), drained
1 large	egg white, beaten
~	caraway seeds

Reuben Bread will turn any soup into a full, robust meal (we especially like it with gumbo). To make a cocktail-sized version, cut dough in half and roll out two 5" x 14" rectangles. Proceed as directed with filling, rising, baking, and slicing.

Dissolve yeast and 1 teaspoon sugar in warm water until bubbly. Combine flour, remaining sugar, salt, and butter in mixer. Add dissolved yeast and beat to make soft dough. Knead 4 minutes and roll out dough to 10" x 14" rectangle. Preheat oven to 400°. Place dough on greased baking sheet and spoon dressing down center. Top with corned beef, cheese, and sauerkraut. Make cuts along sides of dough, from filling to outer edge, at 1" intervals. Alternating sides, fold strips across filling. Cover and allow to rise 30 minutes. Brush surface of dough with egg white and sprinkle with caraway seeds. Bake 25 minutes, then slice and serve warm.

Smoked Turkey Sandwiches with Chutney and Alfalfa Sprouts

Yields 12

½ cup	mayonnaise
3 Tbs	Major Grey chutney, finely chopped
~	thinly sliced whole-wheat bread, crusts removed, cut into fun shapes
~	smoked turkey, thinly sliced
~	alfalfa sprouts

Combine mayonnaise and chutney, mixing well. Spread small amount of chutney on bread shapes. Add turkey slices and alfalfa sprouts and top with matching bread shape.

Mushroom-Stuffed Veal Paté

Serves 8

4 oz	fresh mushrooms, chopped
¼ cup	onion, finely chopped
2 cloves	garlic, minced
¾ tsp	dried thyme
1 Tbs	unsalted butter
2 Tbs	sour cream
~	salt and pepper to taste
3 Tbs	milk
1 large	egg
¾ cup	fresh bread crumbs
1 lb	ground veal
¼ cup	chopped fresh parsley
½ tsp	grated lemon zest
1 tsp	salt
½ tsp	black pepper

Over medium-high heat, cook mushrooms, onion, garlic, and thyme in butter until most liquid has evaporated and mushrooms begin to brown, 5 minutes. Stir in sour cream and cook until syrupy, 2 to 3 minutes. Season to taste with salt and pepper and allow to cool. Preheat oven to 350°. Thoroughly combine milk and egg in large bowl. Add bread crumbs and soak 5 minutes. Mix in veal, parsley, and lemon zest and season with salt and pepper. Place half of veal mixture in 8" x 3" loaf pan. Spoon mushrooms evenly over veal and cover with remaining veal, pressing down evenly over mushrooms. Bake 1 hour, drain off any fat or juices, and allow to stand at room temperature 15 minutes. After baking, allow the terrine to cool thoroughly, then top it with a second loaf pan that has been weighted with small, heavy cans. Refrigerate overnight for a firm texture.

You can serve this rather sophisticated meatloaf hot, perhaps with a light tomato sauce, but we think it's even more delicious cold. It makes terrific picnic fare, served plain or with assorted mustards and breads.

Tuna Stuffed Pita Pockets

Serves 4

8 oz	mozzarella cheese, in ½" cubes
1 can	tuna in water (6½ oz), drained, flaked
1 cup	cherry tomatoes, quartered
1 small	red onion, halved, sliced in thin rings
2 stalks	celery, diced
¼ cup	extra virgin olive oil
3 Tbs	red wine vinegar
1 Tbs	dried basil, crumbled
½ tsp	salt
¼ tsp	crushed red pepper flakes
⅛ tsp	black pepper
4	whole-wheat pitas, heated

Tuna can be marinated in dressing 24 hours in advance. Add cheese and tomatoes one hour before serving.

Combine cheese, tuna, tomatoes, onion, and celery in large bowl. Whisk together oil, vinegar, basil, salt, red pepper flakes, and black pepper. Pour dressing over tuna mixture and toss to coat. Cover with plastic wrap and refrigerate for at least 1 hour. To serve, cut pita bread into halves and spoon marinated salad into each pita pocket.

Grilled Broccoli Cheese Sandwich

Serves 1

4 large	fresh broccoli florets, chopped
1 Tbs	water
1 tsp	unsalted butter
~	garlic salt to taste
2 slices	whole grain bread, toasted
2 slices	Swiss cheese, sandwich-sized
~	unsalted butter for browning

Combine broccoli and water in covered dish and microwave on HIGH 1 minute. Drain and season with 1 teaspoon butter and garlic salt to taste. Place one slice cheese on each toasted bread slice. Spoon broccoli onto one of the toast slices with cheese, then top with second slice to form sandwich. Spread top of sandwich with butter and brown in toaster or oven. Turn sandwich, spread second side with butter, and brown. Cut sandwich in half and serve warm.

Scallion-Stuffed Eggs

Yields 8

4 large	eggs, hard-cooked, peeled
1 Tbs	minced fresh parsley
2 tsp	minced fresh chives
1	green onion, minced
2 Tbs	mayonnaise
2 tsp	Dijon mustard
¼ tsp	salt
~	freshly ground black pepper to taste
~	chopped chives for garnish

Cut eggs in half lengthwise and remove yolks. In food processor, combine egg yolks with parsley, chives, green onion, mayonnaise, mustard, salt, and pepper. Process to blend. Spoon mixture into egg white halves and chill. Garnish with chopped chives.

Dill-Stuffed Eggs

Yields 16

8	hard-cooked eggs, peeled
½ cup	finely chopped purple onions
⅓ cup	chopped fresh dill (2 Tbs dried)
¼ cup	mayonnaise
¼ cup	sour cream
¼ cup	Dijon mustard
~	salt and freshly ground black pepper to taste

Slice eggs in half lengthwise and remove yolks. Mash yolks with fork until smooth. Blend in onions, dill, mayonnaise, sour cream, mustard, salt, and pepper. Spoon mixture into egg white halves and chill.

Pimiento Cheese

A civilized Civil War still rages in the South between devotees of Sweet or Savory Pimiento Cheese. Choose either side and victory will be yours.

Sweet Pimiento Cheese

Yields 1 ½ qts

2 lbs sharp cheddar cheese, coarsely shredded
2 jars pimientos (8 oz total), drained, diced
1 ½ cups mayonnaise, or less
4 Tbs sugar

~

Thoroughly combine all ingredients, using just enough mayonnaise to achieve desired consistency.

Savory Pimiento Cheese

Yields 1 ½ qts

2 lbs sharp cheddar cheese, coarsely shredded
2 jars pimientos (8 oz total), drained, diced
1 ½ cups mayonnaise, or less
1 small white onion, finely chopped
1 tsp coarsely ground black pepper

~

Thoroughly combine all ingredients, using just enough mayonnaise to achieve desired consistency.

Boiled Peanuts

Yields 3 lbs

*3 lbs raw peanuts
in shells
1 gallon water
¹/₂ cup salt
2 Tbs sugar*

-

*Rinse peanuts very
thoroughly in several
changes of water,
making sure they are
clean. Pour water into
6-quart stock pot and
stir in salt and sugar.
Add peanuts, cover
lightly, and bring to boil
over medium heat. Boil
peanuts 2 to 4 hours,
depending on size of
nuts. After 2 hours
cooking time, check
periodically for
doneness. Add addi-
tional boiling water, if
needed, but do not add
extra salt. When
peanuts are done,
remove from heat and
allow to cool in cooking
water to absorb salt, 45
minutes to 1 hour or
longer, depending on
taste. Drain peanuts but
do not rinse or refriger-
ate.*

*There was a time when
community "peanut boilings"
were nearly as common as
barbecues and fish fries in the
Deep South.*

Chinese Nachos
Yields 24

3 oz	Monterey Jack cheese, shredded
2 Tbs	green chilies, drained, chopped
24	won ton skins
~	peanut oil for frying
~	salsa

Mound 1 ¹/₂ teaspoons cheese and ¹/₄ teaspoon green chilies in center of each won ton skin. Brush edges of won ton lightly with water, fold in half diagonally, and press edges together to seal. Heat 1 ¹/₂" oil to 375° in wok or large skillet. Fry 6 wontons at a time until golden brown, 30 seconds on each side. Drain on paper towels. Serve immediately with salsa for dipping. May also be made ahead and reheated in 400° oven.

Pita Bread Crisps
Serves 4-6

1 pkg	pita bread pockets
¹/₂ cup	unsalted butter, melted
~	garlic salt to taste
~	lemon pepper seasoning to taste
~	basil or dill to taste
~	freshly grated Parmesan cheese

Preheat oven to 275°-300°. Tear pita bread apart and arrange on baking sheet. Brush melted butter over bread and sprinkle with garlic salt, lemon pepper, basil or dill, and cheese (or your own favorite combination of seasonings). Bake until brown, watching care-fully to avoid burning. Cool and break into pieces. Serve with cocktails, soups, or salads.

Soft Pretzels
Yields 20

1 pkg	dry yeast
1/2 cup	warm water (105°-115°)
1/2 cup	sugar, divided
2 cups	milk, scalded, cooled to lukewarm
3 1/2 Tbs	salt, divided
1/4 cup	vegetable oil
6 3/4 cups	bread flour, divided
3/4 tsp	baking powder
1 large	egg
1 Tbs	water
4 tsp	coarse salt
~	sesame or poppy seeds, optional

In a large bowl, sprinkle yeast over warm water, add 1 teaspoon sugar, and allow to dissolve until bubbly. Add remaining sugar, lukewarm milk, 1 1/2 teaspoons salt, and oil. Beat in 3 cups flour to make smooth batter. Cover and allow to rise until doubled in bulk and spongy, 45 minutes. Stir down batter. Mix baking powder with 3 cups flour. Stir into batter, one cup at a time, to form stiff dough. Turn dough out onto well-floured surface. Knead until smooth and elastic, 5 to 10 minutes, adding only enough flour to prevent sticking. Lightly flour surface and roll dough out to 10" x 16" rectangle. Cut dough into 20 strips, each 16" long and 1/2" wide. Keep strips covered with damp paper towels while shaping pretzels. With palms of hands, roll one strip back and forth to form a 24" rope. Holding one end in each hand, twist rope into pretzel shape. Repeat with remaining dough strips. Allow pretzels to rise 30 minutes, uncovered, on lightly floured board. In large sauce pan, heat 2 quarts water to boiling. Stir in remaining 3 tablespoons salt. Preheat oven to 400 °. Using large slotted spatula, lower one pretzel at a time into gently boiling water for 2 seconds. Lift out and drain off all water. Place pretzels 1/2" apart on well-greased baking sheet. Beat egg with one tablespoon water, then brush lightly over pretzels. Sprinkle with coarse salt and sesame or poppy seeds, if desired. Bake 18 to 20 minutes or until crust is golden brown. Serve immediately or cool on wire racks.

Baked pretzels can be frozen and reheated. This recipe may seem a bit complex, but we bet your youngsters will be glad to help, especially with the shaping. You'll find that, with a little encouragement, the imaginations of children can leap well beyond the conventional pretzel form.

Glazed Crackers

Yields 72

½ cup	margarine
½ cup	unsalted butter
½ cup	sugar
1 tsp	vanilla extract
1 cup	chopped pecans
2 pkgs	buttery-flavored crackers (8 oz total)

Preheat oven to 325°. Combine margarine, butter, and sugar and boil 3 minutes. Add vanilla and pecans. Arrange crackers on two cookie sheets and spoon butter mixture over crackers. Bake 8 minutes. Remove from oven and allow to cool briefly. Remove crackers from cookie sheets with spatula.

Two-Chocolate Tiger Butter

Yields 72

1 lb	white chocolate
1 jar	chunky peanut butter (12 oz)
1 lb	semi-sweet chocolate, melted

Since white chocolate contains no chocolate liquor, calling it "chocolate" may be fudging the truth just a bit. It is true, however, that white chocolate is not always readily available in some areas. This recipe works best with the ingredients as called for, but almond bark can be substituted if white chocolate proves to be elusive.

Combine white chocolate and peanut butter in top of double boiler. Bring water to boil, then reduce heat to low. Cook, stirring constantly, until chocolate and peanut butter melt. Line 15" x 10" x 1" jelly-roll pan with wax paper and spread peanut butter mixture on pan. Pour melted semi-sweet chocolate over peanut butter mixture and swirl through with knife. Chill until firm, then cut into 1 ½" x 1" pieces and store in refrigerator.

Gathering at The Grove

The Grove—an expanse of green on the campus of the University of Mississippi at Oxford—has been a traditional game-day gathering place for generations of Ole Miss football fans.

Vehicles ranging from tiny sports cars to four-wheel-drive behemoths and customized vans begin to arrive at The Grove in the early dawn, since space is limited, and accommodations are strictly first come, first served. Once a suitable location has been claimed, the occupants start breaking out the provisions. Some bring traditional picnic baskets packed with sandwiches and salads. Others set out elaborate portable kitchens, fire up their bottled gas burners, and proceed to prepare tempting gourmet meals. Along with the food, visiting is the order of the day, with old friends and classmates catching up on current events and waxing nostalgic over days gone by.

PHOTO:
This picnic basket has traveled with Lee Threadgill's family to every University of Mississippi football picnic for the past 35 years.

FOOTBALL TAILGATE PARTY

Daddy's Bloody Mary's

~

Boiled Peanuts

~

Soft Pretzels

~

Caramelized Onion Dip

~

Salmon and Vegetable Smorgasbord

~

Reuben Bread

~

Lou Lou's Cookies

~

Miss Kate's Frozen Tea

Almond Crusted Bars

Yields 30

1 2/3 cups	all-purpose flour
1 1/2 cups	sugar
1/2 cup	unsalted butter, melted
1/8 tsp	salt
2 large	eggs, lightly beaten
1 1/2 Tbs	almond extract
1 cup	sliced almonds

Preheat oven to 350°. Mix together flour and sugar. Add butter, salt, eggs, and almond extract. Spread mixture into lightly greased 13" x 9" pan. Sprinkle sliced almonds over top and press lightly into batter. Bake until lightly browned, 15 to 20 minutes. Cool slightly and slice into bars.

For a thinner, crispier bar, spread batter in a jelly-roll pan. Reduce cooking time and be careful not to over-brown.

Apricot Bars

Yields 30

1 1/2 cups	all-purpose flour
1 tsp	baking powder
1/4 tsp	salt
1 1/2 cups	quick-cooking oatmeal
1 cup	brown sugar
3/4 cup	unsalted butter
1 cup	apricot preserves or jam

Preheat oven to 375°. Sift together flour, baking powder, and salt. Stir in oats and sugar. Cut in butter until crumbly. Pat 2/3 of mixture into 11" x 7 1/2" pan. Spread with apricot preserves and crumble remaining mixture on top. Bake until golden brown, 25 minutes. Cool and cut into 3" x 1" bars.

Grand Marnier Custard Squares
Yields 60

Bottom layer:

1/2 cup	powdered sugar
1/4 tsp	salt
2 cups	unbleached all-purpose flour
1 cup	unsalted butter, room temperature

Top layer:

1 1/2 cups	sugar
~	zest of 3 oranges
1 1/4 tsp	baking powder
1/4 tsp	salt
6 large	eggs
3 Tbs	orange juice
3 Tbs	Grand Marnier liqueur
1 tsp	orange extract

Icing:

2 1/2 cups	powdered sugar, sifted
3 Tbs	Grand Marnier liqueur
3 Tbs	orange juice, or less

Preheat oven to 350°. To prepare bottom layer, blend sugar, salt, and flour and cut in butter. Spread mixture in buttered and floured 10" x 15" baking pan. Bake until very lightly browned, 20 minutes. For the top layer, blend sugar and zest in food processor until zest is finely chopped. Mix in baking powder, salt, eggs, orange juice, Grand Marnier, and orange extract. Pour mixture over bottom layer in pan and bake until firm, 20 minutes. Allow to cool. Prepare icing by blending powdered sugar and Grand Marnier with just enough orange juice to produce a spreadable consistency. Spread icing over cooled cake and cut into squares.

§

Granny's Walnut Bourbon Balls
Yields 42

2 1/2 cups finely crushed
vanilla wafer crumbs
2 Tbs cocoa
1 cup powdered sugar
1 cup finely chopped
walnuts
1/4 cup bourbon
3 Tbs corn syrup
powdered sugar for
coating

~

Thoroughly combine
crumbs, cocoa, powdered
sugar, and nuts.
Stir in bourbon and
syrup and mix until
dough holds together.
Form into
1" balls and roll in
powdered sugar.
Cover and allow to ripen
1 or 2 days.

*Christmas at Granny's
was never complete without these
Bourbon Balls, although she did
occasionally vary them by
substituting coconut for half the
chopped walnuts.*

*2 cups unsalted butter
1 cup dark brown sugar
1 cup light brown sugar
3 large eggs, beaten
1 Tbs vanilla extract
2 Tbs cinnamon
1/2 tsp ginger
2 cups white sugar
2 cups all-purpose flour
2 tsp salt
2 tsp baking soda
3 cups instant oatmeal
2 cups walnut pieces
1 cup raisins*

~

*Preheat oven to 350°.
Cream together butter
and brown sugars.
Add beaten eggs and
vanilla. Combine
cinnamon, ginger, and
white sugar, and add
slowly to creamed
mixture. Sift together
flour, salt, and baking
soda and slowly add to
sugar mixture. Blend in
oatmeal, then stir in
walnut pieces and raisins.
Drop by rounded
teaspoonfuls onto
ungreased cookie sheets.
Bake 9 to 13 minutes.
Remove cookie sheets
from oven, bang sharply
on counter, and
immediately place cookies
on brown paper bag
to cool.*

Molasses Snaps
Yields 48

3/4 cup	unsalted butter
1 cup	sugar
1/4 cup	molasses
1/4 tsp	salt
1 tsp	cinnamon
2 tsp	soda
1 tsp	cloves
1 tsp	ginger
2 cups	all-purpose flour, sifted
~	sugar for coating

Preheat oven to 350°. Cream together butter and sugar. Add molasses and continue to cream. Combine salt, cinnamon, soda, cloves, and ginger and add to molasses mixture, blending well. Slowly add flour and mix until blended. Form dough into 1" balls, roll in sugar, and bake on greased cookie sheet 8 to 10 minutes.

Lemon Glazed Cookies
Yields 36

Cookies:

1 cup	unsalted butter, room temperature
1/3 cup	sifted powdered sugar
1 cup	all-purpose flour
2/3 cup	cornstarch

Lemon Glaze:

2 1/2 cups	sifted powdered sugar
1/2 cup	unsalted butter, melted
2 Tbs	fresh lemon juice
1 Tbs	grated lemon zest

Preheat oven to 350°. Using an electric mixer at medium speed, beat butter and powdered sugar 1 minute. Sift together flour and cornstarch. Add to batter and continue mixing until dough is softened, 1 minute. Drop batter by teaspoonfuls onto ungreased baking sheet and bake 12 to 15 minutes (tops of cookies will not brown). Prepare glaze by combining powdered sugar, butter, lemon juice, and zest. Remove cookies to rack and frost with glaze while warm.

Almond Crescent Cookies

Yields 48

½ cup	powdered sugar
1 cup	unsalted butter
1 Tbs	brandy
2 Tbs	water
1 cup	chopped whole almonds
2 cups	all-purpose flour
⅓ cup	crushed almonds (optional)
~	powdered sugar for dusting

Cream together sugar and butter until light. Add brandy, water, almonds, and flour. Chill 30 minutes. Preheat oven to 350°. Shape small pieces of dough into crescents and roll in crushed almonds, if desired. Bake 12 to 15 minutes, cool, then dust with powdered sugar.

Contemporary Tea Cakes

Yields 24

½ cup	unsalted butter
1 cup	sugar
½ cup	vegetable oil
1 large	egg
1 tsp	white vinegar
2 ½ cups	all-purpose flour
½ tsp	salt
½ tsp	baking soda
1 tsp	vanilla extract

Preheat oven to 350°. Cream together butter, sugar, and oil. Beat together egg and vinegar and combine with butter mixture. Sift together flour, salt, and soda. Stir into butter mixture and add vanilla. Dough will be stiff. Pinch off small balls of dough and arrange on greased cookie sheets. Flatten dough balls with fork and bake until edges are light brown, 5 to 7 minutes.

§

*Dida's
1898
Tea Cakes*
Yields 24

*2 tea cups sugar
2 large eggs
1 tsp baking soda
1 qt flour
2 tsp cream of tartar
½ tsp salt
1 tsp cinnamon
1 large spoonful lard
2 tea cups milk*

~

*Mix sugar and eggs.
Blend soda, flour,
cream of tartar, salt, and
cinnamon and add lard.
Combine with sugar/egg
mixture and milk
to make a stiff dough.
Roll thin and
cut out cookies.
Bake 5 minutes
at 350°.*

*Lida Coffman's friends
called her "Dida." This is her
recipe, dated 1898.*

Celebration Sugar Cookies

Yields 36

Decorator Icing

Yields 1 cup

2 ½ cups	powdered sugar
¼ tsp	cream of tartar
2 large	egg whites, room temperature
~	food coloring, as desired

Beat together powdered sugar, cream of tartar, and egg whites until stiff. The longer this icing is beaten, the thicker it will become. A thin consistency makes a nice glaze; a thicker frosting works well for decorating. Add food coloring as desired and use pastry bag to pipe your choice of decorations.

1 cup	unsalted butter, room temperature
½ cup	sugar
1 tsp	vanilla
2 ½ cups	all-purpose flour
½ tsp	salt
½ tsp	ground mace (optional)
~	powdered sugar and all-purpose flour for dusting
~	Decorator Icing (see accompanying recipe)

Using an electric mixer, cream together butter and sugar. Add vanilla and beat well. Sift together flour, salt, and mace. Combine flour mixture with butter mixture and mix well, but do not overwork. Divide dough in half, cover, and chill 1 hour. Preheat oven to 375°. Dust work surface with 1 part powdered sugar and 1 part flour. Roll out cookie dough to desired thickness—do not over-roll or cookies will be tough. Cut into desired shapes and bake 7 to 8 minutes for ⅛" cookies or 10 to 12 minutes for ¼" cookies. Frost cooled cookies with Decorator Icing.

Chocolate Toffee Cookies

Yields 24

Chocolate Almond Glaze

Yields 1 cup

1 large	egg white
1 cup	sifted powdered sugar
⅓ cup	cocoa
2 Tbs	unsalted butter, room temperature
1 Tbs	hot water
1 Tbs	amaretto
¼ tsp	almond flavoring

In electric mixer, beat egg white at medium speed until frothy. Gradually add powdered sugar and cocoa. Add butter, water, amaretto, and almond flavoring and beat until blended.

½ cup	unsalted butter, room temperature
⅓ cup	sugar
1 large	egg
¾ tsp	vanilla extract
1 ¼ cups	all-purpose flour
⅔ cup	finely chopped pecans, toasted
1 cup	finely chopped almond brickle chips, divided
~	Chocolate Almond Glaze (see accompanying recipe)

Preheat oven to 350°. Cream butter and gradually add sugar, beating until light and fluffy. Add egg and vanilla, beating until blended. Add flour gradually, beating until smooth. Fold in pecans and ⅔ cup brickle chips, reserving ⅓ cup for garnish. Shape dough into 2" sticks, ½" to ¾" in diameter. Place sticks on lightly greased cookie sheets and bake until lightly browned, 10 to 12 minutes. Cool cookies on rack. Dip one end of cookie into Chocolate Almond Glaze, then into reserved brickle chips, and allow to set.

Kathy's Chocolate Chip Cookies
Yields 48

1 ¼ cups	sifted all-purpose flour
½ tsp	salt
½ cup	margarine, room temperature
½ cup	firmly packed light brown sugar
⅓ cup	granulated sugar
1 large	egg
½ tsp	vanilla extract
½ tsp	baking soda
1 Tbs	hot water
1 cup	semi-sweet chocolate chips
½ cup	chopped pecans

Preheat oven to 350°. Sift together flour and salt. In food processor, cream together butter, sugars, egg, and vanilla. Combine soda and hot water and add to batter. Add flour mixture and process to blend. Fold in chocolate chips and nuts. Drop batter by teaspoonfuls onto greased cookie sheet and bake 10 minutes.

Pecan Cocoa Cookies
Yields 66

1 cup	unbleached all-purpose flour, less 2 Tbs
½ tsp	baking soda
¼ tsp	salt
3 oz	sweet cooking chocolate, in pieces
2 oz	unsweetened chocolate, in pieces
1 Tbs	unsweetened cocoa
½ cup	sugar
½ cup	firmly packed light brown sugar
½ cup	unsalted butter, softened, quartered
1 large	egg
2 tsp	vanilla extract
¼ cup	finely chopped pecans

Preheat oven to 375°. In food processor, combine flour, soda, and salt and pulse 3 times to blend. Remove and reserve. Combine chocolates, cocoa, and sugars in processor. Pulse briefly to chop, then process continuously until chocolate is as fine as sugar, 1 minute. Add butter, egg, and vanilla and process 20 seconds, stopping once to scrape bowl. Spoon reserved flour mixture onto batter in circle and pulse just until ingredients are combined, 3 or 4 times—do not overprocess. Refrigerate dough 20 minutes. Shape dough into 1" balls and dip tops in pecans. Space dough balls 2 inches apart on ungreased cookie sheet. Bake 8 minutes for chewy cookies, 9 minutes for crisp.

For ease of handling and better shaped cookies, after baking let cookies rest 2 minutes before carefully transferring to wire rack and cooling completely.

Holiday Macaroon Cookies

Yields 30

2 1/2 cups	all-purpose flour, sifted
1/4 tsp	baking powder
1/2 tsp	salt
1 cup	vegetable shortening
2 tsp	vanilla extract
1/2 cup	powdered sugar, sifted
3 Tbs	milk, divided
1 can	almond paste (8 oz)
1 cup	sugar
2 large	egg whites
1 can	cherry or blueberry pie filling (16 oz)

Sift together flour, baking powder, and salt and set aside. With electric mixer at medium speed, blend shortening, vanilla, and powdered sugar until creamy. Reduce mixer speed to low and add flour mixture and 2 tablespoons milk. Refrigerate dough until easy to handle. Preheat oven to 350°. On lightly floured surface, roll dough to 1/4 " thickness and cut into 2 1/2" rounds. Place rounds on ungreased cookie sheets, spaced 1/2" apart. Bake 15 minutes. Blend almond paste with sugar and egg whites until smooth, then add up to 1 tablespoon milk to reach stiff but manageable consistency. Spoon mixture into pastry bag with large tipped pastry tube in place. Pipe border of almond mixture around top outer edge of cookie. Place teaspoon of cherry or blueberry pie filling in center of each cookie. Bake 20 minutes longer, then cool and store in tightly covered container.

Plantation Almond Tea

Yields 1/2 gallon

3 cups	boiling water
5	tea bags
1 cup	sugar
~	ice and water
1/2 cup	fresh lemon juice
1/2 tsp	almond extract
1 tsp	vanilla

Pour boiling water over tea bags, steep to desired strength, then remove bags. Add sugar and stir to dissolve. Add ice and water to make 1/2 gallon. Stir in lemon juice, almond extract, and vanilla.

Miss Kate's Frozen Tea

Yields 1 gallon

3 lemons
2 oranges
9 family-size tea bags
1 cup chopped fresh mint leaves
3 cups sugar
$^1/_4$ cup muraschino cherry juice
fresh mint for garnish
maraschino cherries for garnish

~

Squeeze lemons and oranges. Chill juices and reserve lemon hulls.
Boil 2 quarts water, remove from heat, and add tea bags, mint leaves, and
reserved lemon hulls. Steep 30 minutes.
Strain, add sugar, and stir until dissolved. Refrigerate up to 24 hours.

When mixture is thoroughly cooled, add lemon, orange, and cherry juices,
plus 1$^1/_2$ quarts more cold water. Stir well, and freeze in 1-gallon ice cream
freezer to slushy consistency.

When serving, garnish with fresh mint and maraschino cherry.

Mrs. John B. Howell, Sr.,
known to her admirers
as Miss Kate,
was a celebrated Canton,
Mississippi, hostess
of three generations ago.
She was a genteel
Southern lady in almost
every respect. But when it
came to guarding the
recipe for her Frozen Tea,
a lioness defending her
young could not match
Miss Kate's ferocity.
The beverage made its
public debut during the
very first Canton Flea
Market (which has since
become an annual event
of national reknown).
Since that time,
magazines, cookbook
publishers, and party-
givers have sought the
secret in vain…until now.
Here, at last,
is the coveted recipe,
in honor of the legendary
Miss Kate.

Café Mocha

Serves 6

1/2 cup	Colombian coffee
4 1/2 cups	cold water
2 Tbs	chocolate syrup
1/2 cup	creme de cacao
~	sweetened whipped cream
~	grated chocolate

Brew coffee with water. Pour brewed coffee into 6 ounce coffee cups. For each serving, add 1 teaspoon chocolate syrup and 1 tablespoon creme de cacao, stirring to blend. Top each serving with sweetened whipped cream and sprinkle with grated chocolate.

Watermelon-Wine Punch

Yields 2 quarts

1/2 large	watermelon
1/2 cup	sugar
1/2 cup	water
1/3 cup	frozen pink lemonade, thawed (3 oz)
3/4 cup	rosé wine (1/4 fifth)
1 bottle	ginger ale (28 oz), chilled

Make 2 cups melon balls from watermelon, then clean out rind for use as serving bowl. Thoroughly chill melon balls and rind. Boil sugar and water together 5 minutes. Blend in lemonade and wine. Chill until thoroughly cold. Blend wine mixture, ginger ale, and melon balls and serve in chilled watermelon rind bowl.

Frozen Fruit Punch

Yields 1 gallon

4 cups	water
3 cups	sugar
5 sprigs	mint
1 can	apricot nectar (12 oz)
1 can	pineapple juice (46 oz)
2 small cans	frozen orange juice (12 oz total), prepared with water
1 bottle	frozen lemon juice (7.5 oz)

Boil together water, sugar, and mint. Strain and remove mint. Stir in nectar, pineapple juice, prepared orange juice, and lemon juice. Freeze until solid, 12 to 24 hours. To serve, thaw mixture slightly and scoop into glasses. Serve with sprigs of mint and spoons.

Hot Tomato-Orange Juice Drink

Serves 6

2 cups	tomato juice
1 cup	beef bouillon
1 cup	orange juice
1 Tbs	Worcestershire sauce
~	garlic powder to taste
~	salt to taste
~	Tabasco Sauce to taste

Combine all ingredients, heat, and serve.

Daddy's Bloody Marys

Serves 8

1 can	tomato juice (46 oz)
3/4 cup	fresh lemon juice
1 Tbs	prepared horseradish
6 dashes	Tabasco Sauce
3 Tbs	Worcestershire sauce
1 tsp	salt
1/2 tsp	pepper
~	parsley flakes (optional)
1 1/2 cups	vodka (1/2 fifth)

When serving 50 or 60 of your closest friends, use these proportions:

7 cans	tomato juice (46 oz each)
1 bottle	Worcestershire sauce (10 oz)
1 bottle	prepared horseradish (10 oz)
1 bottle	Tabasco Sauce (6 oz)
24 large	lemons, squeezed
~	salt, pepper, and parsley flakes to taste
3 bottles	vodka (fifths)

Blend tomato juice, lemon juice, horseradish, Tabasco, Worcestershire, salt, pepper, and parsley, if desired. Refrigerate mixture up to one week. Mix in vodka just before serving.

Blonde Sangria

Yields 2 gallons

4 large	lemons
4 large	oranges
2/3 cup	sugar
1 gallon	Mountain Rhine wine
2 bottles	club soda (2 liters or 2 qts total)
~	lemon and orange slices for garnish
~	crushed ice

Squeeze lemons and oranges and mix juices with sugar. When ready to serve, blend juice mixture with wine and club soda. Serve over crushed ice. Garnish with lemon and orange slices.

PHOTO (left): *Before the days of air-conditioning, homes in the South were*
constructed to catch any available breezes and conduct them through the interior.
Mrs. Ed Nichols' dogtrot-style house on the Nichols farm at Canton, Mississippi,
was built in 1896 by her relatives, the Smith-Vaniz family.

PHOTO (overleaf):
Green Tomato Pickles
Zucchini Relish
Muscadine Hot Pepper Jelly
Summer Squash Relish
Pear Relish
Peach Chutney
Pepper Relish

CONDIMENTS

Tomato Jam
Yields 5-6 cups

2	cinnamon sticks, in pieces
1/2 tsp	whole allspice
1 tsp	whole cloves
1/8 tsp	grated fresh nutmeg
~	*cheese cloth or spice bag*
4 1/2 lbs	ripe summer tomatoes, peeled, quartered
4 1/2 cups	sugar
1 1/2 cups	vinegar (white or cider)
5 drops	Tabasco Sauce

Mix cinnamon, allspice, cloves, and nutmeg and tie in cheesecloth. In non-aluminum pot, combine tomatoes, sugar, vinegar, Tabasco, and bag of spices. Simmer slowly over medium-low heat, stirring frequently, until thick—may require several hours. Keep refrigerated or seal in hot, sterilized jars and process in boiling water bath.

Tomato Jam—a paradox to be sure, but a tasty one at that. This chutney-like concoction makes a delightful glaze for ham, a great accent on sandwiches, and a fun surprise on biscuits or brioche.

This recipe can be doubled, but your results will be better if you prepare two separate batches. For a sweeter jam, add a 20-ounce can of crushed pineapple, drained, during the last 10 minutes of cooking.

Muscadine Hot Pepper Jelly
Yields 12 cups

4	jalapeño peppers, skins removed
1/4 cup	water
2 qts	muscadines, washed, drained
1 pkg	powdered fruit pectin (1 3/4 oz)
7 cups	sugar

You can produce a softer jelly by using 1/4 cup more juice or a stiffer jelly with 1/4 cup less juice. Fewer jalapeño peppers, of course, will yield a milder flavor, and, if you want plain muscadine jelly, you can eliminate the peppers entirely.

Puree jalapeños in food processor with 1/4 cup water, then strain, reserving liquid. Place muscadines in 6- to 8-quart saucepan with cold water to cover. Add reserved jalapeño liquid. Bring to boil and simmer, covered, 15 minutes. Crush muscadines and simmer 5 minutes longer. Place muscadine mixture in jelly bag and squeeze out juice. Strain and measure juice—if less than 6 cups is produced, add water to make 6 cups. Mix fruit pectin with juice in saucepan over high heat. Stirring constantly, bring mixture to hard, rolling boil that cannot be stirred down. Add sugar slowly and boil 1 minute. Remove from heat and skim off foam with metal spoon. Seal immediately in hot, sterilized jars. Allow jelly to rest 24 hours before moving to storage.

Blueberry Jam
Yields 8 cups

3 cups	blueberries
3 cups	water
1 pkg	powdered fruit pectin (1 3/4 oz)
2 Tbs	fresh lemon juice
7 cups	sugar

Pectin:
Natural or Artificial
You can make jellies and jams without artificial fruit pectin. Using 1/4 underripe fruit with 3/4 ripe fruit will provide the pectin required.

Simmer blueberries and water 20 minutes. Measure out 5 cups berries with liquid and place in large pot with powdered pectin and lemon juice. Bring to boil. Add sugar and bring to rolling boil that cannot be stirred down. Seal in hot, sterilized jars.

Date Nut Spread
Yields 3 cups

2 pkgs	cream cheese (16 oz total), room temperature
2 Tbs	honey
3/4 cup	chopped dates
3/4 cup	chopped walnuts

Serve this unbelievably simple recipe with wheat crackers. We would tell you to store it refrigerated, but that's not necessary, as there won't be any left.

Combine cream cheese, honey, dates, and walnuts until well mixed.

Shirley's Fruit Butter
Yields 3 cups

1/2 cup	unsalted butter
2 pkgs	cream cheese (16 oz total)
2 Tbs	Grand Marnier liqueur
1/3 cup	powdered sugar
1 jar	preserves (10 oz)

In food processor with steel blade in place, blend butter, cream cheese, liqueur, and powdered sugar. Add preserves and pulse to blend.

Shirley Corriher, food chemist and cooking instructor, Atlanta, GA

Pear Honey
Yields 12 cups

8 cups	Keiffer pears, ground, drained
6 cups	sugar
1 1/2 cups	crushed pineapple in heavy syrup, drained

Cook ground pears with sugar until mixture looks clear and begins to thicken, 1 1/2 hours. Add pineapple and cook 10 to 15 minutes longer. Seal in hot, sterilized jars and process in boiling water bath.

Keiffer Pears

Keiffer pears are hard, "sand" pears with a grainy texture. They grow throughout Mississippi, and the fruit ripens from mid-August to early September.

Pear Relish
Yields 6 pts

2	chili peppers, finely ground
1 gallon	ground Keiffer pears
1/2 gallon	ground onions
7	red bell peppers, ground
7	green bell peppers, ground
1/3 cup	canning salt
4 cups	sugar
1 qt	white vinegar
2 tsp	mustard seed
3 tsp	turmeric

Combine chili peppers, pears, onions, and bell peppers and cover with canning salt. Allow to stand overnight, then drain thoroughly. Place mixture in large preserving kettle (non-aluminum pot) and add sugar, vinegar, mustard seed, and turmeric. Bring to boil and cook 20 minutes. Refrigerate or seal in hot sterile jars and process in boiling water bath.

Watermelon Rind Chutney

Yields 8 cups

Spiced Vinegar

Yields 2 cups

5 Tbs   whole cloves

5 Tbs   whole allspice

5 Tbs   whole cinnamon

2 cups cider vinegar, heated

Add spices to hot vinegar. Heat without boiling, then allow to stand one week.

2 qts	watermelon rind, white part only, in ⅛" chunks
1	green bell pepper, chopped
2 large	onions, chopped
2 cloves	garlic, chopped
2 Tbs	salt
2 cups	fresh lime juice
2 cups	Spiced Vinegar (see accompanying recipe)
1 lb	light brown sugar
3 ½ cups	white sugar
2 Tbs	white mustard seed
3 ½ tsp	ground ginger
1 pkg	raisins (15 oz)
~	zest from 5 limes

Mix watermelon rind, bell pepper, onions, garlic, and salt. Allow mixture to stand 1 hour, then drain. In a large, non-aluminum pot, combine watermelon rind mixture with lime juice, Spiced Vinegar, sugars, mustard seed, ginger, raisins, and zest. Cook to desired consistency. Refrigerate or seal in hot, sterilized jars and process in boiling water bath.

The Chutney Story

Chutney—a spicy blend of chopped and pickled fruits and vegetables—brings a bit of sparkle to those too familiar vegetable dishes that we serve too often. Generally, chutney is served separately, and diners can add as much or as little as they like to their black-eyed peas, butter beans, turkey, ham, or game.

Peach Chutney

Yields 2 pints

¾ cup	sugar
½ cup	white wine vinegar
½ tsp	minced garlic
3 Tbs	Worcestershire sauce
3 Tbs	water
2 cups	frozen unsweetened sliced peaches, thawed
2 tsp	minced fresh ginger (1 tsp dried)
¼ tsp	crushed red pepper flakes
1 small	onion, finely chopped
¼ cup	white raisins

Combine sugar, vinegar, garlic, Worcestershire, and water and cook over low heat, stirring constantly, until sugar dissolves. Add peaches and continue cooking until peaches look almost clear. Drain peaches, returning sauce to pan. To sauce, add ginger, red pepper flakes, onion, and raisins. Cook gently until thickened. Return peaches to sauce and heat to boiling. Remove from heat and allow to cool. Cover and refrigerate.

Harvest Pecan Chutney

Yields 8 cups

12 cloves	garlic
1	4" piece fresh ginger, peeled, chopped
2 cups	cider vinegar, divided
4 cups	firmly packed light brown sugar
1 medium	onion, chopped
3 lbs	Granny Smith apples, peeled, cored, in 1" cubes
1/2 cup	raisins
1 cup	coarsely chopped pecans
2 tsp	cayenne pepper
1 Tbs	sweet paprika
1 Tbs	dry mustard
1 1/2 tsp	salt

In food processor, puree garlic and ginger with 1 cup vinegar. Transfer mixture to large, non-aluminum saucepan. Mix in brown sugar, onion, and remaining 1 cup vinegar. Bring mixture to boil, stirring until sugar dissolves. Reduce heat to medium and cook, stirring occasionally, until slightly thickened, 10 minutes. Add apples, raisins, pecans, cayenne, paprika, mustard, and salt. Cook, stirring occasionally to prevent scorching, until mixture resembles thick jam, 1 hour. Refrigerate or seal in hot, sterilized jars and process in boiling water bath. Serve with roast beef, chicken, or pork.

Pepper Relish

Yields 10 pints

12	red bell peppers, in chunks
12	green bell peppers, in chunks
12	small cayenne peppers, in chunks
6 large	onions, in chunks
1 head	cabbage, in chunks
1/2 cup	salt
1 qt	cider vinegar
1 qt	sugar
1 pkg	pickling spice (2 1/4 oz), tied in cheesecloth
1 Tbs	celery seed

Combine bell peppers, cayenne peppers, onions, and cabbage in food processor. Pulse to chop, being careful not to overprocess. Place vegetable mixture in large bowl. Stir in salt and allow to stand 30 minutes. Rinse and drain well. In a large non-aluminum pot, combine vegetable mixture with vinegar, sugar, pickling spice, and celery seed. Mix well, then simmer 30 minutes. Refrigerate or seal in hot, sterilized jars and process in boiling water bath.

§

Chapel Chow Chow

Yields 8 cups

6 lbs ripe tomatoes, peeled, quartered
1 small head cabbage, coarsely chopped
2 medium bell peppers, chopped
3 medium onions, chopped
3/4 cup kosher salt
1/2 Tbs celery seed
1 1/2 tsp ground cloves
1 1/2 tsp cinnamon
1 1/2 tsp allspice
1 1/2 tsp ginger
1/4 tsp cayenne pepper
2 1/2 cups sugar
3 cups cider vinegar

Mix tomatoes, cabbage, bell peppers, onions, and kosher salt. Place mixture in jelly bag or pillow case and hang 3 hours to drain. In large, non-aluminum pot, combine drained vegetables with all remaining ingredients. Cook until thickened, 2 hours. Refrigerate or seal in hot, sterilized jars and process in boiling water bath.

~

The historic Chapel of the Cross Episcopal Church in Madison County, Mississippi, dates back to 1848. Every year, the ladies of the congregation prepare huge quantities of Chapel Chow Chow in their church kitchen to sell at "A Day in the Country," the Chapel's fall fundraiser.

Miss Dot's Tomato Relish

Yields 6-8 pints

2 sticks	cinnamon, broken
2 tsp	mustard seed
2 tsp	whole cloves
~	*cloth bag*
25	very ripe tomatoes, peeled, quartered
2 cups	sugar
4 Tbs	salt
4 cups	white vinegar
4	bell peppers, chopped
1 large	onion, chopped
$^1/_8$ tsp	ground ginger
~	cayenne pepper to taste

Combine cinnamon, mustard seed, and cloves and tie in a cloth bag. Place spice bag with all remaining ingredients in large, non-aluminum pot. Cook, stirring frequently, until thick, 2 to 3 hours. Refrigerate or seal in hot, sterilized jars and process in boiling water bath.

Easy Chili Sauce

Yields 5 cups

1 can	tomatoes, chopped (16 oz)
1 can	Rotel tomatoes (10 oz), chopped
1 cup	brown sugar
1 cup	white vinegar
1 large	onion, chopped
$^1/_2$ tsp	cinnamon
1 tsp	ground allspice
$^1/_8$ tsp	ground ginger

Combine all ingredients and cook, uncovered, over low heat, stirring occasionally with wooden spoon, until dark and thick, 1 $^1/_2$ to 2 hours. Store in jars in refrigerator. Serve with okra, peas or beans.

Tips on Canning and Preserving

Use only standard jars and lids that are free from dents, chips, cracks, or rust. Wash jars, rims, and lids in hot, soapy water, and rinse thoroughly.

Sterilization method #1:

Place jars, rims, and lids in large pot. Fill with water and bring to a boil. Boil, uncovered, 15 minutes, then hold in hot water until ready to use.

~

Sterilization method #2:

Place clean, hot jars in preheated 300° oven. Heat 20 minutes, then turn heat off and leave jars in oven until ready to use. Boil lids and rims in water 15 minutes and leave in hot water until ready to use.

~

Fill hot, sterile jars to within $^1/_4$" from top. Wipe rims and threads of jars clean with damp cloth. Place hot lid on jar and screw metal band down evenly and firmly—do not force.

Zucchini Relish

Yields 6 pints

5 lbs	zucchini, unpeeled, chopped
4 medium	white onions, chopped
2 large	green bell peppers, chopped
2 large	red bell peppers, chopped
1/3 cup	salt, non-iodized or pickling
1/4 tsp	turmeric
1 tsp	nutmeg
1 tsp	celery salt
1 tsp	black pepper
1 Tbs	cornstarch
1 1/2 cups	white vinegar
4 1/2 cups	sugar

In non-aluminum pan, combine zucchini, onions, bell peppers, and salt and let stand overnight. Drain, rinse in cold water, and drain again. Mash all water out. Return vegetable mixture to pan, add all remaining ingredients, and simmer 30 minutes. Refrigerate or seal in hot, sterilized jars and process in boiling water bath.

Summer Squash Relish

Yields 6 pints

5 lbs	yellow squash, finely chopped
2 large	onions, chopped
1 large	bell pepper, chopped
6 Tbs	salt
2 1/2 cups	cider vinegar
3 1/2 cups	sugar
1/2 tsp	pepper
1 Tbs	celery seed
2 tsp	turmeric
1 Tbs	dry mustard
1 Tbs	cornstarch
1 Tbs	ground nutmeg

Combine squash, onions, and bell pepper. Mix in salt and refrigerate overnight. Drain and rinse squash mixture and place in non-aluminum pot with all remaining ingredients. Bring mixture to boil, then reduce heat and simmer 15 minutes. Refrigerate or seal in sterilized jars and process in boiling water bath.

*Tips on Canning
and Preserving*

(continued)

Water Bath Processing:

Immerse sealed jars in actively boiling water, making sure jars do not touch each other. Water must cover jars by 1 to 2 inches. Cover and return to boil over high heat. If product contains vinegar, jars should be processed 10 minutes. Without vinegar, jars should be processed 15 minutes for 1/2-pints and pints; 20 minutes for quarts. Jars are properly sealed if lid has "popped down" after contents have cooled. Store in dark, dry, cool place.

~

Preserves, pickles, relishes, and chutneys should be processed in water bath according to above instructions. Jellies, however, do not need water bath processing, and paraffin is no longer recommended for sealing. Use jars that require a 2-piece metal top (lid and screw band).

Green Tomato Pickles

Yields 8 pints

1 cup lime
1 gallon water
7 lbs green tomatoes, washed, sliced
5 lbs sugar
2 qts white vinegar
1 pkg pickling spices (1 ½ oz), tied in cheesecloth

~

In earthenware pot, dissolve lime in water. Add tomato slices and allow to soak in lime water overnight. Wash tomatoes gently but thoroughly through several changes of water, being careful not to break slices.
Boil tomatoes in sugar, vinegar, and pickling spices until tomatoes can be pierced with a broom straw, 2 hours. Seal in sterilized jars and process in boiling water bath.

~

"So I merely slammed the door behind me and went down and made some green-tomato pickle. Somebody had to do it."

from "Why I Live at the P.O."
by Eudora Welty

Sweet Red Pepper and Zucchini Relish

Yields 1 cup

½ cup	water
¼ tsp	ground allspice
⅛ tsp	dried red pepper flakes
1	bay leaf
¼ cup	balsamic vinegar
¼ cup	extra virgin olive oil
3 cloves	garlic, minced
1 large	onion, chopped
1 large	red bell pepper, chopped
2 medium	zucchini, chopped
1 cup	beef stock
~	salt and freshly ground pepper to taste
6	green onions, trimmed, with 2" green tops for garnish

In non-aluminum saucepan over medium-high heat, bring water, allspice, red pepper flakes, and bay leaf to boil. Reduce heat and simmer 5 minutes. Add vinegar and simmer 5 minutes more. Discard bay leaf and set vinegar sauce aside. Heat oil in large, heavy skillet over medium heat. Add garlic and onions and stir 4 minutes—do not brown. Add red bell pepper and stir 3 minutes. Add zucchini and stir 3 minutes. Blend in ¼ cup stock and 2 tablespoons of vinegar sauce and cook until liquid has evaporated. Repeat three more times, adding stock and vinegar sauce in same amounts and letting liquids cook down until almost evaporated. Season with salt and pepper and cool to room temperature. Spoon relish into glass bowl, cover, and refrigerate at least 2 days but not longer than 5 days. Garnish with green onions.

Nick Apostle, owner, Nick's and 400 East Capitol Restaurants, Jackson, MS

Rivers' Sweet Pickles

Yields 1 gallon

1 gallon	whole sour pickles
~	vegetable oil
1 pkg	pickling spices (1 ½ oz)
5 lbs	sugar
15 cloves	garlic, sliced

Thoroughly rinse pickles and jar. Lightly coat bottom of jar with oil. Sprinkle thin layer of sugar over oil. Slice pickles into ¼" slices. Place a layer of pickles in jar and cover with sugar, pickling spices, and a few slices of garlic. Repeat layers until jar is half full, then pour in oil to cover. Resume layering until jar is filled with pickles, then top off with oil. Invert jar and allow to stand 3 days. Store refrigerated or seal in sterile jars for up to six months of unrefrigerated storage.

Hot Mustard

Yields 3 cups

1 cup	tarragon vinegar
2 cans	dry mustard (4 ¾ oz total)
1 cup	sugar
3 large	eggs, beaten

Blend together vinegar and mustard. Store in closed container 24 hours. Mix in sugar and eggs. Cook mixture in double boiler while beating with portable mixer, 20 minutes.

Homemade Mayonnaise

Yields 1 pint

1 large	egg, room temperature
1 Tbs	fresh lemon juice
1 tsp	white vinegar
1 Tbs	Dijon mustard
¼ tsp	salt
¼ tsp	paprika
1 ½ cups	vegetable oil, divided

In food processor, blend egg, lemon juice, vinegar, mustard, salt, paprika, and 1 tablespoon oil, 60 seconds. With machine running, pour in remaining oil in steady stream. Cover and refrigerate as long as 3 to 4 days.

Basil-Garlic Mayonnaise

Yields 1 pint

1 large	egg, room temperature
1 tsp	salt
1 tsp	pepper
1 ⅓ cups	corn oil
⅓ cup	chopped fresh basil leaves
2 cloves	garlic, minced
2 Tbs	fresh lemon juice
⅛ tsp	cayenne pepper

In food processor, blend egg, salt, and pepper. With machine running, add oil in slow, thin stream. After oil is incorporated, blend in basil, garlic, lemon juice, and cayenne.

Herbal Vinegars

Herb vinegars are fabulous to cook with. The most flavorful are made by pouring warm vinegar over fresh herbs and letting them steep at least a week. Strain and bottle with fresh herb sprigs. Some of our favorites include tarragon in cider vinegar, green basil mint in red wine vinegar, and any of these in white wine vinegar: dill flowers, lemon garlic, or red basil.

Herbal Spreads

Herb butters and herb mayonnaise are easily made with a little butter, mayonnaise, or yogurt and a lot of finely minced herbs.
After flavoring, allow the mixture to stand several hours for the flavors to blend.
Keep a supply in your freezer to top eggs, fish, poultry, vegetables, and meat.
Use them in sandwiches and hors d' oeuvres.

*"In water one sees
one's own face;
in wine one beholds the
heart of another."*

FRENCH PROVERB

WINE GUIDE

Many food lovers agree that an appropriate wine of good quality can enhance the experience of a fine meal, yet few would pretend to be wine connoisseurs. In that spirit, we offer a simple and practical guide to wine selection.

The names on our lists of suggestions refer to types of wine not brand names. A knowledgeable sales person in a good wine shop will help you choose specific wines to meet your needs and budget. And remember—a high-priced wine is not necessarily your best choice.

Generally, white wines, rosés, and light, semi-dry red wines should be slightly chilled before serving. Full-bodied red wines are usually best enjoyed at room temperature. But in the appreciation of wine—as in the other fine arts—there are always exceptions to the rules. The best way to educate yourself about wine is to experiment…and enjoy.

EF	VEAL	HAM AND PORK	CHICKEN, TURKEY, AND COLD MEATS	GRILLED CHICKEN

VEAL
Consider sauce and stuffing

HAM AND PORK
Consider sauce and stuffing

CHICKEN, TURKEY, AND COLD MEATS

GRILLED CHICKEN

EF (cut off)

DRY
temperature
aresco
(Italy)
era
(Italy, California)
lo
(Italy)
rnet
ignon
(California)
nti Riserve
(Italy)
s-du-Rhone
(France)
Rotie
(France)
gaux
(France)
loc
(France)
lot
(California, France, Italy)
llac
(France)
te Sirah
(California)
ot Noir
(California)
nerol
(France)
Emillon
(France)
oseph
(France)
rasi
(Italy)
fandel
(California)

/SEMI-DRY
m temperature
ujolais
(France)

RILLED EEF
th a spicy ce or marinade

D/DRY
om temperature
rbera
(Italy)
aujolais
(France)
tes-du-Rhone
(France)
lcetta
(Italy)
eisa
(Italy)
tite Sirah
(California)
ssella
(Italy)
nfandel
(California)

VEAL

WHITE/DRY
Slightly chilled
Folle Branche
(California)
Graves
(France)
Sylvaner Riesling
(California, France, Germany)

RED/DRY
Room temperature
Bardolino
(Italy)
Cabernet Sauvignon
(California)
Freisa
(Italy)
Lago di Caldaro
(Italy)
Nebbiolo
(Italy)

RED/SEMI-DRY
Slightly chilled
Beaujolais
(France)
Chinon
(France)
Cotes-du-Rhone
(France)

LAMB

WHITE/DRY
Slightly chilled
Hockheimer
(Germany)

WHITE/SEMI-DRY
Slightly chilled
Johannisberg Riesling
(California, France, Germany)
Rhine Wines
(Germany)

RED/DRY
Room temperature
Beaune Villages
(France)
Cabernet Sauvignon
(California)
Hermitage
(France)
St. Estephe
(France)
St. Julien
(France)

LIGHT RED/DRY
Slightly chilled
Bardolino
(Italy)

HAM AND PORK

RED/DRY
Room temperature
Chateauneuf-du-Pape
(France)
Chinon
(France)
Cotes-du-Rhone
(France)
Dole du Valais
(Switzerland)
Falerno
(Italy)
Moulin-a-Vent Beaujolais
(France)
Nuits St. Georges
(France)
Rioja
(Spain)

RED/SEMI-DRY
Slightly chilled
Beaujolais
(France)

GAME
Venison, duck, etc.

RED/DRY
Room temperature
Barolo
(Italy)
Brouilly
(France)
Brunello di Montalcino
(Italy)
Chianti Riserva
(Italy)
Cote Rotie
(France)
Egri Bikaver
(Hungary)
Ghemme
(Italy)
Hermitage
(France)
Petite Sirah
(California)
Pinot Noir
(California)
Pomerol
(France)

CHICKEN, TURKEY, AND COLD MEATS

WHITE/DRY
Slightly chilled
Cortese
(Italy)
Dézaley
(Switzerland)
Forster
(Germany)
Frascati
(Italy)
Gewurztraminer
(France, Germany, California)
Hermitage Blanc
(France)
Macon-Villages
(France)
Meursault
(France)
Orvieto
(Italy)
Pinot Blanc
(California)
Pinot-Grigio
(Italy)
Pouilly-Fuissé
(France)
Vouvray
(France)

WHITE/SEMI-DRY
Slightly chilled
Chenin Blanc
(California)

If a heavy, spicy stuffing is used, try a light-bodied red wine.

GRILLED CHICKEN

WHITE/DRY
Slightly chilled
Soave
(Italy)

RED/DRY
Room temperature
Valpolicella
(Italy)

LIGHT RED/DRY
Slightly chilled
Bardolino
(Italy)

LIGHT RED/DRY
Room temperature
Chenas
(France)
Mercury
(France)

ROSÉ/DRY
Slightly chilled
Tavel Rosé
(France)

Any choices from the appetizers list are also appropriate.

FISH AND SEAFOOD
With a light butter sauce

WHITE/DRY
Slightly chilled
Chablis
(France)
Chardonnay
(California, Italy)
Chenin Blanc
(California)
Emerald Dry Riesling
(California)
Frascati
(Italy)
Moselle
(Germany)
Orvieto
(Italy)
Piesporter
(Germany)
Pinot Blanc
(California, France, Italy)
Pouilly Fuissé
(France)
Sylvaner
(California)
Vouvray
(France)

WHITE/SEMI-DRY
Slightly chilled
Chablis
(California)

APPETIZERS

WHITE/DRY
Slightly chilled
Chenin Blanc
(France)
Dézaley
(Switzerland)
Lavaux
(Switzerland)
Pinot Blanc
(Italy, California)
Sancerre
(France)
Soave
(Italy)
Sauvignon Blanc
(California)
Verdicchio
(Italy)
Vouvray
(France)

WHITE/SEMI-DRY
Slightly chilled
Piesporter
(Germany)
Johannisberg Riesling
(California, France, Germany)

ROSÉ/DRY
Slightly chilled
Grenache Rosé
(California)
Tavel Rosé
(France)

SHERRY/DRY
Cool room temperature
Amontillado Sherry
(Spain)

NOTE:
Accompany oyster appetizers with slightly chilled French Chablis, French Muscadet, or California Chardonnay.

COLD BUFFETS
Choose any from the appetizer list above, or:

LIGHT RED/DRY
Slightly chilled
Bardolino
(Italy)
Valpolicella
(Italy)

Wine Guide by
Pegge Drennan Gates

The home of the Junior League of Jackson, at 805 Riverside Drive, was completed in 1963. Before that time, the Junior League met in private homes and at Jackson's Municipal Art Gallery.

THE JUNIOR LEAGUE OF JACKSON

1927 was a year for headlines: Babe Ruth hits 60 home runs! Al Jolsen stars in *The Jazz Singer*! Charles Lindbergh flies solo across the Atlantic!

Also in 1927, eleven young women established the Jackson, Mississippi, Junior Auxiliary—not to make headlines, but to make a difference in their community through volunteer service.

Today, that same organization—known since 1940 as the Junior League of Jackson—boasts more than a thousand members who contribute volunteer hours and money to health care, education, and social service projects. Financial support has been generated through countless fundraisers over the years—from State Fair hamburger stands and professional tennis tournaments to gala balls and Christmas market-place extravaganzas. In addition, the Junior League's widely acclaimed *Southern Sideboards* cookbook has raised over a million dollars since 1978.

This new collection, *Come On In!*, is neither a sequel to nor a substitute for *Southern Sideboards*. Instead, the two books are companion pieces which celebrate the hospitality and cuisine of Mississippi and the South, from richly traditional dishes to contemporary recipes tailored to save time and improve nutrition.

Even in the contemporary South, however, our traditional hospitality is as strong as ever. The Junior League of Jackson hopes you've enjoyed sharing that tradition with us.

Cookbook Committee

Chairman
Martha Stevens McIntosh

Vice-Chairman
Becky Dickinson Wooley

Vice-Chairman
Kelley Walton Fenelon

Recipe Development
Karen Rutcliff Varner

Testing
Angelyn Atkins Cannada

Finance
Creed Coker Ridgway

Computer and Compiling
Lee Buford Threadgill

Proofing and Indexing
Sally Fortenberry North

Creative Coordinator
Dan Ellen Brock Maples

Corporate Sponsors
Leila Bogy Lane

Marketing
Sally Taylor Hensley

Sustaining Advisor
Sandra Rainwater Underwood

LEAGUE PRESIDENTS
(1989-1991)

Carol Puckett Daily
Paula Pruet James
Tish Callender Hughes

COOKBOOK COMMITTEE
CO-CHAIRMEN

Leslie Gruber Bingham
Mary Alice Primos Blackmon
Shannon Lurate Collins
Katy Smith Houston
Anne Russ Marion
Scottie McCord Russ
Kathy Stransky Scott
Doug Yarbrough Strahan
Anne Richardson Wells
Linda Rabb Williams

COOKBOOK MARKETING

Jan McMurtray Costas
Mona Morehart Evans
Beth Kahlmus Graham
Julie Gorman Levanway
Courtney Hammond Love
Hermine Herring McLarty
Susan Bee McNamara
Debbie Miller Westbrook

Special Thanks

The Junior League of Jackson expresses grateful appreciation to the following:

David Adcock

Patricia Brabant

Henri Minor Burnham

Charlotte Capers

Earl Duggan's Seafood Market

The Everyday Gourmet

Pegge Drennan Gates

Hood Furniture Manufacturing Company

Barbara Newman Kroeze

Robert Lambert

Curtis Mohundro

M. J. Murphy

Hilda Stauss Owen

Brantley and Ann Pace

W.K. Paine

Chan Shivers Patterson

Susan Moak Sheldon

Beth Wagner Stevens

Stephanie Strickland
WJTV Studio

ViComm Productions International

Billy and Frances Walton

Come On In! *represents a labor of love that could never have been realized without generous contributions of time, energy, expertise, and resources from countless individuals. Our deepest gratitude goes to all those listed here and to anyone we may have inadvertently failed to mention. We hope you share our pride.*

ACKNOWLEDGMENTS

RECIPE CONTRIBUTORS

Nosa Agho
Claire Williams Aiken
Leesa Crim Allred
Ginger Haddow Amoni
Dorothy Hunter Anderson
Gwen O'Neal Anderson
Lomax Anderson
Martha Yerger Andre
Mary Lynn Andrews
Nick Apostle
Ruby Nickey Assaf
Ouida Barnett Atkins
Barbara Austin
Sarah Peets Avery
Maury McRoberts Ball
Helen Fant Ballew
Susan Travis Barkley
William Donald Barkley, Jr.
Lee Barnes
Mary Lois Dickerson Barnett
Patty Owen Barry
Ellen Conrad Bear
Marion Irish Bell
Leslie Gruber Bingham
Mary Alice Primos Blackmon
Darryl Borden
Liz Waldrop Bradford
Tamara Moore Brahan
Missye Rhee Brickell Breazeale
Betty Lyons Brewer
Barbara Henry Brinson
Jane Ivens Brock
Sandy Speed Brooks
Jessica Barton Brown
Butch Bryan
Sarah Yelverton Buffington
Gwin Pryor Buford
T.C. Buford
Martha Kabbes Burns
Pat Alexander Burrow
Annette Coker Busbice
Kim Tillman Busche
Charles C. Bush
Karen Gordon Bush
Mary Alice Garner Bush
Nancy Reese Bush
Virginia Rankin Campbell
Angelyn Atkins Cannada
Inez Chisolm Cannada
Joy Sudduth Cannada
Rachel Earheart Cannada
Tara Warner Cannada
Marsha Nestor Cannon
Emily Alford Carlisle
Barbara Chesney Carney
Leslie Andrews Carpenter
Ruth Ann Milner Carpenter

Dorothy Poore Cates
Ann Broyles Cavett
Gloria McWilliams Chancellor
Winifred Green Cheney
Jeannie Johnson Chunn
Janet Hendrick Clark
Margaret Evans Clark
Victoria Baugher Clark
Rebecca Peteet Cleland
Martha Croley Click
Lois Smith Clover
Robin Fulcher Coco
Mary Robinson Coker
Nancy Spencer Coker
Gwen Walker Cole
Cissy Wagner Coleman
Shannon Lurate Collins
George H. Constance
Barbara Jones Cook
Elizabeth Wise Copeland
Nan Wideman Copeland
Doris May Corley
Elizabeth Taylor Cossar
Jan McMurtray Costas
Elizabeth Courtney
Alexine Albritton Covington
Cary Lynn Cox
Mildred Gould Creekmore
Sallie Lloyd Crim
Inez Crocker
Ruth Wroten Crouch
W. Lewis Crouch, M.D.
Allie Watkins Cunningham
Barb Miller Currie
Debbye Moore Dabbs
Betsy Caldwell Dale
Dorothy Edwards Dale
Julie Dannenbaum
Dorothy Smith Davis
Beth Green Dean
Judy Quinn Decker
Pat Bracken Decker
Opal Shake Dees
Bette Manske Dickinson
Ouida Creekmore Drinkwater
Dixie Hervey Duddleston
Florence Ratcliff Duett
Earl Duggan
Laura Duggan
Susan Barry Duke
Robin Jones Durham
Helen Mary Doumit Elzen
Gail Crosthwait England
Sarah Hamilton Enochs
Ann Carruth Este
Donna Dale Evans
Margaret Bailey Evans

Mona Morehart Evans
Susan Hofmann Evans
Mary Ann Underwood Faries
Dee Rosenblatt Farrell
Sally Kireker Faulkner
Della Rose Harris Faust
Brenda Greer Fellinger
Doris Stephani Fenelon
Kelley Walton Fenelon
Fran Hall Finch
Tell Lucas Flowers
Eleanor Haldeman Fontaine
Suzie Blackwood Foote
Ellen Mann Ford
Ann Quin Fournet
Dorothy Wilkins Fraley
Kathy Hymers Frye
Beth Pearson Fulghom
Mary Leigh Hendee Furrh
Shelley Muirhead Furrh
Cherry Dean Fyke
Alice Toy Gandy
Craig R.H. Gates
Pegge Drennan Gates
Anne Toy Clark Gathings
Barbara Bush Gatlin
Jane Vaughan Gerber
Jill Dianne Giddens
Fran Watts Ginn
Mary Lewis Herndon Golden
Pryor Buford Graeber
Beth Kahlmus Graham
Margaret Reimers Graves
Linda Thompson Greaves
Francine Lowe Greenlee
Betsy Ellis Greer
Katharine Howell Griffith
Kevin Stevens Guice
Catherine Fisher Hames
Emma George Carr Hamilton
Jo Ann Hanson
Hildegarde McPherson
  Harrington
Frances Foose Harris
Susan Snelling Harris
Terre Blanton Harris
Rosemary Hester Harrison
Carol Gfroerer Hazard
Sally Holloman Hederman
Debby Johnson Hendrick
Sally Taylor Hensley
Frances Johnson Hewitt
Evelyn McLaurin Hinton
Mae Yandell Hitchcock
Sondra Southerland Holman
Amy Knox Hopkins
Katy Smith Houston

Joyce Henne Howard
Hazel Martin Howell
Mary Brown Hudgins
Adelaide Murdock Hunt
Sheila Dollar Hunt
Charles Hyneman
Marsha Pearce James
Mildred Gresham James
Cappie McLean Jeffreys
Erin Conner Johnson
Elta Posey Johnston
Lucia Jones Jones
Kathleen Flanagan Keeton
Judy Entrican Kirkpatrick
Mindy Rice Kitchings
Barbara Newman Kroeze
Holley Westbrook Lacey
Linda Johnson Lambeth
Elise Alford Lambuth
Mary E. Land
Leila Bogy Lane
Maude McLean Lane
Lawana Rouse Lawrence
Julie Gorman Levanway
Henrietta Crosby Levings
Jane Riddell Lewis
Irene Robertson Long
Steven D. Long
Nell Shelton Loper
Carmel Lopez-Lampton
Mary Evelyn Hand Lotterhos
Nancy Dunn Louis
Courtney Hammond Love
Jane F. Lusk
Tracy W. Lusk
Helen Williford Lynch
Irene Gayden Mangum
Darri Dubberly Mansel
Dan Ellen Brock Maples
Grace MacKenzie Marland
Kay Abernathy Martin
Margery Luck Martin
Gloria Bomar Martinson
Bettye West Mason
Carol Lane May
Cathy Thomas May
Marty Hederman May
Reuel May, Jr., D.D.S.
Susan Duquette Mayfield
Lucy Cerhart Mazzaferro
Libby Nance McCammon
Grace Jean Gillespie McClendon
Marilyn M. McClendon
Doris Clark McCullen
Jane Crawford McInnis
Debra Ward McIntosh
Martha Stevens McIntosh

RECIPE CONTRIBUTORS (cont.)

RECIPE TESTERS

Carolyn Newman McIntyre
Anne Stallworth McKeown
Merrill Tenney McKewen
Charlotte Truitt McKinnon
Ermine Herring McLarty
Jane Herring McLarty
Charline Gerrard McLellan
Kay Speake McMurtray
Marissa Walton McNair
Susan Bee McNamara
Nora Frances Stone McRae
Emily Slappey McVey
Joe Middleton
Minnie Miller
Tricia Toler Miller
Marcelle Gruber Milner
Judith Deavenport Mitchner
Estelle Noel Mockbee
Hugh Cameron Montgomery, Jr.
Diane Manning Morse
Gene Deloney Morse
Kay Halterman Mortimer
Formastel Ford Mosby
Frances Jean Rowland Neely
Olivia Watson Neill
Susie Newburn
Anne Gayden Newton
George W. Newton, Jr.
Lynn Stietenroth Newton
Betsy West Nicholas
Betty Martin Nichols
Jane Scott Nichols
Grant Nooe
Sally Fortenberry North
Sally Dahlberg Norton
Gina Gillespie O'Connell
Alice Gandy O'Ferrall
Frances McGowan Overstreet
Vicki Rueseler Overstreet
Anne Elizabeth Henderson Ozier
Lisa Redditt Paris
Jerry Barnett Parker
Donna Neunlist Patrick
Jhan Shivers Patterson
Lucille Rhymes Patterson
Mae Coe Patton
Marion Parham Peaks
Karen Sue Peklo
Marilyn Murdoch Peklo
Barbara Hall Phillips
Cathy Phillips
Nancy Price Porter
Annelle Primos
Jonelle Green Primos
Peter McDonald Primos
Mary Lee Maddin Puckett
Rebecca Allen Raggio
Carol Graves Ratcliff
James Charles Ratcliff, Sr., M.D.
Marvin Lavelle Ratcliff, Jr.
Elizabeth Bass Raulston
Barbara Mason Redmont
Cindy Smith Reed
Susan Stevens Reeder
Maggie Conner Reeves
Creed Coker Ridgway
Melissa Grant Ridgway
Nita Wallace Ridgway
Peggy Garrity Rives
David Alvin Roberts
Jill Guess Robinson
Clarice Johnson Rogers
Betsy Gernert Rosenblatt
Judy Clinton Rosenblatt
Pat Thompson Ross
Ruby B. Rowell
Catherine McGowan Rueseler
Sherry Holland Rula
Scottie McCord Russ
Anne Clarke Sanders
Bernard Sarme
Sally Spencer Sarme
Carlene Myers Scanlon
Kathy Stransky Scott
Becky Wells Seay
Jennifer Jenkins Segrest
Virginia Nelson Self
Virginia Carmichael Shackelford
Janet Keith Shands
Cynthia Strahan Sheridan
Jennie Fyfe Short
Ann Atkinson Simmons
Jean Frazer Simmons
Kandy Stockstill Sims
Sophie Weston Sistrunk

Mary Elizabeth
  Witherspoon Smith
William F. Sneed, M.D.
Doris T. Spain
Jane Proctor Spencer
Carrie Ann Kirkpatrick Stallings
Sara C. Steel
Martha Allred Stennis
Beth Wagner Stevens
Patricia Land Stevens
Pam Partridge Stricklin
Lila Kabbes Strode
Anne Williamson Stubblefield
Jeanette Sullivan
Martha Neblett Summerford
B.J. Odom Swafford
Jo Lynn Rhoades Swayze
Connie Hawkins Taylor
Frances Walton Taylor
Jan Foster Taylor
Mary E. N Lauderdale Teague
Carolyn McRae Temple
Elaine Elias Thomas
Mary Evalyn Antoon Thomas
Lee Buford Threadgill
Grace Brown Toler
Ruth E. Toler
Poppy Tooker
Becky G. Turner
Patsy Patterson Turner
Nadia Aboussouan Tyson
Sandra Rainwater Underwood
Mollie Magee Van Devender
Henri van Goethem
Virginia Bradley Vardaman
Joel Paul Varner
Karen Ratcliff Varner
Karen Varney
William J. Vrazel
Jan Jacks Wade
Deery Mott Walker
Patricia Fugua Walker
Sarah Buford Walker
Estelle Rhymes Wallace
Tricia Putnam Walters
Frances Patterson Walton
Christine Fox Warren
Vivian Curtis Watson
Binny Frederic Webb
Evelyn Sillers Pearson Weems
Susan Long Weems
Anne Pope Wells
Cheryl Blatt Wells
Debbie Miller Westbrook
Kieta Thompson Westbrook
A. Barnes White
Gale Thorne White
Jim White
Harriet Lumpkin Whitehouse
Posey Humphrey Wideman
Catherine Brandon Williams
Baiba Strautins Wilson
Beth Robertson Wilson
Cynthia Curtiss Wise
Elizabeth Powell Wise
Charles Welborn Witt
Jan Roby Wofford
Flora Mae Arant Womack
Charlotte Tolley Womack
Sally Muire Wood
Tracy Carruthers Woods
Becky Dickinson Wooley
Easie Mercier Wooley
O.B. Wooley, Jr., M.D.
Lelia Wallender Wright
Nancy Strahan Wright
Julia Shannon Yandell
Rida Garrett Yates
Linda Biggers Yerger
Beth Spain Young
Cynthia White Youngblood

TESTING COORDINATORS

Mary Alice Primos Blackmon
Melissa Wilson Bondurant
Ellen Cochran Brown
Cherry Dean Fyke
Pamela Palmer Houchins
Marty Hederman May
Deetsa Lowry Molpus
Kerry Barnett Parker
Jan Roby Wofford
Marita Pace Walton
Beth Spain Young

Claire Williams Aiken
Jo Ann Dale Alford
Cheryl Dubard Allen
Dreen Blakeslee Allen
Leesa Crim Allred
Martha Yerger Andre
Carole Sanders Bailey
Dea Dea Adams Baker
Helen Fant Ballew
Brenda Belcher Bethany
Leslie Gruber Bingham
Mary Alice Primos Blackmon
Lydia Berryhill Bolen
Melissa Wilson Bondurant
Martha Hamrick Boshers
Fontaine Hutchins Bowie
Missye Rhee Brickell Breazeale
Betty Lyons Brewer
Jane Ivens Brock
Ellen Cochran Brown
Jessica Barton Brown
Monica Blaise Browne
Barbara Ledbetter Brunini
Grace Atkinson Buchanan
Irma Paris Buchanan
Sarah Yelverton Buffington
Cris Burns
Lind Robinson Bussey
Virginia Rankin Campbell
Angelyn Atkins Cannada
Inez Chisolm Cannada
Joy Sudduth Cannada
Sally Wakefield Carmichael
Leslie Andrews Carpenter
Alice Barnes Carroll
Jean Johnson Chunn
Victoria Baugher Clark
Lois Smith Clover
Robin Fulcher Coco
Meredith Foose Coleman
Barbara Jones Cook
Retta K. Cook
Elizabeth Wise Copeland
Becky Vance Cowart
Katherine Bonney Cox
Meridith Wilson Creekmore
Wanda Wilkinson Crosby
Barb Miller Currie
Betsy Caldwell Dale
Kathryn McKee Davis
Beth Green Dean
Judy Quinn Decker
Pat Bracken Decker
Barbara Carraway Dogan
Dottie Foster Donaldson
Dixie Hervey Duddleston
Susan Barry Duke
Robin Jones Durham
Mel Crooks Evans
Donna Dale Evans
The Everyday Gourmet
Mary Ann Underwood Faries
Dee Rosenblatt Farrell
Kelley Walton Fenelon
Suzie Blackwood Foote
Kay Garraway French
Beth Pearson Fulghom
Mary Leigh Hendee Furrh
Cherry Dean Fyke
Susan Lowry Garner
Anne Toy Clark Gathings
Jane Vaughan Gerber
Darian Green Gibson
Edwina McDuffie Goodman
Pryor Buford Graeber
Beth Kahlmus Graham
Margaret Reimers Graves
Linda Thompson Greaves
Rhonda Plummer Green
Vickie Love Greenlee
Pat Hopkins Grenfell
Julie Critchlow Gresham
Emma George Carr Hamilton
Marilyn McIntosh Harris
Terre Blanton Harris
Jerri Jeter Harvey
Sally Holloman Hederman
Merle Masters Henderson
Mary Margaret Taylor Hickman
Madalyn Cunningham Hindman
Jean Ridley Hines
Loicka Coisne Hodges
Virginia Cavett Hogan
Paula Jennings Hood
Pamela Palmer Houchins
Dorothy Molpus Howorth

Mary Galbreath Jabaley
Marsha Pearce James
Paula Pruet James
Judy Williams Jernigan
Sara Margaret Edwards Johnson
Lucia Jones Jones
Susan Shivers Kellum
Libby Whitaker Kendall
Sally Kireker
Willie Sampson Krooze
Phoebe Kelley Kruger
Linda Johnson Lambeth
Elise Alford Lambuth
Laura Kilpatrick Lampton
Maggi Callen Lampton
Leila Bogy Lane
Rebecca Holmes Long
Carmel Lopez-Lampton
Nina Dunnam Lott
Margaret Smith Lowery
Courtney Hammond Love
Nell Inda Breed Lutken
Irene Gayden Mangum
DeAnn Lewis Manning
Darri Dubberly Mansell
Sandra Vaughey Maris
Margery Luck Martin
Bettye West Mason
Carol Lane May
Marty Hederman May
Susan Duquette Mayfield
Lucy Gerhart Mazzaferro
Susan Elliott McAllister
Lynda Graham McCarty
Grace Jean Gillespie McClendon
Judy Hale McCollum
Anne Harris McDaniel
Jane Crawford McInnis
Debra Ward McIntosh
Martha Stevens McIntosh
Carolyn Newman McIntyre
Anne Stallworth McKeown
Carol Noel McLaurin
Tammy Harris McLaurin
Sarah Hamlin McMillan
Susan Bee McNamara
Nora Frances Stone McRae
Emily Slappey McVey
Ashley Creekmore Meena
Tricia Toler Miller
Mary Carraway Mills
Elizabeth Fair Minor
Muffy Hess Mitch
Pat Goetz Moak
Estelle Noel Mockbee
Deetsa Lowry Molpus
Noni Ward Montague
Leslie Williams Moore
Frances Peake Morse
Patsy Graham Mounger
Melissa Russell Murphree
Olivia Watson Neill
Jane Scott Nichols
Sally Fortenberry North
Sally Dahlberg Norton
Sophia Fox Owen
Lisa Redditt Paris
Kerry Barnett Parker
Betse Brashier Parsons
Donna Neunlist Patrick
Charlotte Gulledge Peets
Karen Sue Peklo
Myrtis Pettis
Gail Jones Pittman
Ann Forrest Porter
Katherine Primos Prewitt
Jonelle Green Primos
Mary Lee Maddin Puckett
Cindy Smith Reed
Maggie Conner Reeves
Creed Coker Ridgway
Melissa Grant Ridgway
Betsy Love Ritter
Peggy Garrity Rives
Joanna Bass Roberts
Cathy Dillon Robinson
Jane Stewart Roper
Joan Hamilton Roper
Sallie L. Roper
Betsy Gernert Rosenblatt
Judy Clinton Rosenblatt
Pat Thompson Ross
Sherry Holland Rula
Scottie McCord Russ
Sue Clayton Russ

Cathey Bass Russell
Anne Clarke Sanders
Carlene Myers Scanlon
Janet Jones Scott
Stephanie Quiriconi Scott
Jennifer Jenkins Segrest
Janet Keith Shands
Kathleene Neblett Shapley
Kathy Shaw
Beverly Melton Shelton
Kandy Stockstill Sims
Lee Wilborn Singletary
Sophie Weston Sistrunk
Mary Elizabeth
  Witherspoon Smith
Pat Pray Sneed
Pat Graham Stevens
Carolyn Matthews Stone
Doug Yarbrough Strahan
Gale Primos Stuart
Anne Williamson Stubblefield
Nancy Shands Studdard
Ingrid Perry Taylor
Jan Foster Taylor
Sandy Steel Temple
Marsha Sherrard Thompson
Sally Bailey Thompson
Lee Buford Threadgill
Grace Brown Toler
Judith Thompson Travis
Becky G. Turner
Sandra Rainwater Underwood
Mollie Magee Van Devender
Carolyn Tabb VanSkiver
Katie Bankston Varner
Karen Ratcliff Varner
Jan Jacks Wade
Deery Mott Walker
Gloria Merry Walker
Tricia Puckett Walker
Frances Patterson Walton
Marita Pace Walton
Cecille Walsh Wardlaw
Debbie Miller Westbrook
Jayne Crisler Westbrook
Kieta Thomson Westbrook
Harriet Lumpkin Whitehouse
Beth Robertson Wilson
Jan Roby Wofford
Celia Farr Wood
Becky Dickinson Wooley
Easie Mercier Wooley
DeVane Farr Yates
Rida Garrett Yates
Mary Montague Yerger
Mary P. Montague Yerger
Beth Spain Young

PROPS

Mary Adams
Suzanne Yates Best
Carleton and Debra Huchel Billups
Mary Alice Primos Blackmon
Jane Patterson Boykin
T. C. and Gwin Buford
Ann Runyon Carter
Anne Manning Cunningham
Dixie Hervey Duddleston
The Everyday Gourmet
Robin Vincent Fiser
Fridge's
Pryor Buford Graeber
Julie Critchlow Gresham
Marsha Pearce James
Jo's Antiques
Governor Ray and Julie Mabus
Eloise Moore McCorkle
Betty Bartling Moore
Jane Scott Nichols
Ed and Mindy Nichols
Hilda Stauss Owen
Nancy Molpus Pace
Gail Jones Pittman
Annelle Primos
Jonelle Green Primos
Dero Todd Puckett
Tommy Rueff, M.D.
Berle Smith
Mildred Primos Smith
Carole Nichols Sneed
Beth Wagner Stevens
Sandra Rainwater Underwood
Gloria Merry Walker
Billy and Frances Walton
John R. Wooley, M.D.
O. B. and Easie Wooley

BIBLIOGRAPHY

Bailey, Tom, and Brown, Ray. *Seafood of the Northern Gulf.* Seacoast.

Davis, Frank. *The Frank Davis Seafood Notebook.* Pelican, 1988.

Herbst, Sharon Tyler. *Food Lover's Companion.* Barron's, 1990.

Kamman, Madeline. *The Making of a Cook.* Atheneum, 1985.

Russo, Julee, and Lukins, Sheila. "Tips for Cooking with Herbs", an information sheet compiled by the authors of *The New Basics Cookbook*.

Excerpt from *A History of the Mississippi Governor's Mansion* by David G. Sansing and Carroll Waller, copyright © 1977, reprinted by permission of University Press of Mississippi.

Excerpt from "June Recital" in *The Golden Apples,* copyright © 1947 and renewed 1975 by Eudora Welty, reprinted by permission of Harcourt Brace Jovanovich, Inc.

Excerpt by Sue Bridwell Beckham from *Encyclopedia of Southern Culture,* coedited by Charles Reagan Wilson and William Ferris, copyright © 1989, reprinted by permission of University of North Carolina Press.

Excerpt from *Southern Food* by John Egerton, copyright © 1987, reprinted by permission of Alfred A. Knopf.

Excerpt from *The Governor's Mansion: A Pictorial History* by David G. Sansing and Carroll Waller, copyright © 1975, reprinted by permission of Mississippi Executive Mansion Commission, Inc.

Excerpt from *The Optimist's Daughter* by Eudora Welty, copyright © 1972, reprinted by permission of Random House.

Excerpt from *Terrains of the Heart and Other Essays on Home* by Willie Morris, copyright © 1981, reprinted by permission of Yoknapatawpha Press.

Excerpt from "Why I Live at the P.O." in *A Curtain of Green and Other Stories,* copyright © 1941 and renewed 1969 by Eudora Welty, reprinted by permission of Harcourt Brace Jovanovich, Inc.

N D E X

Equivalent Measures

dash	=	less than $1/8$ tsp
1 tsp	=	60 drops
1 Tbs	=	3 tsp
2 Tbs	=	1 fl oz
4 Tbs	=	$1/4$ cup
1 cup	=	$1/2$ pt or 8 fl oz
2 cups	=	1 pt
1 pt	=	16 oz
1 qt	=	2 pts
2 qts	=	$1/2$ gal
4 qts	=	1 gal
1 lb	=	16 oz
1 lb	=	2 cups liquid

Come On In!

JUNIOR
LEAGUE
OF JACKSON

P.O. Box 4709
Jackson, MS
39296-4709

601-948-2357

N.

JUNIOR LEAGUE of JACKSON

P.O. Box 4709
Jackson, MS
39296-4709

601-948-2357

Ship to:

Name

Street
Address

City
State/Zip

Daytime
Phone

Nighttime
Phone

Payment by ☐ CHECK   ☐ MONEY ORDER   Total Amount Enclosed

Charge to ☐ MASTERCARD   ☐ VISA   Expiration Date

Account
Number

Name as it
appears on card

Signature

Book	Qty	Total
Come On In! $24.95 each		
Southern Sideboards $14.95 each		
Sub Total		
MS Deliveries Add 7% Sales Tax		
Giftwrap $1.00 each		
Shipping and Handling $2.75 each		
Total		

N.

JUNIOR LEAGUE of JACKSON

P.O. Box 4709
Jackson, MS
39296-4709

601-948-2357

Ship to:

Name

Street
Address

City
State/Zip

Daytime
Phone

Nighttime
Phone

Payment by ☐ CHECK   ☐ MONEY ORDER   Total Amount Enclosed

Charge to ☐ MASTERCARD   ☐ VISA   Expiration Date

Account
Number

Name as it
appears on card

Signature

Book	Qty	Total
Come On In! $24.95 each		
Southern Sideboards $14.95 each		
Sub Total		
MS Deliveries Add 7% Sales Tax		
Giftwrap $1.00 each		
Shipping and Handling $2.75 each		
Total		

N.

JUNIOR LEAGUE of JACKSON

P.O. Box 4709
Jackson, MS
39296-4709

601-948-2357

Ship to:

Name

Street
Address

City
State/Zip

Daytime
Phone

Nighttime
Phone

Payment by ☐ CHECK   ☐ MONEY ORDER   Total Amount Enclosed

Charge to ☐ MASTERCARD   ☐ VISA   Expiration Date

Account
Number

Name as it
appears on card

Signature

Book	Qty	Total
Come On In! $24.95 each		
Southern Sideboards $14.95 each		
Sub Total		
MS Deliveries Add 7% Sales Tax		
Giftwrap $1.00 each		
Shipping and Handling $2.75 each		
Total		

**JUNIOR
LEAGUE
OF JACKSON**

P.O. Box 4709
Jackson, MS
39296-4709

601-948-2357

**JUNIOR
LEAGUE
OF JACKSON**

P.O. Box 4709
Jackson, MS
39296-4709

601-948-2357

**JUNIOR
LEAGUE
OF JACKSON**

P.O. Box 4709
Jackson, MS
39296-4709

601-948-2357

JUNIOR
LEAGUE
ᵒᶠJACKSON
PUBLICATIONS

Come On In! : Recipes from the Junior League of Jackson, Mississippi

DEVELOPMENT

Junior League of Jackson, Mississippi PRESIDENTS		*Come On In !* Cookbook Committee CHAIRMEN
Carol Puckett Daily	1989 - 1990	Martha Stevens McIntosh
Paula Pruett James	1990 - 1991	Martha Stevens McIntosh
First Printing, September 1991 (60,000 copies)		
Tish Callender Hughes	1991 - 1992	Martha Stevens McIntosh
Tricia Putman Walters	1992 - 1993	Becky Dickinson Wooley
Second Printing, September 1993 (75,000 copies)		
Patricia Goodman Ammons	1993 - 1994	Beth Kahlmus Graham

AWARDS

National First Place
Tabasco Community Cookbook Awards
1991

Certificate of Excellence
American Institute of Graphic Arts Book Show
1991